Memories of Hawthorne

By

Rose Hawthorne Lathrop

AMS PRESS
NEW YORK

Reprinted from the edition of 1897, Boston
First AMS EDITION published 1969
Manufactured in the United States of America

Library of Congress Catalogue Card Number: 79-96474

AMS PRESS, INC.
NEW YORK, N. Y. 10003

PREFACE

IT will be seen that this volume is really written by Sophia Hawthorne; whose letters from earliest girlhood are so expressed, and so profound in thought and loveliness, that some will of sterner quality than a daughter's must cast them aside. I have tried to weed out those written records of hers (even from 1820) reaching to her last year in 1871, that could give no especial pleasure to any descendant who might come upon them; and I have been astonished to find that there was scarcely one such page. This is the explanation of my return, in the company of the friends of my father and mother, to an old garden, a familiar discourse, and a circle of life that embraced so much beauty.

ROSE HAWTHORNE LATHROP.

NEW YORK, *February 20th, 1897.*

CONTENTS

CHAPTER I

THE HAWTHORNES AND THE PEABODYS

THE Hawthornes summoned from their quietude by the Peabodys. Sophia Peabody's mother and grandmother, the latter wife of General Palmer, who was prominent in the Revolution. Characteristics of the Misses Peabody. Letters to the Hawthornes from the Peabodys, though so close at hand, because of the difficulty of seeing the former at any time. The dignity of George Peabody's nature. Sophia's fondness for profound books. The great affection of friends for her, who bring rare flowers to the little studio where she is often imprisoned. Elizabeth Hawthorne consents to walk with the Peabodys. Dr. Channing's regard for Sophia's artistic talent and motive. Miss Burley's literary club, to which Hawthorne liked to go with Sophia. The wooing not a moment delayed. Visits from Emerson and Very. Elizabeth goes forth among the most interesting people of Boston, and

CHAPTER II

THE DAYS OF THE ENGAGEMENT

Hawthorne and Sophia become engaged, but defer the announcement for a year. Sophia visits friends in Boston, and Hawthorne visits Boston also. Washington Allston's deep approval of Sophia's talents. Elizabeth visits the Emersons in Concord, and writes as if from heaven. Mr. Bancroft remarked to Emerson that Hawthorne was exceptionally thorough in business. Sophia draws and

CONTENTS

CHAPTER III

THE EARLY DAYS OF THE MARRIAGE

CHAPTER IV

LIFE IN SALEM

CONTENTS

CHAPTER V

FROM SALEM TO BERKSHIRE

CHAPTER VI

LENOX

CHAPTER VII

FROM LENOX TO CONCORD

CONTENTS

CHAPTER VIII

THE LIVERPOOL CONSULATE

CHAPTER IX

ENGLISH DAYS : I

CONTENTS

CONTENTS

CHAPTER XII

ITALIAN DAYS: I

CHAPTER XIII

ITALIAN DAYS: II

CONTENTS

CONTENTS

xii

MEMORIES OF HAWTHORNE

CHAPTER I

THE HAWTHORNES AND THE PEABODYS

To my lot have fallen sundry letters of my mother's, received in youth by her sisters and friends, and by her husband and others in later life. I have often read over these magic little pictures of old days, and each time have felt less inclined to let them remain silently in the family. The letters are full of sunshine, which is not even yet in the least dimmed ; and there is a pleasant chatter of persons of whom we have heard widely in the most refined atmosphere this country knows.

The scene surrounds a soul, my father's, whose excellence grows more and more evident, and who enriches every incident and expression that comes in contact with him. The tone of the life depicted is usually glad ; but even where discomfort and sorrow break it, Hawthorne's unflinching endurance suggests unsoured activity and a brave glance.

I will preserve, as well as I can by selections,

the effect produced upon me by the many packages of letters which I opened some years ago. What Hawthorne cared for is somewhat clearly shown by side-lights; and there is also some explanation from my mother, as unintentionally given as the rest, of why he cared.

It was a genial and vivid existence which enveloped her family always; and it became an interesting problem to the Peabodys to entice the reticent Hawthornes into it, from the adjacent Herbert Street, — by gentle degrees, well-adjusted baits, and affectionate compliments. Trout-fishing comes to mind, — and the trout were very skillful in keeping aloof. Nevertheless, Hawthorne liked all he heard and saw at the Peabodys' in Charter Street; and Sophia, his future wife, gleams near him as the unwitting guide to the warm contact with his kind for which he searched, though with delicacy of choice.

Sophia's mother had strong intellect and great refinement, as well as a strength of character which gave her the will to teach school for many years, while her own children were growing up. She was very well connected in various directions; in other words, she had sprung from cultivated intelligences.

Mrs. Peabody's mother was the wife of Judge Cranch, of Boston, whose sister, the wife of General Palmer, wrote to her in Revolutionary days the following letter, wherein very mild words stand for very strong emotions: —

2

GERMANTOWN, February 12, 1775.

DEAR SISTER, — It is a long time since we
have heard from you, except by transient reports
that your family was pretty well. I suppose you
are all anxious about publick affairs as well as
other folks. 'T is a dreadful dull time for writing; this suspense that we are in seems to absorb
every Faculty of the mind, especially in our situation where we seldom see anybody from the
busy world.

Mr. Palmer has been gone a fortnight to Congress, and we have never heard a word from him.
The folks are almost impatient to hear what they
are about.

Certainly we at this time want every motive of
Religion to strengthen our souls and bear up our
spirits, that we may not faint in the evil time.
Why should not there be religious as well as Political correspondencies? I believe much good
might be done by such means, as those who are
sincerely good would be able to strengthen each
other — oh dear! I am so stupid! I wonder whether you feel so, too; but you have little ones
about you that will keep you rousing. My Love
to them all, together wth my Brother.

Your affectionate sister, M. PALMER.

Literature, art, and intercourse were the three
gracious deities of the Peabody home, and many
persons came to join the family in worshiping
them; so that the pages of all the letters and
journals, from which but a fragmentary gleaning

3

has been made, blossom daily with name after name of callers. Elizabeth was profoundly interesting, Mary was brilliant, and Sophia was lovely in her studio, to which everybody eagerly mounted. At about the time when I begin to levy upon the letters, the efforts of these young ladies to establish common ground of friendship with the Hawthornes peep forth in small messages, bequeathed to me by my recluse aunt Ebie Hawthorne.

Elizabeth Peabody was the first and most frequent angler at the brookside, and actually succeeded in establishing a sturdy friendship with the young author, who was being sought for by the best people in Salem. His mother and sisters, walks and books, were the principal factors in his capture by the admiring enemy. Elizabeth had already a high intercourse upon high themes with the best minds among manly American thought. Her perfect simplicity of motive and abandonment of selfish, vain effeminateness made her the delight of the great men she met. She was a connoisseur in this field. To such a genial cultivator of development it seemed folly for the women of the Hawthorne family so to conceal their value; it was positively non-permissible for the genius of the family to conceal *his*, and so this New World Walton fished him forth. She sends a note to Herbert Street: —

MY DEAR MRS. HAWTHORNE, — I have taken the liberty to have your book bound before I returned it to you, as it was somewhat abused at the

4

printing-office. And besides, I thought there should be some attempt at harmony between the outside and the inside; and more than that, I wanted in some slight degree to express my respect for it. How happy you must be in reading these tales! For if the genius which produced them is independent of all source but the divine bounty, the holiness and virtue which breathe on every page may be fairly attributed to the sacred influences of a pure New England home, in no small degree. But to enter upon the satisfactions of a mother in such a case I feel to be intruding upon consecrated ground. Yet you will easily pardon the feeling that impels me.

With the greatest respect, yours,

ELIZABETH P. PEABODY.

My mother joins in the pursuit, though interested only in catching a glimpse of the widow and the shy eldest daughter. It must have been worth many experiments to gently succeed in putting their skill in hiding to naught. She slaps a dainty fishing-line through the leaves: —

MY DEAR ELIZABETH, — I send you a volume of Carlyle, lately published. It is well worth reading; and your mother — will she like to read it? I shall charge Bridget to inquire how your mother's and Louisa's headaches are. I should have gone myself to-day to ask, had not the wind been east. Won't you come to walk to-morrow afternoon with my mother, dear Elizabeth, and then I shall see you a few minutes ? I want very much to see you, and to show you a certain white vase filled with brilliant flowers, which would charm your eye. I hope you enjoyed the music last evening.

Truly yours and Louisa's,

S. A. PEABODY.

I can imagine nothing more curious to the Peabodys than people who withdrew themselves from choice. My mother was often hidden, because of great delicacy of health, which her ardent pursuance of art constantly fatigued ; but she saw so many people that there was scarcely a whole day of isolation. At the Hawthornes', on the contrary, quiet prevailed : caused partly by bereavement, partly by proud poverty, and no doubt not a little by the witch-shadow of Judge Hawthorne's unfortunate condemnation of Rebecca Nurse, whose dying curse was never ignored ; partly also by a sense of superiority, which, I think, was the skeleton in every Hawthorne's body at that time.

For a year one of the brothers at the Peabodys', George, remained in his room, slowly dying from the effects of over-exertion in athletic sports. He was of large frame and of noble appearance, and was referred to by my mother in after-life with the deepest admiration. She writes : —

" It is difficult to realize how ill he is. He has none of the ways of sick people. His voice is as cheerful as ever, with no whine in its tones. He has no whims. He is always ready to smile, and reads constantly. . . . Mary and I spent the evening with the beloved one. He was pretty cheery, and told a comical anecdote of Dean Swift. He stood up on Friday much more firmly than formerly. Elizabeth Hawthorne sent him Miss Martineau's book, after tea, which was certainly very kind and attentive in her. I am determined to go and see her this week. I spent the morning upon my bed, reading Herodotus. . . . I found that mother had taken James and gone to Paradise after a *hawthorne* bush. It is a bush for which she has had a longing for several years, but never could get any kind friend to uproot it for her."

The highest principles of thought and action are constantly danced about and caressed by my mother in all her letters, as we imagine a Greek maiden paying cheerful homage to beautiful statues of the gods. For instance, in writing to the brother already mentioned, before his illness, she says : —

"I do not like to have you say that you enjoy despising people, George. It would be a little better to say you cannot help it sometimes ; and even that is a dangerous attitude of mind. It is better to sorrow over than to despise. You know, Wordsworth says, 'He that feels contempt for any living thing hath faculties which he has never used.' "

A message from Mary Peabody shows how intimate Herbert and Charter streets were growing : —

My dear Elizabeth, — I am very sorry to have been prevented from walking, but I hope to be able to go by Tuesday. George is fast growing weaker, and we do not know what a day may bring forth. Still, I feel it is necessary to take exercise when I can. We do not tell all our fears to Sophia, whom we wish to keep cheerfully employed as long as we can. Will you ask your brother to dine with us to-morrow? Elizabeth [who was then teaching school in Boston] depends upon the pleasure of seeing him when she comes. We dine as early as twelve on Sunday.

Yours very truly,

MARY T. PEABODY.

From this point, the letters and fragments of journals bring to view what Hawthorne saw, and make real to us the woman he soon loved.

SALEM, October 22, 1832.

I have been in old native Salem for ten days. Betty and I returned by seven o'clock to our minimum of a house, and upon entering I really felt a slight want of breath to find the walls so near together and the ceiling nearly upon my head. But there stood my beloved mother, all in white, her face radiant with welcome and love, and in her arms there was no want of room. In September or October I live *par excellence*. I feel in the abstract just as an autumn leaf *looks*. I step abroad from my clay house, and become

8

a part of the splendor and claritude and vigor around.

DEAR BETTY, — I forgot to tell you that mother's garden has been arranged. She is quite happy in it. Father presided over a man as he uprooted and planted. The man was quite an original. He came looking very nice, very gentlemanly, in broadcloth and cambric cravat. But after disappearing into the barn for several minutes, he came forth transformed into a dirty workman, though still somewhat distinguished by his figure and air. He expressed himself in very courtly phrase, also, and was quite sentimental about the shrubbery round the tombs. [A graveyard was close to the house.] I should much like to know the history of his mind and career. . . . The clematis which climbs into my window is all sprouting. My glorious tree — my hieroglyphic for the everlasting forests — is also putting forth leaves, and the robins sing among the branches.

Ellen Barstow came with an exquisite crimson rose for me, which she wished to present herself ; and as I was lying down, she went away to come again So towards tea-time I saw her and Augusta running along. Ellen discovered me at the window, and shouted and flew on. As they were ascending the stairs I heard Ellen say, "Now hold your hand behind you, Augusta!" They entered with hands concealed and gleaming faces, and when they were within reach suddenly the concealed hands were thrust towards my face, each adorned with a crimson rose. My exclamation of delight seemed to fulfill their desires; and now I want to know if it is not worth fifteen years of bodily pain and discomfort to be the cause of such divine sentiment in the souls of so many children as I am? I feel perfectly consecrated by it, and bound over to be worthy of such pure emotions. Oh, *not* mysterious Providence! How even are thy golden scales — sweetest compensations poising exactly the ills! It is not suffering which I think beautiful or desirable, but what suffering brings along with it, and *causes*. My door was open, and who should unexpectedly come out of Mary's room but Miss Elizabeth Hawthorne, going to walk with Mary. I was very glad to see her, and wanted her to come into my studio, but Mary was in haste to be walking. Miss Hawthorne looked very interesting. They had a delightful ramble, and she sent me a bunch of seaweed fastened to a rock, which she stepped into the sea to get for me. It looks like a drooping plume if it is held up, and I went into George's room to get his admiration; but he persisted in declaring it hideous. I was delighted by her thinking of sending it to me.

I happened to be up in the third story just as the children were going home [Mary was teaching two or three little girls], and they went into my studio with Mary. I was very much impressed with what I heard said in tones of reverence. "*Look* at that hammock! *Oh*, that pic-

THE HAWTHORNES AND THE PEABODYS

ture! And there are the flowers! Oh, *I* gave her those! Miss Peabody, is that a *bed? Oh,* how beautifully everything looks! Is Sophia gone out?" I cannot convey to you the intonations of affection and interest which made these sentences so touching.

This morning Mary came in and threw at me a beautiful handful of flowers, which I crowed over for a time, and then arose. I worked a little while at my painting, and then Mary Channing came gliding in upon me, like a dream, with more flowers, the Scotch rose and many rare things among them. Mr. Doughty [the artist, who had consented to give Sophia lessons] came, as bright as possible. The cool breezes, the flowers, etc., put him into excellent humor. He said it was luxury to sit and paint here. He created a glowing bank in broad sunshine. Mr. Russell called, and came up into my studio. He thought such a studio and such an occupation must cure the headache. Then I prepared to make several calls, but on my way was arrested by Mr. George Hillard, who was altogether too agreeable to leave. He is amazingly entertaining, to be sure. He remarked what a torment of his life Mr. Reed, the postmaster in Cambridge, was. He is an old man, about a hundred and forty years old, who always made him think of the little end of nothing sharpened off into a point. He had but one joke — to tell people sometimes when they asked for a letter that they must pay half a dollar for it; and then, if in their simplicity they gave it, he would laugh, and say it was a joke. After Mr. Hillard went away, Sally Gardiner came in with an armful of roses, which she poured upon me, taken from Judge Jackson's garden. She had just returned from Milton, and was overflowing with its grandeur and beauty.

Yours affectionately,

SOPHIE.

The somewhat invalided little artist was highly and widely admired; and to illustrate the happy fact I quote this letter, written by her spirited sister Mary : —

BOSTON, June 19, 1833.

MY DEAREST, — I went to Dr. Channing's yesterday afternoon and carried him your drawings, with which he was so enchanted that I left them for him to look at again. He gathered himself up in a little striped cloak, and all radiant with that soul of his, said with his most divine inflection, "This is a great and noble undertaking, and will do much for us here." And then he rolled his orbs upon me in that majestic way of his, which, when it melts into loveliness as it sometimes does, so takes captivity captive. In short, he was quite in an ecstasy with you and your notions. [Probably drawings illustrating auxiliary verbs.] He inquired very particularly for you, and showed me all the new books he had just received from England, which he thought a great imposition, they being big books. Edward [his brother] came in, and they greeted affection-

ately. After a long survey of the Professor, he
exclaimed, "Why, Edward, you look gross —
take care of the intellect!" Then he handed
him one of the great books, just arrived, which
was an edition of Thomas Belsham's works, with
a likeness of the author. "There," said he, "is
a man who had not quite the dimensions of a
hogshead; but he was the largest man I ever
saw." Edward looked rather uneasy. "William,"
he replied, "I don't think you are any judge of
large men. Last week I looked quite thin, but
to-day my head and face are very much swelled."
The Doctor, in the simplicity of his heart, never
thinks of feelings, only of things, as Plato would
say.   Your affectionate sister,
                                        MARY.

Sophia writes to Elizabeth in Boston, in 1838,
of her daily life, as follows : —

"I went to my hammock [in the studio] with
Xenophon. Socrates was divinest, after Jesus
Christ, I think. He lived up to his thought. . . .
After dinner, Mary went out 'to take the fresh,'
intending to finish the afternoon by a walk with
Miss Hawthorne, and I commissioned her to
bring home both her and her brother, if he should
go, that I might give him my fragrant violets. . . .

"Miss Hawthorne came to walk, and remarked
to Mary how beautiful the crocuses were which I
had given to her brother. Mary told her that I
sent them *to her.* 'That is a pretty story,' she
replied. 'He never told me so.'

"Just after seven Mr. Hawthorne came. He looked very brilliant. . . . His coming here is one sure way of keeping you in mind, and it must be excessively tame for him after his experience of your society and conversation ; so that, I think, you will shine the more by contrast."

One evening, she says, she "showed him Sarah Clarke's picture of the island, and that gorgeous flower in the Chinese book of which there is a mighty tree in Cuba. And then I turned over the pictures of those hideous birds, which diverted him exceedingly. One he thought deserved study. . . .

"I was to go to see his sister Elizabeth that afternoon, and he had heard about it. He asked if I could go, and said he should have waited for me to come if he had not supposed the east wind would prevent me. I said that it would. He wanted to know if I would come the next day. I meant to call Mary, but he prevented me by saying he could not stay long enough. . . . [He seldom stayed unless he found Sophia alone.]

"Last evening Mr. Hawthorne came for Mary to go with him to Miss Burley's [to a club which met every week]. Mary could not go. It seemed a shame to refuse him. I came down to catch a glimpse of him. He has a celestial expression which I do not like to lose. . . .

"The children have just come in, and brought me a host of odorous violets. I made George a visit in the afternoon, in the midst of my battle with headache, and to my question of 'How dost?' he replied, for the first time, 'Pretty fair,' instead of the unvarying 'Middling.' Skeptics surely cannot disbelieve in one thing that is invisible, and that is Pain."

May, 1838.

After my siesta I went down to Herbert Street with the book I wished to leave, and when I opened the gate [of the Hawthornes' house] the old woman with her hood on [an aunt of the Hawthornes] was stooping over a flower-bed, planting seeds. She lifted her smiling face, which must have been very pretty in her youth, and said, "How do you do, Miss Peabody?" Yet I never saw her in my life before. She begged me to walk in, but I refused, and gave her my message of thanks for the book.

Ever thine wholly,
SOPHIECHEN.

May 14, 1838.

To-day I was tempted to trot about the room and arrange all my vases, and give an air to the various knickknacks. I am much more easily tired than ever before. My walk to Castle Hill before February did not make me feel so hopelessly tired as it now does to walk as far as the Hawthornes'. Mr. Hawthorne had declined to come to dine with you on your arrival, but was to be here directly after dinner. When he came I happened to be the only one ready to go down. His first question was, "Where is Elizabeth?" He was not at all inclined to bear the disappointment

15

of your not being here, after all. He thought it "too bad," "insufferable," "not fair," and wondered what could be the reason. I told him your excuse, and that there was a letter for him, which Mary soon brought. He put it into his pocket without breaking the seal. He looked very handsome, and was full of smiles. I assured him the morning was the best time to do creative work. He said he believed he would go and take a walk in South Salem. "Won't you go?" he asked of me. But the wind was east.

My dear Lizzie, — I can think of nothing now but Charles Emerson. A sudden gloom seems to overshadow me. I hope you will tell us to-morrow whether he is dangerously ill. We had an exquisite visit from Waldo. It was the warbling of the Attic bird. The gleam of his *diffused* smile; the musical thunder of his voice; his repose, so full of the essence of life; his simplicity — just think of all these, and of my privilege in seeing and hearing him. He enjoyed everything we showed him so much. He talked so divinely to Raphael's Madonna del Pesce. I vainly imagined I was very quiet all the while, preserving a very demure exterior, and supposed I was sharing his oceanic calm. But the next day I was aware that I had been in a very intense state. I told Mary, that night after he had gone, that I felt like a *gem;* that was the only way I could express it. I don't know what Mary hoped to get from him, but *I* was sure of drinking in that which would make me paint Cuban skies better than even my recollections could have made me, were they as vivid as the rays of the sun in that sunniest of climates. He made me feel as Eliza Dwight did once, when she looked uncommonly beautiful and animated. I felt as if her beauty was all about the room, and that I was in it, and therefore beautiful too. It seemed just so with Waldo's soul-beauty. Good-by,

SOPHY.

June 1, 1838.

One afternoon Elizabeth Hawthorne came to walk with Mary, and mother went with her instead. She first came up into my chamber, and seemed well pleased with it, but especially admired the elm-tree outside. She looked very interesting. Mother took her to the cold spring, and they did not return till just at dark, loaded with airy anemones and blue violets and a few columbines. They had found Mr. John King and his daughter at the spring, looking for wild-flowers, and mother introduced Miss Hawthorne; but she hung her head and scarcely answered, and did not open her lips again, though Mr. King accompanied them all the way home. He gave mother some columbines, and after a while said, "I must make your bunch like Mrs. Peabody's, my dear," and so put some more into Miss Hawthorne's hand.

The day before Mr. Hawthorne had called at noon to see our ladyships, and I never saw him

17

look so brilliantly *rayonnant*. He said to me, " *Your story* will be finished soon, Sophia — to-morrow or next day." I was surprised to have the story so appropriated, and I do long to see it. [Probably Edward Randolph's Portrait.] He proposed to Mary to go to the beach the same day, and she consented. He said that he had not spoken to his sister about it, but would do so as soon as he went home. He wished to go early, and have a good walk. Only think what progress! To come and propose a walk at mid-day!

He said he had a letter nearly written to you, but should not finish it till you wrote. He seemed quite impatient to hear from you, and remarked that he had not heard since you were here. Mary went to Herbert Street to join Miss Haw-thorne for the walk, but did not see her. Her mother said Elizabeth did not want to go because it was windy, and the sun was too hot, and clouds were in the south! (It was the loveliest day in the world.) Was it not too bad to disap-point her brother so? I could have whipped her. When Mary went the next day with the tulips, Louisa told her that Elizabeth was very sorry afterwards that she did not go.

A successful visit, almost accidental, upon Ebie Hawthorne pleased Sophia very much, and she writes : —

" She was very agreeable, and took the trouble to go and get some engravings of heads to show me, Wordsworth among the number, which I had never seen before.

"Elizabeth also inquired particularly for George, and gave me more books for him. She asked if we did not miss you exceedingly. I should like to have stayed for two or three hours. She came downstairs with me, and out of the door, and talked about the front yard, where her aunt is going to make a garden."

Elizabeth Peabody's letters are always delightfully direct, and varied in quality of emotion, being equally urgent over philosophy or daily bread, as the ensuing one will show in part :—

53 MYRTLE STREET, BOSTON, 1838.

MY DEAR SOPHIA, — Your beautiful letters require an answer, but I cannot possibly answer them in kind. This evening, notwithstanding the storm, George and Susan Hillard have gone to a singing-school, and left me to amuse myself. I hoped Mr. Hawthorne would come in. I have not seen him yet. Last night I took tea with Sally Gardiner and Miss Jackson, who are still enjoying your Flaxman drawings. Why do not you Salem folks have a hencoop and keep hens! five or six hens would *overwhelm* you with eggs all the year round. I like to hear the little items about Hawthorne. I had a nice talk with Mr. Capen about him to-day. He has him in his mind, and I hope it will come to some good purpose for the public.

Yours truly and ever,   E. P. P.

Sophia writes : —

July 23, 1838.

William White arrived on Saturday. Why did not you send Stuart's Athens by him? He said that he had heard it remarked that Mr. Emerson expected another Messiah. Your slight account of Mr. E.'s "Address" is enough to wake the dead, and I do not know what the original utterance must have done. I told Mary I thought Mr. Emerson was the Word again. She exclaimed, "You blasphemer!" "Do you really think it blasphemy?" said I. "Oh no," she replied. "It is the gospel *according to you.*" Was not that a happy saying? While the maid was at Miss Burley's on an errand, she saw Mr. Hawthorne enter, probably for a take-leave call. He was here also, looking radiant. He said he took up my Journal [written in Cuba] to bring it back, but my "works were so voluminous that he concluded to send them!"

Elizabeth Peabody makes, upon her return to Salem for the winter, an heroic move towards gaining a still more affectionate advantage over the solitaries in Herbert Street. A little smile must have given her face its most piquant expression as she wrote : —

Saturday, November 10, 1838.

DEAR LOUISA, — You know I want to knit those little stockings and shoes, — I think I will do it in the course of time *at your house,* — and would thank you to buy the materials for me, and

20

I will pay you what they cost, when I know what it is. I suppose the four or five evenings which I shall anticipate spending with you (in the course of the winter!) will complete the articles.

When Elizabeth wakes, please give her this note and rose and book; and when Nathaniel comes *to dinner* please give him the note I wrote to him. He said he was going to write to-day, and therefore I should prefer that he should not be interrupted on purpose to read it. We will not interrupt the bird in his song. I *wonder* what sort of a preparation he finds an evening of whist, for the company of the Muse!

Yours ever truly,

E. P. PEABODY.

It is delightful to picture the commotion in the fernlike seclusion which enveloped the women of the Hawthorne household when this note was opened and read. Squirrels aroused, owls awakened, foxes startled, would have sympathized. Louisa, the only really active member of the trio, wonderfully deft in finest sewing and embroidery, generously willing to labor for all the relatives when illness required, may not have felt faint or fierce. But Mrs. Hawthorne, even in the covert of her chamber, where she chiefly resided, no doubt drew back; and Elizabeth's beautiful eyes must have shone superbly. However, to prove that the trio among the ferns (guarding, as testimony proves, Hawthorne himself with unasked care) could serve the needs of others on occasion,

I will insert a little letter of a much earlier date, from Louisa.

TO MISS MARY MANNING, RAYMOND, MAINE, CARE OF RICHARD MANNING, ESQ.

SALEM, March 3, 1831.

MY DEAR AUNT, — Uncle Sammie has returned from Boston, and has taken up his abode for the present at uncle Robert's [his brother, who befriended Hawthorne in his early youth], and is much better than we expected to see him. We should have been glad to have him with us, and would have done everything in our power to make him happy. We are so near that he can at any time command our services and our company. Nathaniel goes in to see him, and I am there a great part of the time. Mother has kept about all winter. There have been worse storms than I ever remember ; the roads were absolutely impassable, and the snow-banks almost as high as the house. I would write more, but my time is much taken up now. I remain yours,

With much affection,
M. L. HATHORNE.

That the reluctance to be genial with very genial folk was bravely overcome (to some extent) the ensuing notes prove : —

DEAR ELIZABETH, — As you were out on Saturday evening, I hope you will be able to come and spend to-morrow evening with us — will you not? I should be extremely happy to see Mary, though I despair of it; and though I cannot venture to ask Sophia, perhaps you can for me. Pray tell me particularly how your father is; we are all anxious to hear; and whether George is as he was when we heard last.

I am, in haste,   E. M. H.

DEAR ELIZABETH, — Shall we go to the beach? If so, I propose that we set off *instanter.* I think a sea-breeze would be most refreshing this afternoon.   Truly yours,

M. T. P.

Don't forget to ask your brother.

MY DEAR E., — I am afraid I shall not be able to go and spend an evening with you while the girls are gone. To-morrow, you know, is the eclipse. I wish you would come here in the afternoon. The graveyard is an open place to see it from, and I should be very glad of your company. Yesterday I heard of Nathaniel. A gentleman was shut up with him on a rainy day in a tavern in Berkshire, and was *perfectly charmed* with his luck.   In haste, yours,

E. P. P.

By and by Elizabeth Peabody returns to Boston, and Sophia goes on with letters: —

I do not think I am subject to my imagination; I can let an idea go to the grave that I see

23

is false. When I am altogether true to the light I have, I shall be in the heaven where the angelic Very now is. I went to see dear Miss Burley, who sent for me to go to her room. She insisted upon accompanying me all the way downstairs, limping painfully, and *would* open the outer door for me, and bow me out with as much deference as if I had been Victoria, or Hawthorne himself! So much for the Word uttering itself through my fingers in the face of Ilbrahim. [She had just finished illustrating "The Gentle Boy" by a drawing which was greatly praised.]

Jones Very came to tea that afternoon. He was troubled at first, but we comforted him with sympathy. His conversation with George was divine, and such level rays of celestial light as beamed from his face upon George, every time he looked up at him, were lovely to behold. We told him of our enjoyment of his sonnets. He smiled, and said that, unless we thought them beautiful because we also heard the Voice in reading them, they would be of no avail. "Since I have shown you my sonnets," said he to me, "I think you should show me your paintings." Mary brought my drawing-book and "Æschylus" [wonderfully perfect drawings from Flaxman's illustrations]. He deeply enjoyed all. I told him of my Ilbrahim. He said he delighted in the "Twice-Told Tales." Yesterday Mr. Hawthorne came in, and said, "I am going to Miss Burley's, but you *must not* go. It is too cold. You certainly must not go." I assured him I should go, and was sorry I was not

wanted. He laughed, and said I *was not*. But
I persisted. He knew I should be made sick ;
that it was too cold. Meanwhile I put on an
incalculable quantity of clothes. Father kept
remonstrating, but not violently, and I gently
imploring. When I was ready, Mr. Hawthorne
said he was glad I was going. Mary was packed
up safely, also. I was very animated, and felt
much better than on either of the previous club
nights. Mr. Hawthorne declared it must be the
spirit of contradiction that made me so ; and I
told him it was nothing but *fact*. We walked
quite fast, for I seemed stepping on air. It was
partly because I had not got tired during the day.
It was splendid moonlight. I was not in the least
cold, except my thumb and phiz. Mr. H. said he
should have done admirably were it not for his
nose. He did not believe but that it would moderate, " For God tempers the wind to the shorn
lamb, and when you go out we may expect mild
weather ! " Was not that sweet ? Mr. H. and
I went into the parlor together, and Miss Burley
looked delighted. He was exquisitely agreeable,
and talked *a great deal*, and looked serene and
happy and exceedingly beautiful. Miss Burley
showed Mary and me some botanical specimens,
and he came to the table and added much to the
lights. But oh, we missed you so much ; Miss
Burley said so, and I felt it. They do not understand Very, there. When we were taking leave,
Mr. Howes said to Mr. Hawthorne that he hoped
nothing would prevent his coming next Saturday.

"Oh no," replied he. "It is so much a custom, now, that I cannot do without it." Was not that delightful for Miss Burley's ears? I was so glad he said it. When we came out it was much more moderate, and we got home very comfortably. Mr. H. said he thought of coming for me to walk on Friday, but was afraid the walking was not good enough. I told him how we were all disappointed at his vanishing that night, and he laughed greatly. He said he should not be able to come this evening to meet Very, because he had something to read, for he was engaged Monday and Tuesday evening and could not read then. I am so sorry.

Yours affectionately,　　　　SOPHIE.

CHAPTER II

THE DAYS OF THE ENGAGEMENT

THE engagement of Hawthorne to his future wife was now a fact, but it was not spoken of except to one or two persons. Sophia had slipped away for a visit to friends in Boston ; but as Elizabeth was at present in Newton, her letters to the latter continued as follows : —

WEST STREET, BOSTON, May 19, 1839.

DEAREST LIZZIE, — Two days ago Mr. Hawthorne came. He said that there was nothing to which he could possibly compare his surprise, to find that the bird had flown when he went to our house. He said he sat for half an hour in the parlor before he knocked to announce his presence, feeling sure I would know he was there, and descend, — till at last he was tired of waiting. "Oh, it was terrible to find you gone," he said. And it was such a loss, to be sure, to me not to see him. I am glad you enjoyed his visit so much. He told me he should be at the picture-gallery the next morning [Sophia went very early to avoid the crowd], and there I found him at eight o'clock. He came home with me through a piercing east wind, which he was sure would make me ill for a week. In the evening he came

to see if it had given me a cold, but it had not.
Caroline [Tappan] was busy with her children,
and did not come down for half an hour. When
she did, she was very agreeable, and so was Mr.
Hawthorne. She admired him greatly. He said
he should be at the gallery this morning, if possible. I went before eight, and found the room
empty, except for Mr. William Russell. Mr. H.
arrived at nine, for, as it was cloudy weather
until then, he thought I would not be there, and
he came with the sunshine. At ten it began to
grow crowded, and we went out. He peremp-
torily declared I should ride.

Washington Allston had a great regard for
Sophia's talent in art. Elizabeth refers to it in a
letter written while visiting the Emersons : —

CONCORD, MASS., June 23, 1839.

Here I am on the Mount of Transfiguration,
but very much in the condition of the disciples
when they were prostrate in the dust. I got terribly tired in Boston. I went to the Athenæum
Gallery on Monday morning, and in the evening
Hawthorne came and said that he went to the
Allston gallery on Saturday afternoon. I went
to Allston's on Tuesday evening. He was in
delightful spirits, but soft as a summer evening.
He seemed transported with delight on hearing
of your freedom from pain, and was eager to know
what you were going to paint. I said you had
several things a-going, but did not like to tell of

your plans. He said, then you would be more
likely to execute them, and that it was a good
thing to have several paintings at once, because
that would save time, as you could rest yourself
by change. I carried to him a volume of "Twice-
Told Tales," to exchange for mine. He said he
thirsted for imaginative writing, and all the family
had read the book with great delight. I am really
provoked that I did not bring "The Token"
with me, so as to have "The Mermaid" and "The
Haunted Mind" to read to people. I was hardly
seated here, after tea yesterday, before Mr. Emerson asked me what I had to say of Hawthorne,
and told me that Mr. Bancroft said that Hawthorne was the most efficient and best of the Custom House officers. Pray tell that down in Herbert Street. Mr. Emerson seemed all congenial
about him, but has not yet read his writings. He
is in a good mood to do so, however, and I intend
to bring him to his knees in a day or two, so that
he will read the book, and all that Hawthorne has
written. He is in a delightful state of mind ; not
yet rested from last winter's undue labors, but
keenly industrious. He has uttered no heresies
about Mr. Allston, but only beautiful things, —
dwelling, however, on his highest merits least.
He says Very forbids all correcting of his verses ;
but nevertheless he [Emerson] selects and com-
bines with sovereign will, "and shall," he says,
"make out quite a little gem of a volume."
"But," says he, "Hawthorne says he [Very] is
always vain. I find I cannot forget that dictum

29

which you repeated; but it is continually con-
firmed by himself, amidst all his sublimities."
And then he repeated some of Very's speeches,
and told how he dealt with him. I am very
stupid. I have been *awake* for about two months!
Mr. Emerson is very luminous, and wiser than
ever. Oh, he is beautiful, and good, and great!

Your sister,   E.

Sophia, once more in Salem, replies : —

June 29, 1839.

I am very sorry you were disappointed by not
meeting Mr. Hawthorne at the galleries. But I
am delighted that you saw Mr. Allston. How
kind and inspiring is his interest about my health.
I am rejoiced that Mr. Emerson has uttered no
heresies about our High Priest of Nature. For
him to think that because a man is born to-day
instead of yesterday he cannot move the soul
seems quite inconsistent with his proclamation
that "the sun shines to-day, also!"

When some other callers had departed, came
Mr. Hawthorne. It was a powerful east wind,
and he would not let me go out ; but we were
both so virtuous that he went alone to Miss Burley's. You never can know what a sacrifice that
was! If you could, you would never again accuse
either of us of disregard of the claims of others.
I told him what Mr. Bancroft said, and he blushed
deeply, and replied, "What fame!" After he
went away, I read "Bettina von Arnim." She
is not to be judged ; she is to be received and

believed. She is genius, life, love, inspiration. If anybody undertakes to criticise her before me, I intend to vanish, if it is from a precipice into the sea. Tuesday, my Demon called upon me to draw some of the Auxiliary Verbs. . . .

July 5. Yesterday was the great day, and this wretched town made no appropriations for celebrating it — not even for the ringing of bells. So the people in wrath hung flags at half-mast, and declared they would toll the bells. Then it was granted that there should be joyful ringing at noon and sunset. They pealed forth jubilantly, and I heard the clash of cymbals in the afternoon. Every soul in America should thrill on the anniversary of the most illustrious event in all history ; and as some souls sleep, these should be stirred with bells, trumpets, and eloquence.

To-day the Demon demanded the completion of St. George and Una; and, alternating with my music, I drew all the morning. A horse has leaped out of my mind. I wonder what those learned in horses would say to him. George says he is superb. My idea was to have St. George's whole figure express the profoundest repose, command, and self-involvedness, while the horse should be in most vivid action and motion, the glory of his nostrils terrible, "as much disdaining to the curb to yield." The foam of power, and the stillness of power. You must judge if I have succeeded. The figure of Una is now far better than the first one. You cannot imagine with what ease I draw ; I feel as if I could and might do anything, now. Next week, if Outlines do not prevail, I shall begin again with oils. I feel on a height. Oh, I am so happy! But I have not ridden horseback since Tuesday on account of the weather. Is it not well that I kept fast hold of the white hand of Hope, dear Betty? For behold where she has led me! My wildest imaginations, during my hours of sickness in the past, never could have compassed such a destiny. All my life long my word has been, "This is well, and to-morrow it will be better; and God knows when to bring that morrow." You mistake me if you thought I ever believed that we should not be active *for others*. That is of course. With regard to our own minds, it seems to me we should take holy care of the present moment, and leave the end to God.

Now I am indeed made deeply conscious of what it is to be loved. Most tunefully sweet is this voice which affirms ever, for negation belongs to this world only. Its breath so informs the natural body that the spiritual body begins to plume its wings within, and I seem appareled in celestial light.

A few paragraphs from letters written by Hawthorne follow: —

Six o'clock, P. M.

What a wonderful vision that is — the dream-angel. I do esteem it almost a miracle that your pencil should unconsciously have produced it; it is as much an apparition of an ethereal being as if the heavenly face and form had been shadowed forth in the air, instead of upon paper. It seems to me that it is our guardian angel, who kneels at the footstool of God, and is pointing to us upon earth, and asking earthly and heavenly blessings for us, — entreating that we may not be much longer divided, that we may sit by our own fireside. . . .

BOSTON, September 9, half past eight P. M., 1839.

I was not at the end of Long Wharf to-day, but in a distant region; my authority having been put in requisition to quell a rebellion of the captain and "gang" of shovelers aboard a coal-vessel. . . . Well — I have conquered the rebels, and proclaimed an amnesty; so to-morrow I shall return to that Paradise of Measures, the end of Long Wharf. Not to my former salt-ship, she being now discharged; but to another, which will probably employ me wellnigh a fortnight longer. The salt is white and pure — there is something holy in salt.

BOSTON, 1839.

Your wisdom is not of the earth; it has passed through no other mind, but gushes fresh and pure from your own, and therefore I deem myself the safer when I receive your outpourings as a revelation from Heaven. Not but what you have read, and tasted deeply, no doubt, of the thoughts of other minds; but the thoughts of other minds make no change in your essence, as they do in almost everybody else's essence. You are still sweet Sophie Hawthorne, and still your

33

soul and intellect breathe forth an influence like that of wildflowers, to which God, not man, gives all their sweetness. . . . If the whole world had been ransacked for a name, I do not think that another could have been found to suit you half so well. It is as sweet as a wildflower. You ought to have been born with that very name — only then I should have done you an irreparable injury by merging it in my own.

You are fitly expressed to my soul's apprehension by those two magic words — Sophia Hawthorne! I repeat them to myself sometimes; and always they have a new charm. I am afraid I do not write very clearly, having been pretty hard at work since sunrise. You are wiser than I, and will know what I have tried to say. . . .

NATHANIEL HAWTHORNE.

Their engagement was not announced for about a year, because it was expected that it would be a very long one; and also to avoid, for as great an interval as possible, causing consternation in Herbert Street, since there, the approach of any permanent change on Hawthorne's part from a quiet sojourn under shadows and through enchantingly mellowed lights was looked upon as a Waterloo.

I go back a little from the last date to give the following fragment of a diary, contained in a small leather-bound memorandum-book, marked on the cover "Scrap-Book, 1839." The period covered is a brief portion of Hawthorne's service as weigher and gauger in the Boston Custom House, a position to which he was appointed by George Bancroft, at that time collector of the port.

February 7, 1839. Yesterday and day before, measuring a load of coal from the schooner Thomas Lowder, of St. John, N. B. A little, black, dirty vessel. The coal stowed in the hold, so as to fill the schooner full, and make her a solid mass of black mineral. The master, Best, a likely young man ; his mate a fellow jabbering in some strange gibberish, English I believe — or nearer that than anything else — but gushing out all together — whole sentences confounded into one long, unintelligible word. Irishmen shoveling the coal into the two Custom House tubs, to be craned out of the hold, and others wheeling it away in barrows, to be laden into wagons. The first day, I walked the wharf, suffering not a little from cold ; yesterday, I sat in the cabin whence I could look through the interstices of the bulk-head, or whatever they call it, into the hold. My eyes, what a cabin! Three paces would more than measure it in any direction, and it was filled with barrels, not clean and new, but black, and containing probably the provender of the vessel ; jugs, firkins, the cook's utensils and kitchen furniture — everything grimy and sable with coal dust. There were two or three tiers of berths ; and the blankets, etc., are not to be thought of. A cooking stove, wherein was burning some of the coal — excellent fuel, burning as freely as wood, and without the bituminous melting of

Newcastle coal. The cook of the vessel, a grimy, unshaven, middle-aged man, trimming the fire at need, and sometimes washing his dishes in water that seemed to have cleansed the whole world beforehand — the draining of gutters, or caught at sink-spouts. In the cessations of labor, the Irishmen in the hold would poke their heads through the open space into the cabin and call "Cook!" — for a drink of water or a pipe — whereupon Cook would fill a short black pipe, put a coal into it, and stick it into the Irishman's mouth. Here sat I on a bench before the fire, the other guests of the cabin being the stevedore, who takes the job of getting the coal ashore, and the owner of the horse that raised the tackle — the horse being driven by a boy. The cabin was lined with slabs — the rudest and dirtiest hole imaginable, yet the passengers had been accommodated here in the trip from New Brunswick. The bitter zero atmosphere came down the companion-way, and threw its chill over me sometimes, but I was pretty comfortable — though, on reaching home, I found that I had swaggered through several thronged streets with coal streaks on my visage.

The wharfinger's office is a general resort and refuge for people who have business to do on the wharf, in the spaces before work is commenced, between the hours of one and two, etc. A salamander stove — a table of the signals, wharves, and agent of packets plying to and from Boston — a snuff-box — a few chairs — etc., constituting the furniture. A newspaper.

February 11. Talk at the Custom House on Temperance. Gibson gives an account of his brother's sore leg, which was amputated. Major Grafton talks of ancestors settling early in Salem — in 1632. Of a swallow's nest, which he observed, year after year, on revisiting his boyhood's residence in Salem, for thirty years. It was so situated under the eaves of the house, that he could put his hand in and feel the young ones. At last, he found the nest gone, and was grieved thereby. Query, whether the descendants of the original builders of the nest inhabited it during the whole thirty years. If so, the family might vie for duration with the majority of human families.

February 15. At the Custom House, Mr. Pike told a story of a human skeleton without a head being discovered in High Street, Salem, about eight years ago — I think in digging the foundations of a building. It was about four feet below the surface. He sought information about the mystery of an old traditionary woman of eighty, resident.in the neighborhood. She, coming to the spot where the bones were, lifted up her hands and cried out, "So! they 've found the rest of the poor Frenchman's bones at last!" Then, with great excitement, she told the bystanders how, some seventy-five years before, a young Frenchman had come from over-seas with a Captain Tanent, and had resided with him in Salem. He was said to be very wealthy, and was gayly appareled in the fashion of those times. After a while the Frenchman disappeared and Captain Tanent gave out that he had gone to some other place, and been killed there. After two or three years, it was found that the Captain had grown rich; but he squandered his money in dissipated habits, died poor — and there are now none left of the race. Many years afterwards, digging near his habitation, the workmen found a human skull; and it was supposed to be that of the young Frenchman, who was all along supposed to have been murdered by the Captain. They did not seek for the rest of the skeleton; and no more was seen of it till Mr. Pike happened to be present at the discovery. The bone first found was that of the leg. He described it as lying along horizontally, so that the head was under the corner of the house; and now I recollect that they were digging a post-hole when the last discovery was made, and at that of the head they were digging the foundation of the house. The bones did not adhere together, though the shape of a man was plainly discernible. There were no remnants of clothing.

Mr. Pike told furthermore how a lady of truth and respectability — a church member — averred to him that she had seen a ghost. She was sitting with an old gentleman, who was engaged in reading the newspaper; and she saw the figure of a woman advance behind him and look over his shoulder. The narrator then called to the old gentleman to look around. He did so rather pettishly, and said, "Well, what do you want me to look round for?" The figure either vanished or went out of the room, and he resumed the reading of his newspaper. Again the narrator saw the same figure of a woman come in and look over his shoulder, bending forward her head. This time she did not speak, but hemmed so as to attract the old gentleman's attention; and again the apparition vanished. But a third time it entered the room, and glided behind the old gentleman's chair, as before, appearing, I suppose, to glance at the newspaper; and this time, if I mistake not, she nodded or made some sort of sign to the woman. How the ghost vanished, I do not recollect; but the old gentleman, when told of the matter, answered very scornfully. Nevertheless, it turned out that his wife had died precisely, allowing for the difference of time caused by distance of place, at the time when this apparition had made its threefold visit.

Mr. Pike is not an utter disbeliever in ghosts, and has had some singular experiences himself: — for instance, he saw, one night, a boy's face, as plainly as ever he saw anything in his life, gazing at him. Another time — or, as I think, two or three other times — he saw the figure of a man standing motionless for half an hour in Norman Street, where the headless ghost is said to walk.

February 19. Mr. Pike is a shortish man, very stoutly built, with a short neck — an apoplectic frame. His forehead is marked, but not expansive, though large — I mean, it has not a broad, smooth quietude. His face dark and sallow — ugly, but with a pleasant, kindly, as well as strong

and thoughtful expression. Stiff, black hair,
which starts bushy and almost erect from his
forehead — a heavy, yet very intelligent countenance. He is subject to the asthma, and moreover to a sort of apoplectic fit, which compels
[him] to sleep almost as erect as he sits ; and if
he were to lie down horizontally in bed, he would
feel almost sure of one of these fits. When they
seize him, he awakes feeling as if [his] head were
swelled to enormous size, and on the point of
bursting — with great pain. He has his perfect
consciousness, but is unable to call for assistance,
or make any noise except by blowing forcibly
with his mouth, and unless this brings help, he
must die. When shaken violently, and lifted to
a sitting posture, he recovers. After a fit, he
feels a great horror of going to bed again. If
one were to seize him at his boarding-house, his
chance would be bad, because if any heard his
snortings, they would not probably know what
was the matter. These two afflictions might
seem enough to make one man miserable, yet he
appears in pretty fair spirits.

He is a Methodist, has occasionally preached,
and believes that he has an assurance of salvation immediate from the Deity. Last Sunday,
he says, he gave religious instruction to a class in
the State's Prison.

Speaking of his political hostilities, he said that
he never could feel ill will against a person when
he personally met him, that he was not capable of
hatred, but of strong affection, — that he always

remembered that "every man once had a mother, and she loved him." A strong, stubborn, kindly nature this.

The City-Crier, talking in a familiar style to his auditors — delivering various messages to them, intermixed with his own remarks. He then runs over his memory to see whether he has omitted anything, and recollects a lost child — "We 've lost a child," says he ; as if, in his universal sympathy for all who have wants, and seek the gratification of them through his medium, he were one with the parents of the child. He then tells the people, whenever they find lost children, not to keep them overnight, but to bring them to his office. "For it is a cruel thing" — to keep them ; and at the conclusion of his lecture, he tells them that he has already worn out his lungs, talking to them of these things. He completely personifies the public, and considers it as an individual with whom he holds converse, — he being as important on his side, as they on theirs.

An old man fishing on Long Wharf with a pole three or four feet long — just long enough to clear the edge of the wharf. Patched clothes, old, black coat — does not look as if he fished for what he might catch, but as a pastime, yet quite poor and needy looking. Fishing all the afternoon, and takes nothing but a plaice or two, which get quite sun-dried. Sometimes he hauls up his line, with as much briskness as he can,

and finds a sculpin on the hook. The boys come
around him, and eye his motions, and make pitying or impertinent remarks at his ill-luck — the
old man answers not, but fishes on imperturbably.
Anon, he gathers up his clams or worms, and his
one sun-baked flounder — you think he is going
home — but no, he is merely going to another
corner of the wharf, where he throws his line
under a vessel's counter, and fishes on with the
same deathlike patience as before. He seems not
quiet so much as torpid, — not kindly nor unkindly feeling — but not to have anything to do
with the rest of the world. He has no business,
no amusement, but just to crawl to the end of
Long Wharf, and throw his line over. He has
no sort of skill in fishing, but a peculiar clumsi-
ness.

Objects on a wharf — a huge pile of cotton
bales, from a New Orleans ship, twenty or thirty
feet high, as high as a house. Barrels of molasses, in regular ranges ; casks of linseed oil. Iron
in bars landing from a vessel, and the weigher's
scales standing conveniently. To stand on the
elevated deck or rail of a ship, and look up the
wharf, you see the whole space of it thronged
with trucks and carts, removing the cargoes of
vessels, or taking commodities to and from stores.
Long Wharf is devoted to ponderous, evil-smell-
ing, inelegant necessaries of life — such as salt,
salt-fish, oil, iron, molasses, etc.

Near the head of Long Wharf there is an old
sloop, which has been converted into a store for

the sale of wooden ware, made at Hingham. It
is afloat, and is sometimes moored close to the
wharf ; — or, when another vessel wishes to take
its place, midway in the dock. It has been there
many years. The storekeeper lives and sleeps
on board.

Schooners more than any other vessels seem
to have such names as Betsey, Emma-Jane, Sarah,
Alice, — being the namesakes of the owner's wife,
daughter, or sweet-heart. They are a sort of
domestic concern, in which all the family take an
interest. Not a cold, stately, unpersonified thing,
like a merchant's tall ship, perhaps one of half a
dozen, in which he takes pride, but which he does
not love, nor has a family feeling for. Now Betsey, or Sarah-Ann, seems like one of the family
— something like a cow.

Long flat-boats, taking in salt to carry it up
the Merrimack canal, to Concord, in New Hampshire. Contrast and similarities between a stout,
likely country fellow, aboard one of these, to
whom the scenes of a sea-port are entirely new,
but who is brisk, ready, and shrewd in his own
way, and the mate of a ship, who has sailed to
every port. They talk together, and take to each
other.

The brig Tiberius, from an English port, with
seventy or thereabouts factory girls, imported to
work in our factories. Some pale and delicate-
looking ; others rugged and coarse. The scene
of landing them in boats, at the wharf-stairs, to
the considerable display of their legs ; — whence

they are carried off to the Worcester railroad in hacks and omnibuses. Their farewells to the men — Good-by, John, etc., — with wavings of handkerchiefs as long as they were in sight.

A pert, petulant young clerk, continually fooling with the mate, swearing at the stevedores and laboring men, who regard him not. Somewhat dissipated, probably.

The mate of a coal-vessel — a leathern belt round his waist, sustaining a knife in a leathern sheath. Probably he uses it to eat his dinner with ; perhaps also as a weapon.

A young sailor, with an anchor handsomely traced on the back of his hand — a foul anchor — and perhaps other naval insignia on his wrists and breast. He wears a sky-blue silk short jacket, with velvet collar — a bosom-pin, etc.

An old seaman, seventy years of age — he has spent seven years in the British Navy (being of English birth) and nine in ours ; has voyaged all over the world — for instance, I asked if he had ever been in the Red Sea, and he had, in the American sloop of war that carried General Eaton, in 1803. His hair is brown — without a single visible gray hair in it ; and he would seem not much above fifty. He is of particularly quiet demeanor — but observant of all things, and reflective — a philosopher in a check shirt and sail-cloth trousers. Giving an impression of the strictest integrity — of inability not to do his duty, and his whole duty. Seemingly, he does not take a very strong interest in the world, be-

ing a widower without children; but he feels
kindly towards it, and judges mildly of it; and
enjoys it very tolerably well, although he has so
slight a hold on it that it would not trouble him
much to give it up. He said he hoped he should
die at sea, because then it would be so little
trouble to bury him. He is a skeptic, — and
when I asked him if he would not wish to live
again, he spoke doubtfully and coldly. He said
that he had been in England within two or three
years — in his native county, Yorkshire — and
finding his brother's children in very poor condition, he gave them sixty golden sovereigns. " I
have always had too many poor friends," he said,
"and that has kept me poor." This old man
kept tally of the Alfred Tyler's cargo, on behalf
of the Captain, diligently marking all day long,
and calling " tally, Sir," to me at every sixth tub.
Often would he have to attend to some call of
the stevedores, or wheelers, or shovelers — now
for a piece of spun-yarn — now for a handspike —
now for a hammer, or some nails — now for some
of the ship's molasses, to sweeten water — the
which the Captain afterwards reprehended him
for giving. These calls would keep him in about
movement enough to give variety to his tallying
— he moving quietly about the decks, as if he
belonged aboard ship and nowhere else. Then
sitting down he would converse (though by no
means forward to talk) about the weather, about
his recent or former voyages, etc., etc., etc., we
dodging the intense sun round the main mast.

Sophia writes to Hawthorne from Milton : —

Sunday A. M., May 30, 1841.

DEAREST, — The chilling atmosphere keeps me from church to-day. . . . Since I saw you at the Farm, I wish far more than ever to have a home for you to come to, after associating with men at the Farm [Brook Farm] all day. A sacred retreat you should have, of all men. Most people would not desire or like it, but notwithstanding your exquisite courtesy and conformableness and geniality there, I could see very plainly that you were not leading your ideal life. Never upon the face of any mortal was there such a divine expression of sweetness and kindliness as I saw upon yours during the various transactions and witticisms of the excellent fraternity. Yet it was also the expression of a witness and hearer, rather than of comradeship. Had I perceived a particle of even the highest kind of pride in your manner, it would have spoiled the perfect beauty and fitness.

M. L. Sturgis, in a little note, gives a glimpse of Sophia's world at that date : —

"I have seen your 'Gentle Boy' to-night. I like it very much indeed. The boy I love already. Do you see Mr. Hawthorne often ? It was a shame he did not talk more that night at the Farm. Just recall that beautiful moon over the water, and those dear trees!"

Ellen Hooper, when the engagement is known, shows how people felt about the new author : —

"Your note seems to require a mood quite apart from the 'every day' of one's life, wherein to be read and answered. . . . I do not know Mr. Hawthorne—and yet I do; and I love him with that eminently Platonic love which one has for a friend *in black and white* [print]. He seems very near to me, for he is not only a dreamer, but wakes now and then with a pleasant 'Good-morrow' for shabby human interests. I am glad to hear that he is *healthful*, for I profoundly admire this quality; and particularly in one who is not entitled to it on the ground of being stupid!"

Sophia's aptness for writing poetry led her to inclose this poem to her future husband in one of her letters:—

> God granteth not to man a richer boon
> Than tow'rd himself to draw the waiting soul,
> Making it swift to pray this high control
> Would with according grace its jars attune.
> And man on man the largest gift bestows
> When from the vision-mount he sings aloud,
> And pours upon the unascended crowd
> Pure Order's heavenly stream that o'er him flows.
> So thou, my friend, hast risen through thought supreme
> To central insight of eternal law.
> Thy golden-cadenced intuitions gleam
> From that new heaven which John of Patmos saw;
> And I my spirit lowly bend to thine,
> In recognition of thy words divine.

From Salem she writes to Elizabeth, her summer jaunt being over:—

"I have not *touched* a pencil since I came home. I cannot be grateful enough that I can be hands and feet to the dearest mother in the world, who has all my life been all things to me, so delicate as I have been. There is pastime, pleasure, and a touch of the infinitely beautiful to me in what is generally considered *drudgery;* and I find there is nothing so inconsiderable in life that the moving of the spirit of love over it does not commute it into essential beauty."

48

CHAPTER III

JUST before her marriage, on July 9, 1842, and her residence in the Old Manse, Sophia wrote to Mrs. Caleb Foote, of Salem : —

July 5.

MY DEAR MARY, — You mistake much when you say you will not hear from me after I have gone to my own home. I shall tell those who are dear to me that I love them still. I feel to-day like a rising Phœnix.

Mr. Hawthorne has been here, looking like the angel of the Apocalypse, so powerful and gentle. It seems as if I were realizing the dreams of the poets in my own person. Just think of the felicity of showing him my inscriptions with pencil and sculpturing-tool — and he so just and severe a critic ! He is far the best critic I ever had. The agent of Heaven in this Concord plan was Elizabeth Hoar ; a fit minister on such an errand, for minister means angel of God. Her interest has been very great in every detail. . . .

Yours affectionately,

SOPHIA.

The following note is descriptive of the real

49

happiness in the marriage, which was felt and often uttered by friends : —

DEAR SOPHIA, — I am not much used to expressing to others what I feel about them, but I will give way to the feeling which prompts me to tell you how much I think about you now. An event like your marriage with Mr. Hawthorne is, like the presence of a few persons in this world, precious to me as an assurance of the good we all long for. I do not know your husband personally, but I care for him so much that I could well do the thought of him a passing reverence, like the young man who, I was told, uncovered his head as he passed Mr. Hawthorne's house. Perhaps you are too much absorbed to recognize now, even in thought, the greeting of a friend ; perhaps we shall meet very little hereafter, as indeed we have hardly been intimate heretofore ; but I shall remember you with interest. Affectionately yours,

E. S. HOOPER.

Mrs. Hawthorne's letters and journals while at the Old Manse now portray a beautiful existence : —

CONCORD, December 18, 1842.

MY DEAR MARY [Mrs. Caleb Foote, of Salem], — I hoped I should see you again, before I came home to our Paradise. I intended to give you a concise history of my elysian life. Soon after we returned, my dear lord began to write in earnest ; and then commenced my leisure, because, till we meet at dinner, I do not see him. I have had to sew, as I did not touch a needle all summer, and far into the autumn, Mr. Hawthorne not letting me have a needle or a pen in my hand. We were interrupted by no one, except a short call now and then from Elizabeth Hoar, who can hardly be called an earthly inhabitant ; and Mr. Emerson, whose face pictured the promised land (which we were then enjoying), and intruded no more than a sunset, or a rich warble from a bird.

One evening, two days after our arrival at the Old Manse, George Hillard and Henry Cleveland appeared for fifteen minutes, on their way to Niagara Falls, and were thrown into raptures by the embowering flowers and the dear old house they adorned, and the pictures of Holy Mothers mild on the walls, and Mr. Hawthorne's Study, and the noble avenue. We forgave them for their appearance here, because they were gone as soon as they had come, and we felt very hospitable. We wandered down to our sweet, sleepy river, and it was so silent all around us and so solitary, that we seemed the only persons living. We sat beneath our stately trees, and felt as if we were the rightful inheritors of the old abbey, which had descended to us from a long line. The treetops waved a majestic welcome, and rustled their thousand leaves like brooks over our heads. But the bloom and fragrance of nature had become secondary to us, though we were lovers of it. In my husband's face and eyes I saw a fairer world, of which the other was a faint copy. I fast ceased to represent Lilias Fay, under the influence of happiness, peace, and rest. We explored the woods. Sarah the maid was very tasty, and we had beautiful order ; and when we ran races down the avenue, or I danced before my husband to the measures of the great music-box, she declared it did her heart good to see us as joyful as two children.

December 30. Sweet, dear Mary, nearly a fortnight has passed since I wrote the above. I really believe I will finish my letter to-day, though I do not promise. That magician upstairs is very potent ! In the afternoon and evening I sit in the Study with him. It is the pleasantest niche in our temple. We watch the sun, together, descending in purple and gold, in every variety of magnificence, over the river. Lately, we go on the river, which is now frozen ; my lord to skate, and I to run and slide, during the dolphin-death of day. I consider my husband a rare sight, gliding over the icy stream. For, wrapped in his cloak, he looks very graceful ; perpetually darting from me in long, sweeping curves, and returning again — again to shoot away. Our meadow at the bottom of the orchard is like a small frozen sea, now ; and that is the present scene of our heroic games. Sometimes, in the splendor of the dying light, we seem sporting upon transparent gold, so prismatic becomes the ice ; and the snow takes opaline hues, from the gems that float above as clouds. It is eminently the hour to see objects, just after the sun has disappeared. Oh, such oxygen as we inhale! Often other skaters appear, — young men and boys, — who principally interest me as foils to my husband, who, in the presence of nature, loses all shyness, and moves regally like a king. One afternoon, Mr. Emerson and Mr. Thoreau went with him down the river. Henry Thoreau is an experienced skater, and was figuring dithyrambic dances and Bacchic leaps on the ice — very remarkable, but very ugly, methought. Next him followed Mr. Hawthorne who, wrapped in his cloak, moved like a self-impelled Greek statue, stately and grave. Mr. Emerson closed the line, evidently too weary to hold himself erect, pitching headforemost, half lying on the air. He came in to rest himself, and said to me that Hawthorne was a tiger, a bear, a lion, — in short, a satyr, and there was no tiring him out ; and he might be the death of a man like himself. And then, turning upon me that kindling smile for which he is so memorable, he added, "Mr. Hawthorne is such an Ajax, who can cope with him ! "

After the first snowstorm, before it was so deep, we walked in the woods, very beautiful in winter, and found slides in Sleepy Hollow, where we became children, and enjoyed ourselves as of old, — only more, a great deal. Sometimes it is before breakfast that Mr. Hawthorne goes to skate upon the meadow. Yesterday, before he went out, he said it was very cloudy and gloomy, and he thought it would storm. In half an hour, oh, wonder ! what a scene ! Instead of black sky, the rising sun, not yet above the hill, had changed the firmament into a vast rose! On every side, east, west, north, and south, — every point blushed roses. I ran to the Study, and the meadow sea also was a rose, the reflection of that above. And there was my husband, careering about, glorified by the light. Such is Paradise.

In the evening we are gathered together beneath our luminous star, in the Study, for we have a large hanging astral lamp, which beautifully illumines the room, with its walls of pale yellow paper, its Holy Mother over the fireplace, and pleasant books, and its pretty bronze vase, on one of the secretaries, filled with ferns. Except once Mr. Emerson, no one hunts us out in the evening. Then Mr. Hawthorne reads to me. At present we can only get along with the old English writers, and we find that they are the hive from which all modern honey is stolen. They are thick-set with thought, instead of one thought serving for a whole book. Shakespeare is preëminent; Spenser is music. We dare to dislike Milton when he goes to heaven. We do not recognize God in his picture of Him. There is something so penetrating and clear in Mr. Hawthorne's intellect, that now I am acquainted with it, merely thinking of him as I read winnows the chaff from the wheat at once. And when he reads to me, it is the acutest criticism. Such a voice, too, — such sweet thunder! Whatever is not worth much shows sadly, coming through such a medium, fit only for noblest ideas. From reading his books you can have some idea of what it is to dwell with Mr. Hawthorne. But only a shadow of him is found in his books. The half is not told there. Your true friend,

SOPHIA A. HAWTHORNE.

P. S. Mr. Hawthorne sends his love to your husband.

CONCORD, April 6, 1843.

MY DEAREST MARY, — I received your letter of April 2 late last evening. It is one, I am sure, which might call a response out of a heart of adamant; and mine, being of a tenderer substance, it answers with all its chords. Dear, sweet, tender, loving Mary, you are more like Herder's Swan than anything else I can think of. The spirits of your translated babes bring you airs from heaven. What a lovely trinity of souls; what a fair star they form, according to Swedenborg's beautiful idea. I doubt not there is a path of descent, like that of Jacob's ladder, from their Father's bosom to your heart, and they ascend and descend, like those angels of his dream.

Dear Mary, just imagine my husband in reality, as faintly shadowed in his productions. Fresh as a young fountain, with childlike, transparent emotions; vivid as the flash of a sword in the sun with sharp wit and penetration; of such an unworn, unworldly observance of all that is enacted and thought under the sun; as free from prejudice and party or sectarian bias as the birds, and therefore wise with a large wisdom that is as impartial as God's winds and sunbeams. His frolic is like the sport of Milton's "unarmed

55

youth of heaven." But I will not pretend to describe his intellect; and I have by no means yet searched it out. I repose in it as upon some elemental force, which always seems just created, though we cannot tell when it began to be. Of his beautiful, genial, tender, and great nature I can still less adequately discourse. His magnanimity, strength, and sweetness alternately, and together, charm me. He fascinates, wins, and commands.

We have passed the winter delightfully, reading to each other, and lately studying German. I knew a little, just enough to empower me to hold the rod, and be somewhat impertinent, and I have entire preëminence in the way of pronunciation. But ever and anon I am made quite humble by being helped out of thick forests by my knight, instead of guiding him. So we teach each other in the most charming manner, and I call it the royal road to knowledge, finally discovered by us. Mr. Hawthorne writes all the morning. Do you see "The Democratic Review"? In the March number is "The Procession of Life." Mr. Jonathan Phillips told Elizabeth he thought it a great production, and immediately undertook to read all else my husband had written. "The Celestial Railroad," for the April number, is unique, and of deep significance. It is a rare privilege to hear him read his manuscript aloud with the true expression.

Elizabeth Hoar has taken tea with us only once this winter, and I have seen her very rarely. The walking is so bad in the country in winter that only tall boots can cope with it. Unawares one foot sinks down to the Celestial Empire, and the other anchors in the moon. I have had to confine myself principally to the avenue, through which our Flibbertigibbet [or Imp] made a clear path for me. Mr. Thoreau has been pretty often, and is very interesting. Mr. Emerson, from January, was at the South; so Sirius was not visible to the eye for nearly three months.

Among other things, I have been very much interested in teaching my Irish angel to read and write. She is as bright as Burke, and repays me an hundredfold by her progress. She is so sweet and generous and gentle, that it is pleasant to happen upon her pretty face about the house.

Mr. Hawthorne says I must tell you that he shall be most happy to meet you in heaven; but he wishes you would as a preliminary come and spend a week with us this summer. He says this is the best way to get acquainted with him.

To Mrs. Peabody, now living in Boston, Sophia writes : —

May.

DARLING MOTHER, — I find my heart cannot rest unless I send you an enormous bunch of columbines; and so I have concluded to take my cake-box and fill it with flowers. My husband and I have gathered all these columbines since dinner, on the bank of the river, two fields off from the battle-ground. Now I think of it, it is Lizzie's favorite wildflower. I cannot bear to think of you as two prisoners in the book-room, at this time. I do not know, however, as Elizabeth would be happy to remain in the country, because men and women are her flowers, and they do not grow on hills and slopes. But you were born to live in a garden, where flowers at your tendance might gladlier grow (according to Milton). We had a letter from Louisa Hawthorne to-day, which says that the cat Beelzebub is dead. We are going to put our Pigwiggin in mourning for her cousin. [Hawthorne was, as all his family were, remarkably fond of cats. He had given Beelzebub his name.]

Another letter now goes to Mrs. Foote : —

August 11.

BELOVED MARY, — I received your long expected letter during a visit from the Hillards. I feared you were ill, but not that you had forgotten me ; for I have an imperturbable faith in the love of my friends which appearances cannot affect.

No influenzas or epidemics of any kind reach our old abbey, though in the village of Concord they often prevail. I think the angel who descended with healing in his wings, and stirred the pool of Bethesda, must purify the air around us. We have had a charming summer. At the first flinging open of our doors my father made us a visit of a week, and, according to his love of order, put everything out of doors in place ; moved patriarchal boards covered with venerable moss, and vividly exercised all his mechanical powers. Among other things he prepared the clay with which I mould men and heroes, so that I began Mr. Hawthorne's bust. Next came Miss Anna Shaw [Mrs. S. G. Ward], in full glory of her golden curls, flowing free over her neck and brows, so that she looked like the goddess Diana, or Aurora. Everything happened just right. The day she arrived, Mr. Emerson came to dine, and shone back to the shining Anna. He was truly "tangled in the meshes of her golden hair," for he reported in several places how beautiful it was, afterwards. It was very warm, and after Mr. Emerson left us, we went out upon the lawn under the shady trees, and Anna extended herself on the grass, leaning her arms upon a low cricket, and "Sydnian showers of sweet discourse" distilled upon us. Towards sunset we went to the terrace on the bank of the river, and then there was a walk to Sleepy Hollow. Afterwards, we again resorted to the lawn, and the stars all came out over our heads with great brilliancy; and Anna, again upon the grass, pointed out the most beautiful constellations. Now we expect Louisa Hawthorne every day. Excepting for the three weeks and a little more occupied by our friends, we have been quite alone. The 9th of July, our wedding-day, was most heavenly, and at night there was a most lustrous moon. That night Mr. Allston died. Nature certainly arrayed herself in her most lovely guise, to bid him farewell.

Mr. Hawthorne has written a little, and cultivated his garden a great deal; and as you may suppose, such vegetables never before were tasted. It is a sober fact, dear Mary, that I never ate any so good. When Apollos tend herds and till the earth, it is but reasonable to expect unusual effects. I planted flowers, which grow pretty well. We have voyaged on the river constantly, harvesting water-lilies; and lately cardinal-flowers, which enrich the borders with their superb scarlet mantles in great conclaves.

I have just finished Ranke's "History of the Popes." I stumbled quite accidentally upon ecclesiastical history, lately. I asked my husband to bring me any book that he chanced to touch upon from his Study, one day, and it proved to be "Luther, and the Reformation." So I have gone on and backwards, upon the same subject. I read several volumes of the Theological Library, fretting all the time over the narrow spirit in which great men were written about. Finally I took Ranke. He is splendid and whole-sided, and has given me an idea of the state of Europe from the first times.

Elizabeth Hoar came while Susan Hillard was here, looking as usual like the Rose of Sharon, though thinner than ever. Ellery Channing and E. live in a little red cottage on the road, with one acre attached, upon which Ellery has worked very hard. E. keeps a small school for little children. They are very happy, and Ellery is a very charming companion. He talks very agreeably.

October 15.

BELOVED MARIE, — I received your requiem for Mrs. Peabody [not a near connection of Mrs. Hawthorne's, but of Mr. George Peabody's, the philanthropist] yesterday, and cannot delay responding to it. We talk a great deal about the reality of Heaven and the shadowiness of earth, but no one acts as if it were the truth. It seems as if the benign and tender Father of men, in whose presence we rejoice and confide, became suddenly changed into a dark power, and curtained Himself with gloom, the instant death laid its hand upon our present bodies, and freed the soul for another condition. And this, too, although Jesus Christ at the hour when His spirit resigned the clay rent the veil from top to bottom, and revealed to all eyes the golden cherubim and the Holy of Holies. God alone knows whether I could act my belief in the greatest of all possible earthly separations. But before I loved as I now do heaven was dim to me in comparison. I cannot conceive of a *separation* for one moment from my transfigured soul in him who is transfused with my being. I am in heaven now. Oh, let me not doubt it, if for a little while a shadow should wrap his material form from my sight.

I am in rejoicing and most vigorous health. After breakfast I paint for two or three hours. I am now copying Mr. Emerson's divine Endymion. After dinner we walk till about five.

The following letter refers to Sophia's sister Mary, who had become Mrs. Horace Mann : —

DEAREST MARY, — I do not know whether you were ever aware of the peculiar love I have felt from childhood for my precious sister, who is now so blest. It has always been enthusiastic and profound. Her still and perfect disinterestedness, her noiseless self-devotion, her transparent truthfulness and all-comprehensive benevolence through life! No words can ever express what a spear in my side it has been to see her year after year toiling for all but herself, and growing thin and pale with too much effort. Not that ever her heroic heart uttered a word of complaint or depreciation. But so much the more did I feel for her. I saw her lose her enchanting gayety, and become grave and sad, yet could do nothing to restore her spirits. I was hardly aware, until it was removed, how weighty had been the burden of her unfulfilled life upon my heart. At her engagement, all my wings were unfolded, and my body was light as air.

Mrs. Mann had been to Europe for her wedding-tour, and was thus welcomed home : —

November 7.

BELOVED MARY, — Yesterday noon my dear husband came home from the village but a few seconds — it seemed even to me — after he left me, shining with glad tidings. They were, that the steamer had arrived with you in it ! Imagine my joy, for I cannot tell it. You will come and see me, I am sure. I am especially commissioned by Mr. Emerson to request my dear and honorable brother, Mr. Mann, to come to Concord to lecture at the Lyceum as soon as he possibly can. He says that Mr. Hoar told him he had never heard such eloquence from human lips as from Mr. Mann's. "Therefore," says he, "this is the place of all others for him to come and lecture." Tell me beforehand whether your husband eats anything *in particular*, that I may have it all ready for him. I am in the greatest hurry that mortal has been in since Absalom ran from his pursuers.　　　　　Your own

SOPHIECHEN.

The record for Sophia's mother goes on unfailingly : —

November 19.

MY DEAREST MOTHER, — This Indian summer is very beautiful. The dulcet air and stillness are lovely. This morning we watched the opal dawn, and the stars becoming pale before it, as also the old moon, which rose between five and six o'clock, and, in the form of a boat of pure silvery-gold, floated up the sea of clear, rosy air. I am so very early a riser that the first faint light usually finds me busy.

I wish you could see how charmingly my husband's Study looks now. As we abandon our drawing-room this winter, I have hung on his

63

walls the two Lake Como and the Loch Lomond pictures, all of which I painted expressly for him ; and the little mahogany centre-table stands under the astral lamp, covered with a crimson cloth. The antique centre-table broke down one day beneath my dear husband's arms, with a mighty sound, astonishing me in my studio below the Study. He has mended it. On one of the secretaries stands the lovely Ceres, and opposite it Margaret Fuller's bronze vase. In the afternoon, when the sun fills the room and lights up the pictures, it is beautiful. Yet still more, perhaps, in the evening, when the astral enacts the sun, and pours shine upon all the objects, and shows, beneath, the noblest head in Christendom, in the ancient chair with its sculptured back [a chair said to have come over in the Mayflower, and owned by the Hawthorne family] ; and whenever I look up, two stars beneath a brow of serene white radiate love and sympathy upon me. Can you think of a happier life, with its rich intellectual feasts? That downy bloom of happiness, which unfaithful and ignoble poets have persisted in declaring always vanished at the touch and wear of life, is delicate and fresh as ever, and must remain so if we remain unprofane. The sacredness, the loftiness, the ethereal delicacy of such a soul as my husband's will keep heaven about us. My thought does not yet compass him.

December. For the world's eye I care nothing; but in the profound shelter of this home I would put on daily a velvet robe, and pearls in my hair, to gratify my husband's taste. This is a true

wife's world. Directly after dinner my lord went
to the Athenæum ; and when he returned, he sat
reading Horace Walpole till he went out to the
wood-house to saw and split wood. Presently I
saw, hastening up the avenue, Mr. George Bradford. He stayed to tea. His beautiful character
makes him perennial in interest. As my husband
says, we can see nature through him straight,
without refraction. My water this morning was
deadly cold instead of livingly cold, and I knew
the Imp must have taken it from some already
drawn, instead of right from the well. The maid
brought for me from Mrs. Emerson's "The Mys-
teries of Paris," which I read all the evening. I
have been to see E. Channing, who looked very
pretty. She has a dog named Romeo, which
Mrs. S. G. Ward gave them. I borrowed a book
of E. about sainted women. In "The Democratic
Review" was my husband's "Fire Worship." I
could not wait to read it ! It is perfectly inimitable, as usual. His wit is as subtle as fire. This
morning I got up by moonlight again, and sewed
till Mary brought my fresh-drawn water. The
moon did not set till after dawn. To-day I pro-
menaded in the gallery with wadded dress and
muff and tippet on. After tea, my lord read Jones
Very's criticism upon "Hamlet." This morning
was very superb, and the sunlight played upon
the white earth like the glow of rubies upon
pearls. My husband was entirely satisfied with
the beauty of it. He is so seldom fully satisfied
with weather, things, or people, that I am always

glad to find him pleased. Nothing short of perfection can content him. How can seraphs be contented with less? After breakfast, as I could not walk out on account of the snow, I concluded to housewife. My husband shoveled paths (heaps of snow being trifles to his might), and sawed and split wood, and brought me water from the well. To such uses do seraphs come when they get astray on earth. I painted till after one o'clock. There was a purple and gold sunset. After dinner to-day Mr. Hawthorne went to the village, and brought back "The Salem Gazette." Some one had the impudence to speak of him in it as "gentle Nat Hawthorne." I cannot conceive who could be so bold and so familiar. Gentle he surely is, but such an epithet does not comprehend him, and gives a false idea. As usual after sunset, he went out to find exercise till quite dark. Then he read aloud part of "The Tempest," while I sewed. In the evening he told me about his early life in Raymond [Maine], and he gave me some of Mr. Bridge's famous wine. To-day my husband partly read "Two Gentlemen of Verona." I do not like it much. What a queer mood Shakespeare must have been in, to write it. He seems to be making fun. I wrote to Mrs. Follen, and made up a budget of a paper from my husband for her "Child's Friend." It was the incident of Mr. Raike's life, with regard to his founding of Sunday-schools, most exquisitely told, and set in a frame of precious jewels. Whatever my husband touches turns to

gold in the intellectual and spiritual world. I
sewed on a purple blouse for him till dusk. We
have the luxury of our maid's absence, and Apollo
helped me by making the fires. I warmed rice
for myself, and had .the happiness of toasting his
bread. He read aloud "Love's Labour 's Lost,"
and said that play had no foundation in nature.
To-day there have been bright gleams, but no
steady sunshine. Apollo boiled some potatoes
for breakfast. Imagine him with that magnificent head bent over a cooking-stove, and those
star-eyes watching the pot boil! In consequence,
there never were such good potatoes before. For
dinner we did not succeed in warming the potatoes effectually; but they were edible, and we
had meat, cheese, and apples. This is Christmas
Day, which I consider the most illustrious and
sacred day of the year. Before sunrise, a great,
dark blue cloud in the east made me suppose it
was to be a dismal day; but I was quite mistaken, for it has been uncommonly beautiful.
Peace has seemed brooding "with turtle wing"
over the world, and no one stirs, as if all men
obeyed the command of the elements, which was,
"Be still, as we are." I intended to make a fine
bowl of chocolate for my husband's dinner, but
he proposed to celebrate Christmas by having no
cooking at all. At one o'clock we went together
to the village, my husband going to the Athenæum, and I to Mrs. Emerson's, where Mr. Thoreau was dining. On the way home I saw in the
distance the form of forms approaching. We

dined on preserved fruits and bread and milk, —
quite elegant and very nice. What a miracle my
husband is! He has the faculty of accommodating
himself to all sorts of circumstances with marvelous grace of soul. In the afternoon he brought
me some letters, one being from E. Hooper, with
verses which she had written after reading "Fire
Worship." The motto is "Fight for your stoves!"
and the measure that of "Scots wha hae." It is
very good. The maid returned. This morning
we awoke to a mighty snowstorm. The trees
stood white-armed all around us. In the afternoon some one knocked at the front door. I was
amazed, supposing no one could overcome the
roads, and thought it must be a government
officer. As the door opened, I heard a voice say,
"Where is the man?" It was Ellery Channing,
who exclaimed, as he appeared at the Study,
where we were, that it was the very time to come,
— he liked the snow. He looked like a shaggy
bear; but his face was quite shining, as usual.
He brought some novels and reviews, which
Queen Margaret [Fuller] had sent to Ellen Channing [her sister] to read. We had to leave him,
while we dined, at three. He would not join us,
and made his exit while we were in the dining-
room. To-day as I painted the wind arose, and
howled and swept about, and clouded the sun,
and wearied my spirits. I was obliged to put
away my palette at half past twelve o'clock, and
then came up, and looked into the Study at my
husband. He was writing, and I was conscience-

stricken for having interrupted him. We went to walk, and a neighbor invited us to drive to town in his sleigh. I accepted, but my husband did not. The Imp sprang on, as we passed his house ; and then I found that the kind old man was Mr. Jarvis of the hill. I went to the post-office, where my husband was reading a letter from Mr. Hillard. We stayed at the Athenæum till after two, and then braved the warring winds homewards. We had no reading in the evening, for the wind was too noisy.

January 1, 1844. A quiet morning at last ; the wind had howled itself dead, as if it were the breath of the Old Year, by midnight. On our way home to-day from the Athenæum, Dr. Bart-lett met us, and offered to take me along. On the way he spoke of George Bradford's worship-ing Mr. Hawthorne. I had a fine time painting, this morning. Everything went right, and I suc-ceeded quite to my mind. I felt sure my husband above me must also be having a propitious morn-ing. When he came to dinner, he said he did not know as he ever felt so much like writing on any one day. Mr. Emerson called.

January 9.

BELOVED MOTHER, — I dated all the docu-ments I sent by Plato [Mr. Emerson] a day too late. My husband will dispatch a budget to Mr. Hillard's care, containing a paper which he is to send to Mr. Griswold, editor of " Graham's Mag-azine." He wrote to my husband, when he took the editorship, and requested him to contribute, telling him he intended to make the magazine of a higher character, and therefore ventured to ask, offering five dollars per page, and the liberty of drawing for the money the moment the article was published. "The Democratic Review" is so poor now that it can only offer twenty dollars for an article of what length soever, so that Mr. Hawthorne cannot well afford to give any but short stories to it ; and it is besides sadly dilatory about payment. The last paper he sent to it was a real gift, as it was more than four pages ; but he thought its character better suited to the grave "Democrat" than for the other publication. Why did not you send the last number ? He is quite impatient for it. I also long to read again that terrific and true picture of a cold heart. [The Bosom Serpent.] I do not know what the present production is about, even ; for I have made it a law to myself never to ask him a word concerning what he is writing, because I always disliked to speak of what *I* was *painting*. He often tells me ; but sometimes the story remains hidden till he reads it aloud to me, before sending it away. I can comprehend the delicacy and tricksiness of his mood when he is evolving a work of art. He waits upon the light in such a purely simple way that I do not wonder at the perfection of each of his stories. Of several sketches, first one and then another come up to be clothed upon with language, after their own will and pleasure. It is real inspiration, and few are reverent and patient

70

enough to wait for it as he does. I think it is in this way that he comes to be so void of extravagance in his style and material. He does not meddle with the clear, true picture that is painted on his mind. He lifts the curtain, and we see a microcosm of nature, so cunningly portrayed that truth itself seems to have been the agent of its appearance. Thus his taste is genuine — the most faultless I ever knew. Now, behold! all unforeseen, a criticism upon the genius of Nathaniel Hawthorne!

Dear mother, Louisa Hawthorne has sent me some exquisite silk flannel for little shirts, but not quite enough. It is a dollar a yard. Mrs. Emerson says that you will find it at Jacobs', on Tremont Street. I could not refuse my child the luxury of feeling such a material over its dear little bosom. I have to spend a great deal of time in darning the small craters in my stockings.

January 21. In the hope of some unoccupied carrier-pigeon's straying this way, I shall write today. The extreme cold freezes the ground, and my lord will not consent to my putting foot out of doors, so I remain a singing-bird in my happy cage, endeavoring by walks in the long upper entry (which is enlivened by sundry winds rushing through a broken window-pane) to make some amends for being deprived of the outward world. Yesterday I felt as if I had dieted upon diamonds and were sparkling with rainbow colors like an icicle in the sun. I painted upon Endymion. My husband blasphemes the fierce winds and extreme cold in a very picturesque manner; but the disapprobation he feels is a moral one, not a physical discomfort. He cleaves the air like a Damascus blade, so finely attempered that he is unharmed. I never knew any person in such fine health as he is; because he is not obtusely well — he has no brute force; but every part of his frame seems in perfect diapason, like a bird's. I should be afraid of him if he were in ferocious health; but his health is heavenly. Endymion will *certainly* be finished this week if I remain alive, and the sun shines. [It is a picture in pale brown monochromes, of the most remarkable perfection of finish and beauty of draughtsmanship.] I shall ask Plato to carry it to Boston in his arms, unless my honorable brother Horace [Mann] will take it when he comes to lecture. It will be perfectly light, but cannot be given up to the stageman. I do not want it shown to any person until it be framed, with a glass over it. Daggett must be made to hasten his work; but he is as obstinate and cross as a mule; yet no one can make such superlative frames. The price must be an hundred dollars independently of the frame; if it be worth one cent, it is worth that. I dearly desire that some one I know should possess it. I shall be glad some day to redeem it, for it has come out of my soul. What a record it is of these happy, hopeful days! The divine dream shining in Endymion's face, his body entranced in sleep, his soul bathed in light, every curve flowing in consummate beauty — in some way it is my life. But, for Endymion, I must look upon a small bit of gold. [Her husband would not let her sell the picture, after all.]

March 16.

MY DEAREST MOTHER, —The sumptuous box-ful arrived, and the dressed beef is most accept-able, and the wafers are very nice, Mr. Hawthorne liking them exceedingly. Una went to see her father yesterday morning, the nurse declaring that she looked as nice as silver and pretty as a white rose. Great was his surprise to see his little daughter coming to him! My husband wishes father would please go to the agents for "The Democratic Review," and tell them he is on the free list. The three last numbers have not been sent to him, they having stopped sending at the printing of "The Christmas Banquet." Will father also look into "Graham's Magazine" for March, and see whether it contains "Earth's Holocaust," and if so, send it to us?

August.

Directly after you left us, baby went to sleep, and slept three hours, during which time I accom-plished wonders. We dined upon potatoes, corn, carrots, and whortleberry pudding, quite sumptu-ously. Our cook was Hyperion, whom we have engaged. He, with his eyes of light, his arched brow, and "locks of lovely splendor," officiated even to dish-washing, with the air of one making worlds. I, with babe on arm, looked at him part of the time. No accident happened, except that a sprigged saucer "came into halves;" and I found that Hyperion, in his new office, had put the ivory handles of the knives into the water, knowing no better, and left the silver to be washed last instead of first. I dragged Una in her carriage in the avenue, and she was very happy. She woke a little after four this morning, and when I first opened my eyes upon her, her feet were "in the sky." I laid the breakfast-table, and prepared everything for Hyperion to cook milk and boil water. At breakfast, baby sat radiant in her coach. George Prescott brought a hot Indian cake from his mother, while we were at table. Before Hyperion had quite finished his kitchen-work, Colonel Hall and his little son came to see him. The Colonel only stayed about an hour, and could not come to dinner. The unhappy lamb was boiled, together with some shelled beans and corn.

August 20. Your packet arrived last evening. I am much inclined to have the black woman. My husband says he does not want me to undertake to keep anybody who is apparently innocent, after my late sore experience. He says the old black lady is probably as bad already as she ever will be. If you find the blackey not disinclined to come to such poor folks, I will take her in September. I cannot well ask dear Mary to visit me while my Hyperion is cook and maid. He will not let me go into his kitchen, hardly; but it is no poetry to cook, and wash dishes; and I cannot let him do it for anybody but myself alone. The only way we can make money now seems to be to save it ; and as he declares he can manage till September, we will remain alone till then. It is beyond words enchanting to be so. But, I assure you, his office is no sinecure. He actually *does* everything. And I sit upstairs, and out of doors with baby, more of a queen than ever, for I have a king to my servitor. It would cost too much to board ; you know we cannot live cheaper anywhere or anyhow than thus.

Again, a letter is sent to Mrs. Caleb Foote : —

The Promised Land.

MY DEAR MARY, — You are the most satisfactory person to draw for of any one I know. [Sophia had sent one of her pictures as a present.] Your letter gave me the purest pleasure, for it made me feel as if I had caused two hearts to be glad, and that is worth living for, if it be done but once in a life. . . . We have passed the happiest winter, the long evenings lifted out of the common sphere by the magic of Shakespeare. Mr. Hawthorne read aloud to me all the Plays. And you must know how he reads, before you can have any idea what it was. I can truly say I never comprehended Shakespeare before ; and my husband was pleased to declare that he never himself understood him so well, though he has pored over the Plays all his life. All the magnificence, the pomp, the cunning beauty, the wisdom and fine wit, and the grace were revealed to me as by a new light. Every character is unfixed from the page, and stands free in life. Meanwhile I

75

sewed, and whenever a little garment was finished, I held it up, and won a radiant smile for it and the never-weary question (with the charming, arch glance) "Pray, who is that for ?"

We breakfast about nine o'clock, because we do not dine till three ; and we have no tea ceremony, because it broke our evenings too much. I break my fast upon fruit, and we lunch upon fruit, and in the evening, also, partake of that paradisaical food. Mr. Emerson, with his sunrise smile, Ellery Channing, radiating dark light, and, very rarely, Elizabeth Hoar, with spirit voice and tread, have alone varied our days from without ; but we have felt no want. My sweet, intelligent maid sings at her work, with melodious note. I do not know what is in store for me ; but I know well that God is in the future, and I do not fear, or lose the precious present by anticipating possible evil. I remember Father Taylor's inspired words, "Heaven is not afar. We are like phials of water in the midst of the ocean. Eternity, heaven, God, are all around us, and we are full of God. Let the thin crystal break, and it is all one." Mr. Mann came to Concord to lecture last week. He looked *happiest*. What can he ask for more, having Mary for his own ? Hold me ever as

Your true and affectionate friend,

SOPHIA.

The Hawthornes left the Old Manse for visits to their relatives. Hawthorne went to Salem in advance of his wife, who writes to him : —

76

BOSTON, August 15.

. . . Yesterday your letter raised me to the eighth heaven — one heaven beyond the imagination of the great poet. . . . I am very sorry you did not come, for Mr. Atherton was to be at home at eight o'clock that evening, hoping to see you, and Mr. Pierce was also in the city, desiring to meet you. Una knew Mr. Atherton directly, when I took her to call, and at once challenged him to run after her. Soon afterwards a fine wooden singing-bird arrived, with a card on which was written "for Una Hawthorne." Mrs. Williams called. She asked me to give you a *great deal* of love. She wished we would visit her in Augusta, Maine. I have taken Una upon the Common several times, and she runs after all babies and dogs. She is so beautiful that I am astonished at her. Frank Shaw says she is perfect, and like Raphael's ideal babies. This morning a letter came to you from the Count [Mr. John O'Sullivan was usually called by this title by the Hawthornes], who has some good proposals. The offer from the "Blatant Beast" [name given by Hawthorne to a certain publisher] of the — But I will send the letter; it will not cost any more than mine alone, thanks to the new law.

Having gone to stay for a few days in Herbert Street, Mrs. Hawthorne writes to her mother : —

SALEM, November 19.

. . . Father took most beautiful care of us, and did not leave us till we were .seated in the cars.

Mr. Dike followed. I told him that if he wished to see Una, he could do it by sitting behind. This he did, and kept up a constant talking with her, all the way. She looked lofty and grave, and unfathomable in her eyes; but finally had compassion on him, and faintly smiled in that way which always makes her father say, "Mightily gracious, madam!" An old man by the side of Mr. Dike asked him whether Una were his grandchild! She liked the old man, and smiled at him whenever he spoke to her. Upon arriving in Salem, Mr. Dike went to find my husband; whom, however, I saw afar off in the crowd of ugly men, showing like a jewel (pearl) in an Ethiop's ear, so fine and pale, with the large lids cast down, and a radiant smile on his lips.

For the first time since my husband can remember, he dined with his mother! This is only one of the miracles which the baby is to perform. Her grandmother held her on her lap till one of us should finish dining, and then ate her own meal. She thinks Una is a beauty, and, I believe, is not at all disappointed in her. Her grandmother also says she has the most perfect form she ever saw in a baby. She waked this morning like another dawn, and smiled bountifully, and was borne off to the penetralia of the house to see Madam Hawthorne and aunt Elizabeth. My husband's muse is urging him now, and he is writing again. He never looked so excellently beautiful. Una is to be dressed as sumptuously as possible to-day, to visit her grandaunt Ruth

[Manning]. Louisa wants her to overcome with all kinds of beauty, outward and inward. I feel just made. All are quite well here, and enjoy the baby vastly.

To Hawthorne in Salem : —

BOSTON, December 19.

. . . If I asked myself strictly whether I could write to you this evening, I should say absolutely no, for ten thousand different things demand the precious moments while our baby sleeps. . . . I bless God for such a destiny as mine ; you satisfy me beyond all things. . . . Una is now downstairs with her aunt Elizabeth, and she shines with perfection of well-being. When she is near a chair, with both hands resting upon it, she will suddenly let go, and for a few glorious seconds maintain her equilibrium, and then down she sits upon the floor. C. Sturgis and Anna Shaw have been to see her. I took her to William Story's yesterday, and he thought her eyes very beautiful, and said he had scarcely ever seen perfectly gray eyes before ; and that such were the finest eyes in the world, capable of the most expression. He added, that her eyes were like those of an exquisite child of Raphael's, which he had seen, in oils.

Mr. Colton has been again to see you. Perhaps it is quite fortunate that you were guarded from an interview, since you would have refused his offers. When will you come back ? Mr. Hillard said you promised to go there again. You can always come here.

Your loving wife,   PHŒBE.

After returning home, Sophia writes : —

CONCORD, January 26, 1845.

BEST MOTHER (I like that Swedish epithet), — The jewel is *precisely* what I wanted. It appears strange for us to make presents of precious stones set in gold ; but the occasion is sufficient to justify it. Mrs. Prescott is perpetually doing for me what she will not allow me to pay for, and often what I cannot pay for. She remains rich in consciousness, but the burden of obligation is too great. She papered my kitchen with her own hands, and would not let me even pay for the paper ; she also employed her man to put up a partition ; and she is stiff-necked as an Israelite on these points. She sends us Indian cakes and milk bread, or any nicety she happens to have. George has the pleasantest way of going of errands about which I cannot employ the Imp, Ben, and he took excellent care of Leo, the dog, during our absence, feeding him so sumptuously that he looked very superb when we returned, only requiring to have an heroic soul to be the Doge of dogs. I never imagined anything so enchanting as Una's rapid development. Every morning, as soon as she is awake, she extends her little hand to the Madonna. Then she points to Loch Lomond (which I have moved to my room), and then to Abbotsford, each time observing something about the pictures, as she gazes into my face. My replies I always feel to be very stupid; but I do as well as I can, considering that I am not now a baby. Another of her acts is to put up her forefinger to my mouth, to be kissed; and often she puts up her own mouth for a kiss, and then smiles with an expression of covert fun — *sub ridens,* her father calls it. The other evening, while the trees were still crystal chandeliers, it grew dusk before the lamps were lighted; and all at once, behold the full moon rose up from behind the hill "over against our house," exactly between the trees at the entrance of our avenue. Picture to yourself the magnificence. The sharp gleam of the crystals made it seem as if the stars had fallen, and were caught by the branches, and a thousand shining scimitars flashed into view. Una happened to be turned towards the scene. How I wish you could have seen the wonder and gleam of her face! As the moon rose higher and higher, she continued to talk about it, her hand extended. We lighted no lamp that evening. The next morning I asked her where the moon was, and she turned towards the window with a questioning tone. Last evening my better than Epaminondas was stretched upon the floor, for her entertainment. It was the prettiest sight that ever was. Una is as strong as a little lion, and I could dance at any moment. The half-hour glass that you gave me is a great enchantment to my husband, and has already suggested some divine production.

To Mrs. Foote, once more: —

Paradise Regained, May 4, 1845.

MY DEAR MARY, — My husband and I will be most happy to receive you, I would say at once, but I must wait till these avenue trees are in leaf, because I want you to see our quiet Eden in its full summer dress. It has begun to array itself; and the Balm of Gilead, a significant tree for us, is already in tender green, and the showerful poplar, so mightily abused, is, this lovely morning, becoming golden with new yellow foliage. But as this is our last year in the blessed old abbey, you must see it in perfection. The lawn beneath the trees is already a rich emerald, and large gold stars begin to spangle it. You shall see my little darling running over the green grass, with a continued song of exultation. She thinks this is the first Paradise, and that her father is the primal Adam, and that she possesses the earth, now that she is out of leading-strings.

December 7, 1845.

I was very glad of an answer to my volume of a letter, and that it gave you satisfaction. Words are a poor portrait of Una, this ray of light. The distinctness and intelligence of her language are a kind of miracle. Her father said one day that she was the book of Revelation. Once, I said for her Mother Goose's " Cushy cow bonny, let down your milk!" and after hearing the whole verse several times she began to repeat it to herself, but said, "Tushy tow bonny, let down *Nona's* milk!" And she always corrects me if I omit her name. She often says, "Bobby Shafto's done to sea; tome back, marry *Nona!*" with a very facetious expression. Her father tells her that he shall not allow Bobby to marry her.

CHAPTER IV

LIFE IN SALEM

THE Hawthornes now moved to Salem, where they remained for several years.

Washington's Birthday, 1846.

TRUE MOTHER, — Through the howling storm your little box of benefits came safely. I was especially grateful to hear from you, because I had read in the paper of Mr. Mann's walking into the dock, and feared he might be very ill after it. I was exceedingly relieved to hear that he was none the worse for such an unexpected baptism. I thought that after getting tired and heated by lecturing, the transition might be almost mortal for his delicate frame. I, in my old-fashioned simplicity of faith, would have it that God saved him. My husband has found " The Christmas Banquet," and he has made up the second volume, which I send with this, for dear father to transmit to New York. The second volume must be printed first, because he has not long enough dreamed over the new tale or essay which is to commence the first volume. From all question as to what this precious web may be, last woven in the loom of his genius, I sacredly abstain till

84

the fullness of time. Oh, I am so glad that these scattered jewels are now to be set together!

"Zuna" is spreading out her painted tea-set upon a little oval tray that came from beyond sea, in her father's childhood. She plays tea-drinking with infinite grace and skill. Last week Louisa Hawthorne and I spent the day with Mrs. Dike, and Una behaved like a consummate lady, although she frolicked like a child. Mrs. Dike gave her some beautiful silver playthings, with which she had a tea-party. Rebecca Manning [a little cousin] was there, and over their airy tea Una undertook to be agreeable, and began of her own accord to converse, and tell Rebecca about her life in Concord. She said, "In Tontord Zuna went out into the orchard and picked apples in her little basket, for papa and mamma to eat." And then, with a countenance and tone of triumph, she exclaimed, "And papa's boat!"

A long letter written by George William Curtis is a bright ray from a beautiful personality, containing these descriptions : —

ROME, January 14, 1847.

MY DEAR FRIENDS, — How often in the long sunny silence of that summer voyage, when in the Atlantic all day the sea rippled as gently about the ship as the waters of Walden pour against their shore, and in the Mediterranean the moon would have no other mirror, but entranced its waves to an oily calmness in which she shone unbroken, did I figure you gliding with us on our fairy way to France, Italy, and in the next summer, Switzerland! One day in our voyage we passed the Straits of Gibraltar — seeing land for the first time in twenty-eight days. We came so near and passed so rapidly, saw so distinctly the dusky gray olive foliage of Spain and the little round towers whence the old Spaniards looked for the Moors; and on the other side, so grim and lonely, the intricate mountain outline of Africa, so distinctly, and at night again, and for many days after, the same broad water; that it lies more dreamily in my memory than anything else. . . . On the forty-fifth day I stepped ashore in France; but not without more regret than I thought possible, for the ship; and one of the crew, of my own age, with whom I had seen the stars fade in the morning during his watch, had become very dear to me. Yet in Marseilles everything was quaint. . . . The same features I had always known in a city, — men, houses, streets, squares; but with an expression unknown before. At night, with my sailor friend, I threaded some of the narrower streets, which were like corridors in an unshapely Titan palace. At the doors of the smallest shops on each side sat the spinsters in the moonlight, gossiping and knitting; while over them bent old French tradesmen, in long yarn stockings and velvet knee-breeches. The street was barely wide enough for a carriage, and they talked across; and all was as gay and happy as Arcadia. Every day [in Flor.

ence], I was in the galleries, which are freely
open to every one, and here saw the grandest
works of Raphael in his middle and best style.
Of the wonderful feminine grace and tenderness
of these, of which no copy can give an idea, I
cannot properly speak. From him only have I received the idea of the Immaculate Mother — the
union of celestial superiority with human mater-
nity. The innumerable other Madonnas are beautiful pictures ; but they are either mere mothers
or mere angels. It is the same union in kind with
what you may observe in his portrait, where mas-
culine character is so blended and tempered with
feminine grace and flexibility. Raphael is the
clear, deep, beautiful eye, in which and through
which is seen the undoubted heaven. . . .

How glad I am that I have a right to send you
a letter ! I have left a small space into which
to squeeze a large love, which I send to Mrs.
H., with my thanks for her kind letter, which
could not come too late, and which I am very
sure highly gratified Mr. Crawford. He desires
to make his especial regards to Mrs. H., and said
that he should write her a note, if it were not too
great a liberty, which he would send in a letter
to Mrs. Howe. Mention my name to Una; for
in some dim remembrance of Concord meadows
I may then figure as a shadowy faun. A long,
pleasant letter from George Bradford, the other
day, gave me the last news from our old home,
which is very placid and beautiful in my memory.
I should love to see Ellery Channing's new book.

But I am sure that he will never forgive himself for coming to Rome for sixteen days. I am sorry to say good-by. G. W. Curtis.

While on a visit to her mother, Mrs. Hawthorne writes to her husband : —

Boston, July.

... I received your most precious letter yesterday. I do not need to stand apart from daily life to see how fair and blest our lot is. Every mother is not like me — because not every mother has such a father for her children ; so that my cares are forever light. Am I not eminently well, round, and rubicund ? Even in the very centre of simultaneous screams from both darling little throats, I am quite as sensible of my happiness as when the most dulcet sounds are issuing thence. I have suffered only for you, in my babydom. You ought not to be obliged to undergo the wear and tear of the nursery ; it is contrary to your nature and your mood. You were born to muse, and through undisturbed dreams to enlighten the world. Una mourns for you. "Oh, I *must* go home to see my papa ! Oh, *when* are we going to Salem ?" Her little heart has enough of mine in it to feel widowed without you. Julian does not walk yet ; but he understands everything, and talks a great deal.

There was a sharp contrast between Mrs. Hawthorne's earlier life of intercourse with trooping, charming friends, and devotion to art and literature, and the toils of motherhood in poverty which now absorbed her days. She refers to this new order of existence with joyful patience in the following letters to Mrs. Peabody : —

SALEM, September, 1848.

Dora Golden [Julian's nurse] takes this to you. She deferred her visit to Boston for my convenience, because Mr. Hawthorne thought of going to Temple, to visit General Miller; but he did not go. Mr. Hawthorne will contribute to Elizabeth's book, but not for pay. Mary Chase took Una and me to Nahant to see Rebecca Kinsman at her cottage. It was a dear little nest, on the brow of a hill commanding the boundless sea. Una flew around like a petrel ; only that her hair floated golden in the sunshine, and the petrel's feathers are gray. You are quite right ; I am so happy that I require nothing more. No art nor beauty can excel my daily life, with such a husband and such children, the exponents of all art and beauty, I really have not even the temptation to go out of my house to find anything better. Not that I enjoy less any specimen of earthly or heavenly grace when I meet it elsewhere ; but I have so much in perpetual presence that I am not *hungry* for such things.

November 19, 1848.

I intended almost every day last week to go to Boston, but was detained by various circumstances. Among other things, Mr. Daniel Webster was to come to lecture, and I thought I must wait to hear him. I am glad I did, for it was a very *useful* lecture, and in some parts quite grand. It was upon the Constitution — a noble subject. You know he is particularly designated as the Expounder of the Constitution. He stood like an Egyptian column, solid and without any Corinthian grace, but with dignity and composed majesty. He gave a simple statement of facts concerning the formation of our united government ; and towards the close, he now and then thundered, and his great cavernous eyes lightened, as he eloquently showed how noble and wonderful it was, and how astonishing the sagacity and insight of those young patriots had been in the memorable Congress. The old Lion walked the stage with a sort of repressed rage, when he referred to those persons who cried out, "Down with the Constitution!" "Madmen! Or most wicked if not mad!" said he, with a glare of fire, as he looked about him. He had risen with his hat in his hand, and held it all the time, making no gestures excepting once, when he referred to the American eagle and flag. He then raised his hand and pointed as if the eagle were cleaving the air ; and he said, "Who calls this the Massachusetts eagle, the Illinois eagle, — or this the Virginia flag, or the New Hampshire flag? Are they not the American eagle and the American flag? And wherever the flag waves, let him touch it who dares!" His voice and glance as he pronounced these words were

the artillery of a storm ; and they were followed
by tremendous rolls of applause. Mr. Hawthorne,
who is one of the managers of the Lyceum (!)
was deputed to go on Monday to West Newton,
to see Mr. Mann about lecturing here.

Sophia writes to Mrs. Mann, then in Washington : —

"Is Congress behaving any worse than usual?
The members are always giving the lie and seiz-
ing each other by the collar, ever since the grave
and majestic days of the first Sessions, it seems
to me. But we have not got to being quite such
monkeys as the French are in their Assemblies.
Mrs. George Peabody, a week or two ago, gave
a great ball, to which she invited us. I heard
that Mr. Peabody had put his magnificent Murillo
picture in the finest light imaginable, having built
a temporary oratory for it, on the piazza upon
which the library opens. The library was dark
as night, and as I entered it, the only object I
could see was this divine Madonna at the end of
the illuminated oratory. It is the Annunciation.
There is not the smallest glory of color in the
picture. The power, the wonder of the picture, is
the beauty of the expression and features. Her
eyes are lifted and her hands crossed upon her
bosom. The features seem hardly material, such
a fineness and spiritual light transfigure them.
It is the greatest picture I ever saw."

A fragment of a letter suggests a lecture and
a great innovation.

" My husband bought a ticket for himself, and went with me ! ! Mr. Alcott spent an evening with us a week or more ago, and was very interesting; telling, at my request, about his youth, and peddling, etc. There were six ladies and six gentlemen present last Monday evening. They assembled at Mr. Stone's. Miss Hannah Hodges, Mrs. J. C. Lee, and two ladies whom I did not know, besides Mrs. Stone and myself; Mr. Frothingham, Mr. William Silsbee, Mr. Shackford, of Lynn, Mr. Pike, Mr. Streeter, and my husband, besides Mr. Stone and his son. Mr. Alcott said he would commence with the Nativity, and first read Milton's Hymn. Then he retreated to his corner, and for about an hour and three quarters kept up an even flow of thought, without a word being uttered by any other person present. Then Mr. Stone questioned him upon his use of the word 'artistic;' which provoked a fine analysis from him of the word 'artist' as distinguished from 'artisan.' I thought the whole monologue very beautiful and clear. This evening Mr. Thoreau is going to lecture, and will stay with us. His lecture before was so enchanting; such a revelation of nature in all its exquisite details of wood - thrushes, squirrels, sunshine, mists and shadows, fresh, vernal odors, pine-tree ocean melodies, that my ear rang with music, and I seemed to have been wandering through copse and dingle! Mr. Thoreau has risen above all his arrogance of manner, and is as gentle, simple, ruddy, and meek as all geniuses should be; and now his great blue eyes fairly outshine and put into shade a nose which I once thought must make him uncomely forever."

Several letters from Mr. and Mrs. Hawthorne break in upon the usual quietude with allusions to the real hardship of public misapprehension; yet no false statements and judgments were ever more coolly received. Still, Mrs. Hawthorne writes with an excited hand : —

June 8, 1849.

MY DEAR FATHER, — Mr. Hawthorne received news by telegraph to-day that he is turned out of office headlong. I have written to mother, and told her, fearing she would hear of it accidentally. We are not cast down at all, and do not be anxious for us. You will see by my letter to mother how we are hopeful and cheerful about it, and expect better things. The cock is crowing the noon of night and I must to bed. I have written a long letter to mother. We are all well.

Your affectionate daughter,

SOPHIA.

The letter to her mother has not been completely preserved, but runs : —

. . . The telegraph to-day brought us news that would have made the cottage [at Lenox] particularly acceptable, because we could have lived there upon our own responsibility — for the Old General has turned Mr. Hawthorne out of the Surveyorship. Do not be troubled; for *we* are not.

93

Mr. Hawthorne never liked the office at all, and is rather relieved than otherwise that it is taken out of his hands, and has an inward confidence that something much better and more suitable for him will turn up. As for me, you know I am composed of Hope and Faith, and while I have my husband and the children I feel as if Montezuma's diamonds and emeralds were spiritually in my possession. But we look forward with a kind of rapture to the possibility of now going into the country somewhere this summer, and setting Una down in *a field*, where she so pines to go. Meantime, the newly appointed Surveyor's commission has not arrived, and so Mr. Hawthorne is not yet out of office.

I have not seen my husband happier than since this turning out. He has felt in chains for a long time, and being a MAN, he is not alarmed at being set upon his own feet again, — or on his *head*, I might say, — for that contains the available gold, of a mine scarcely yet worked at all. As Margaret [Fuller] truly said once, "We have had but a drop or so from that ocean." We are both perfectly well, too, and brave with happiness, and "a credence in our hearts, and espérance so absolutely strong, as doth outvie the attest of eyes and ears." (So Shakespeare somewhere speaks for us, somewhat so — but not verbatim, for I forget one or two words.)

Above all, it has come in the way of an inevitable Providence to us (whatever knavery some people may have to answer for, who have been the agents in the removal), and I never receive inevitable Providences with resignation merely; but with *joy*, as certainly, undoubtedly, the best possible events that can happen for me — and immediately I begin to weave the apparent straw into gold, like the maiden in the fairy tale.

Good-by now, dear mother. Do not be anxious. I should not have told you this *now* — fearing you might be troubled — but I was afraid you might see the removal in the papers, or hear of it; and I thought it best to let you know just how it is with us, so that you might not have a shock.   Your most affectionate child,

SOPHIA.

June 10.

MY DEAR FATHER, — Here is a pretty business, discovered in an unexpected manner to Mr. Hawthorne by a friendly and honorable Whig. Perhaps you know that the President said before he took the chair that he should make no removals, except for dishonesty and unfaithfulness. So that all who voted for him after that declaration pledged themselves to the same course. You know also doubtless that there has never been such a succession of removals of honorable and honest men since we were a nation as since the accession of President Taylor, — not even under Jackson, — who, however, always removed people because they were Whigs, without any covert implication of character. This has been Democratic conduct — to remove for political reasons.

95

This conduct the Whigs always disapproved, and always said that no one ought to be removed but from disability or dishonesty. So that now when any one is removed, it is implied that the person is either a shiftless or a dishonest man. It is very plain that neither of these charges could be brought against Mr. Hawthorne. Therefore a most base and *incredible* falsehood has been told — written down and signed and sent to the Cabinet in secret. This infamous paper certifies among other things (of which we have not heard) — that Mr. Hawthorne has been in the habit of writing political articles in magazines and newspapers!

This he has never done, as every one knows, in his life — not *one word* of politics was ever written by him. His townsfolk, of course, know it well. But what will surprise you more than this fact is to hear who got up this paper, and perjured his soul upon it; who followed his name with their signatures, and how it was indorsed. It was no less a person than Mr. C. W. U.!!! who has thus proved himself a liar and a most consummate hypocrite; for he has always professed himself the warmest friend. He certifies the facts of the paper; and *thirty* other gentlemen of *Salem* sign their names! Among whom are G. D. and young N. S., and Mr. R. R.! Can you believe it? Not one of these gentlemen knew this to be true, because it is *not* true; and yet, for party ends, they have all perjured themselves to get away this office, and make the President believe there were plausible pretexts; they had no idea it could be found out. But the District Attorney *saw* the paper. He is a Whig, but friendly to Mr. Hawthorne, on literary grounds; and the District Attorney told a Salem gentleman, also a Whig and a *personal* friend of Mr. Hawthorne's. Thus, the "murder" is out, through better members of the same party.

Mr. Hawthorne took the removal with perfect composure and content, having long expected it on account of his being a Democrat. But yesterday, when he went to Boston and found out this, the lion was roused in him. He says it is a cowardly attack upon his character, done in such secrecy; and that he shall use his pen now in a way he never has done, and expose the lie, addressing the public.   Your cnild,

SOPHIA.

June 17.

MY BLESSED MOTHER, — Your most welcome and beautiful letter of the 11th I very gladly received. You take our reverse of fortune in the way I hoped you would. I feel "beyond the utmost scope and vision of calamity" (as Pericles said to Aspasia), while my husband satisfies my highest ideal, and while the graces of heaven fill the hearts of my children. Everything else is very external. This is the immortal life which makes flowers of asphodel bloom in my path, and no rude step can crush them. I exult in my husband. He stands upon a table-land of high behavior which is far above these mean and false proceedings, with which a party of intriguers are now concerning themselves, and covering themselves with the hopeless mud of Dante's Inferno. The more harm they try to do, deeper down they plunge into the mire; and I doubt if ever in this world some of them will be able to wash their faces clean again. My husband supposed he was removed because he was a Democrat (and you know very well how he has always been a Democrat, not a Locofoco — if that means a lucifer match). Therefore he took it as a matter of course in the way of politics; though it surprised me, because General Taylor had pledged himself not to remove any person for political *opinions*, but only for dishonesty and inefficiency. This was why all Mr. Hawthorne's Whig as well as Democrat friends were sure he would not be disturbed. He could not even have provoked hostility by having taken any active part in politics, — never writing, never speaking, never moving for the cause. But these intriguers secretly carried out their plan. They wrote in letters false charges which they sent to Washington, and thirty gentlemen signed their names to a paper requesting the appointment of Mr. Putnam.

June 21, Thursday.

MY OWN DEAR MOTHER, — I am truly disappointed that you have not had this letter before, but the tide of events has hurried me away from it. Now I must write a few words. You never

heard of such a time about any one as there has
been about Mr. Hawthorne. The whole country is up in arms, and will not allow Mr. Hawthorne to be removed. And now I have the good
news to tell you that his removal is *suspended* at
Washington, and he is either to be reinstated if
he will consent, or to be presented with a better
office. At Washington the Government was de-
ceived, and were not told that the person to
be removed was *Mr. Hawthorne* — so secret and
cunning were these four gentlemen of Salem !
I cannot tell you all the abominable story now ;
and it is no matter, since they are caught in their
own toils, and defeated. Mr. Hawthorne's name
is ringing through the land. All the latent feeling about him now comes out, and he finds himself very famous. Mr. Samuel Hooper has been
very active for him. Mr. Howes has done nothing else for ten days but go back and forth to
Boston, and come here to see my husband, upon
the subject. It has wholly roused him out of
his deep affliction for the death of Frederic [his
brother], for whom he feels as if he were acting
now, so deep was Frederic's love and admiration
for Mr. Hawthorne. I wrote the above on my lap,
following Julian about, this hottest day. Now
I can only say good-by, and implore you to stay
through July among the mountains. It is too
hot in West Street for you. We are all well,
here, and there. When I see you, I will tell you
this long story about the removal, which has
proved no removal, as Mr. Hawthorne has not

left the Custom House, and the commission of
the new officer has not arrived.

Your loving child,
SOPHIA.

P. S. Just to show to what a detail of meanness and cunning the reverend person descends,
I must tell you that he brought from Washington
a paper which he copied from the original memorial there ; which memorial was a testimony
of the merchants of Salem in favor of Colonel
Miller's being Collector. This memorial Mr.
Hawthorne, in official capacity as Surveyor of
the Port, and acquainted therefore with the merchants, indorsed, — saying that, "to the best of
his recollection," these were all the principal
merchants, and that they were responsible persons. In the copy which Mr. U. made he left
out "to the best of his recollection," and made it
read that these were *all* the merchants of Salem.
Stephen C. Phillips's name was not signed. And
so Mr. U. brings this to prove that Mr. Hawthorne is impeachable for want of veracity ! He
tried hard to find that my husband acted politi-
cally with regard to Colonel Miller's appointment;
and as this was impossible, he thought he would
try to prove him a false witness. Did you ever
know of such pitiful evasions ? But there is no
language to describe him. He is, my husband
says, the most satisfactory villain that ever was,
for at every point he is consummate. The Government had decided to reinstate Mr. Hawthorne
before Mr. U.'s arrival at Washington, and his

representations changed the purpose. I trust Mr. Everett will be enlightened about the latter, so as to see what an unjust act he has committed by retracting his first letter. "What!" said Charles Sumner of Mr. U., "that smooth, smiling, oily man of God!"

Hawthorne has occasion to write to the

HON. HORACE MANN, M. C., WEST NEWTON, MASS.

SALEM, June 26, 1849.

MY DEAR SIR, — I have just received your note, in which you kindly offer me your interest towards reinstating me in the office of Surveyor.

I was perfectly in earnest in what I told Elizabeth, and should still be very unwilling to have you enter into treaty with Mr. K., Mr. U., or other members of the local party, in my behalf. But, on returning here, after an absence of two or three days, I found a state of things rather different from what I expected, the general feeling being strongly in my favor, and a disposition to make a compromise, advantageous to me, on the part of some, at least, of those who had acted against me. "The Essex Register," of yesterday, speaks of an intention to offer me some better office than that of which I have been deprived. Now, I do not think that I can, preserving my self-respect, accept of any compromise. No other office can be offered me that will not have been made vacant by the removal of a Democrat ; and, even if there were such an office, still, as charges

101

have been made against me, complete justice can be done only by placing me exactly where I was before. This also would be the easiest thing for the Administration to do, as they still hold my successor's commission suspended. A compromise might indeed be made, not with me, but with Captain Putnam, by giving him a place in this Custom House — which would be of greater emolument than my office ; and I have reason to believe that the Collector would accede to such an arrangement. Perhaps this idea might do something towards inducing Mr. Meredith to make the reinstatement.

I did not intend to involve you in this business ; nor, indeed, have I desired any friend to take up my cause ; but if, in view of the whole matter, you should see fit to do as Mr. Mills advises, I shall feel truly obliged. Of course, after consenting that you should use your influence in my behalf, I should feel myself bound to accept the reinstatement, if offered. I beg you to believe, also, that I would not allow you to say a word for me, if I did not know that I have within my power a complete refutation of any charges of official misconduct that have been, or may be, brought against me.

Sophia and the children are well. The managers of the Lyceum desire to know if you will deliver two lectures for them, before the session of Congress.

Very truly yours,

NATHANIEL HAWTHORNE.

SALEM, July 2, 1849.

MY DEAR SIR, — I am inclined to think, from various suspicious indications that I have noticed or heard of, between the Whigs and one or two of my subordinate officers, that they are concocting, or have already concocted, a new set of charges against me. Would it not be a judicious measure for you to write to the Department, requesting a copy of these charges, that I may have an opportunity of answering them? There can be nothing (setting aside the most direct false testimony, if even that) which I shall not have it in my power either to explain, defend, or disprove. I had some idea of calling for these charges through the newspapers, but it would bring on a controversy which might be interminable, and would only, however clearly I should prove my innocence, make my reinstatement the more difficult; so that I judge it best to meet the charges in this way — always provided that there are any.

It grieves me to give you so much trouble; but you must recollect that it was your own voluntary kindness, and not my importunity, that involves you in it. Very truly yours,

NATHANIEL HAWTHORNE.

The following letter is fragmentary, because of the demands of some autograph-hunter.

. . . It occurred to me, after sending off those documents, yesterday, that I ought to have given

you some particulars as to the political character
and standing of the gentlemen who signed them.
B. Barstow, Esq., is Vice-President of the Hick-
ory Club, and a member of the Democratic Town
Committee. William B. Pike is Chairman of the
Democratic County Committee. T. Burchmore,
Jr., Esq., is Chairman of the Democratic Congres-
sional District Committee. Dr. B. F. Browne
signs in his own official character as a member of
the Democratic State Committee. They have all
been active in our local politics, and thoroughly
acquainted with the political . . . [mutilated for
autograph signature].

As respects the letter from T. Burchmore, Jr.,
to myself, I wish to say a few words. Mr. Burchmore has, for twenty-five years past, occupied a
situation in the Custom House ; and for a long
time past, though nominally only head clerk, has
been the actual head of the establishment, ow-
ing to his great business talent and thorough acquaintance with all matters connected with the
revenue. He is an upright and honorable . . .
[mutilated] . . . in my behalf ; and I would wish,
therefore, in communicating with the Department, that you would use him as tenderly as possible. Of course, his letter may be sent on, but
it would be best not to advert to his being connected with the Custom House ; and as he holds
his office from the Collector, it is very probable
that the Department may not know him in an
official character.

My successor's commission has not yet arrived.

The enemy is very quiet, and I know little or nothing about their motions.

Mrs. Mann's letter to Sophia arrived this morning.

P. S. The gentlemen above mentioned have a high social standing, as well as a political one. Mr. Barstow, for instance, you may recollect as Vice-President of the Salem Lyceum, where he was introduced to you.

SALEM, August 8, 1849.

MY DEAR SIR, — My case is so simple, and the necessary evidence comes from so few sources, and is so direct in its application, that I think I cannot mistake my way through it ; nor do I see how it can be prejudiced by my remaining quiet, for the present. I will sketch it to you as briefly as possible.

Mr. U. accuses me of suspending one or more inspectors for refusing to pay party subscriptions, and avers that I sent them a letter of suspension by a messenger, whom he names, and that — I suppose after the payment of the subscription — I withdrew the suspension.

I shall prove that a question was referred to me — as chief executive officer of the Custom House — from the Collector's office, as to what action should be taken on a letter from the Treasury Department, requiring the dismissal of our temporary inspectors. We had two officers in that position. They were Democrats, men with large families and no resources, and irreproachable as officers; and for these reasons I was unwilling that they should lose their situations. In order, therefore, to comply with the spirit of the Treasury order, without ruining these two men, I projected a plan of suspending them from office during the inactive season of the year, but without removing them, and in such a manner that they might return to duty when the state of business should justify it. I wrote an order (which I still have in my possession) covering these objects, which, however, was not intended to be acted on immediately, but for previous consultation with the Deputy Collector and the head clerk. On consulting the latter gentleman, he was of opinion, for various reasons which he cited, that the two inspectors might be allowed to remain undisturbed until further orders from the Treasury; to which, as the responsibility was entirely with the Collector's Department, I made no objection. And here, so far as I had any knowledge or concern, the matter ended.

But it is said that I notified the inspectors of their suspension by a certain person, who is named. I have required an explanation of this person, and he at once avowed that, being aware of this contemplated movement, and being in friendly relations with these two men, he thought it his duty to inform them of it; but he most distinctly states that he did it without my authority or knowledge, and that he will testify to this effect whenever I call upon him so to do. I did not inquire what communication he had with the two inspectors, or with either of them; for I look upon his evidence as clearing me, whatever may have passed between him and them. But my idea is (I may be mistaken, but it is founded on some observation of the manœuvres of small politicians, and knowing the rigid discipline of custom houses as to party subscriptions) that there really was an operation to squeeze an assessment out of the recusant inspectors, under the terror of an impending removal or suspension; that one of the inspectors turned traitor, and was impelled, by the threats and promises of Mr. U. and his coadjutors, to bring his evidence to a pretty direct point on me; and that Mr. U., in his memorial to the Treasury Department, defined and completed the lie, in such shape as I have given it above. But I do not see how it can stand for a moment against my defense.

The head clerk (the same Mr. Burchmore whose letter I transmitted to you) was turned out a week ago, and will gladly give his evidence at any moment, proving the grounds on which I acted. The other person who is said to have acted as messenger is still in office, a weigher and gauger, at a salary of $1500 per annum. He is a poor man, having been in office but two years, and expended all his income in paying debts for which he was an indorser, and he now wishes to get a few hundred dollars to carry him to California, or give him some other start in life. Still, he will come forward if I call upon him, but, of course, would rather wait for his removal, which will doubtless take place before the session of Congress. Meantime, I have no object to obtain, worth purchasing at the sacrifice which he must make. My surveyorship is lost, and I have no expectation, nor any desire, of regaining it. My purpose is simply to make such a defense to the Senate as will insure the rejection of my successor, and thus satisfy the public that I was removed on false or insufficient grounds. Then, if Mr. U. should give me occasion, — or perhaps if he should not, — I shall do my best to kill and scalp him in the public prints ; and I think I shall succeed.

I mean soon to comply with your kind invitation to come and see you, not on the above business, but because I think of writing a schoolbook, — or, at any rate, a book for the young, — and should highly prize your advice as to what is wanted, and how it should be achieved. I mean, as soon as possible, — that is to say, as soon as I can find a cheap, pleasant, and healthy residence, — to remove into the country, and bid farewell forever to this abominable city ; for, now that my mother is gone, I have no longer anything to keep me here.

Sophia and the children are pretty well. With my best regards to Mrs. Mann, I am,

Very truly yours,

NATHANIEL HAWTHORNE.

P. S. Do pardon me for troubling you with this long letter : but I am glad to put you in possession of the facts, in case of accidents.

I will insert here some letters that relate to this time, though written in 1884 : —

PROVIDENCE, RHODE ISLAND, September 15.

DEAR MRS. LATHROP, . . . That matter of the memorial fountain, or monument [in honor of "The Town Pump"], which the death of Mrs. Brooks prevented our going on with, I trust may yet in the fullness of time be accomplished. I have a plan which may fructify, although some years may intervene before any decided steps can be taken. Perhaps it will be just as well to wait, after all, until some of those wretches who delight in vilifying your father perish from the face of the earth. Let us have patience. They are fast becoming superannuated, and the "venom of their spleen" will perish with them. They comprehend him not, and are willfully blind and deaf. Dr. Wheatland estimates that less than a score of these strange malignants are now to be met with on the streets of Salem. But he has not like me

> "Unaware,
> Ranging the woods to start a hare,
> Come to the mouth of the dark lair,
> Where growling low, a fierce old bear,
> Lies amid bones and blood."

By the bye, I found once that Miss Savage had wholly forgotten Hawthorne's reference to the Town Pump which closes his Custom House chapter, and so I put "The Scarlet Letter" into my valise (she having lost her copy), and two or three weeks ago I called at her house and read her the passage. Afterwards, I dropped in to see Mullet, and I left the book with him, as he had not read it for many years. I think you will like to see a note he has written me, so I inclose it.

Faithfully yours,

GEORGE H. HOLDEN.

February 5.

MY DEAR MRS. LATHROP, — Rummaging among my papers, last evening, I ran across another letter from our "bright-eyed" and noble-hearted friend Mullet, which I think you will be glad to read, because Mullet wrote it. I therefore inclose the letter. Mullet is very hard of hearing, and on that account goes out but little. During the twelve years that I lived in Salem I am sure I never once met him on the street. In fact, I think I never heard of him, even, till after I moved to Providence. I heard of him one day at the "Gazette" office, and forthwith dug him out. He is a great reader. The Harpers have sent me all of Rolfe's Shakespeare, and I found that I have duplicate copies of three or four of the Plays. These duplicates I shall ask Mullet to oblige me by accepting. Mullet is *not* the chap who bored your father so fearfully by endless talk about Shakespeare and Napoleon, but he is a prodigious admirer of the great dramatist. He has the Plays in one huge, unwieldy volume, and for that reason reads them less than he would if they were in a more handy form. Mullet is a great reader of the old English poets (I don't mean so far back as

Chaucer and Spenser), and I suppose he can repeat from memory thousands of lines. I have found no chance to call upon him since I fruitlessly rang his doorbell, as stated in his letter.

Please remind me to tell you about an African fetich which Mullet gave me one day, and a reminiscence of your father linked therewith.

Ever faithfully,

GEORGE H. HOLDEN.

SALEM, September 10, 1884.

DEAR MR. HOLDEN, — It was my good fortune during the year 1850 to be presented with a copy of " The Scarlet Letter," together with " the compliments of the author." Of course, the gift was highly prized ; but its fate was that of many other volumes, borrowed and never returned. A volume of the same, from the late edition issued last year, proved a most welcome visitor to my enforced seclusion. After the lapse of many years I once more had the *real* pleasure of reading over that popular work. The enjoyment derived from a fresh perusal of the introductory chapter on the Custom House was great indeed. It seemed like living over that period of my existence again. The scenes described in such a masterly manner were vividly before me ; and while reading I frequently stopped to laugh at the scrupulously nice delineation. The zest with which I read was heightened by the reproduction of the characters in that superlative picture of word-painting, for they together with the artist were vividly — I had almost said palpably — before me, as though it were a thing of yesterday. How real the "*patriarchal* body of veterans" appeared, "tipped back in chairs," and "at times asleep; but occasionally might be heard talking together in voices between speech and a snore. There was no more vivacity than in the drowsy drone of so many bumblebees." However much others may be entertained by reading that chapter of exquisite humor, those who were the daily witnesses of the scenes for several years can best appreciate its nicety and drollery. The "veteran shipmaster," concerning whom Hawthorne says, "scarcely a day passed that he did not stir me to laughter and admiration by his marvelous gift as a story-teller," was Captain Stephen Burchmore, the public storekeeper. The stories of themselves were generally extravagant and grotesque. It was "the *marvelous gift*" of narration that carried people off their legs. I have known the company present to roar with laughter, and not one more convulsed than Mr. Hawthorne.

Truly yours,

GEORGE W. MULLET.

SALEM, October 1, 1883.

DEAR MR. HOLDEN, — You request me to "write the particulars about the good turn I had done Hawthorne in sacrificing my own interests in his behalf."

Mr. Hawthorne had not been thought of in connection with any office in the Custom House

until after arrangements were made to have them
filled with others. Richard Lindsay was sup-
ported for the surveyorship and myself for the
naval office. All necessary documents had been
forwarded to Washington, duly authenticated, and
tidings of the appointments daily looked for.

At this late stage Hawthorne was first suggested
for Surveyor. The matter was urgently pushed.
To accomplish it, Lindsay must be prevailed upon
to withdraw. All were agreed that I was the one
to engineer the matter, Lindsay and myself being fast friends, and our relations uninterruptedly
pleasant. That he would willingly consent was
not expected, and indeed it was problematical if
he would at all. I felt exceedingly delicate about
suggesting the business, as I had in person been
through the country obtaining signatures from
resident committees favoring his appointment. I
therefore voluntarily offered to withdraw my application for the naval office in favor of Hawthorne,
but that found no favor.

Finally, to secure the desideratum, I proposed
that Lindsay and self both withdraw, and have
the offices filled with others. I desired my friend
should understand that I asked for no sacrifice I
was not willing to share. My withdrawal was
stoutly opposed as entirely unnecessary, but it
was my *ultimatum;* on no other condition would
I move in the matter. The business was then
broken by me to Lindsay, and it required all the
persuasion I could exercise to reconcile him to
the arrangement. The expedient of my own

withdrawal brought it about; otherwise it would not have been accomplished.

It now only remained for us to write to Washington, withdrawing our candidatures, and transferring all our support to the applications of Hawthorne for Surveyor and Howard for Naval Officer. Soon their commissions came, and Lindsay and myself were subsequently appointed as inspectors under Hawthorne.

At that time I regarded Hawthorne's appointment as decidedly popular with the party, with men of letters, and with the increasing multitude who admired him as one of the brightest stars in the literary firmament.

Never have I experienced the least regret for waiving my own advantage to bring the pleasing result about. For nearly four years it brought me almost daily into proximity with him, either officially or casually. The recollection well repays the little sacrifice made. His port, his placidity, his hours of abstraction, his mild, pleasant voice, — no sweeter ever uttered by mortal lips, — are all readily recalled. Truly yours,

G. W. MULLET.

CHAPTER V

PLANS for retiring into the depths of the country were made, and Horatio Bridge was requested
to see what chance there was for a home near the
ocean, to which Hawthorne always turned as to
the most desirable neighbor. Mr. Bridge responds
in part : —

UNITED STATES NAVY YARD, PORTSMOUTH, N. H.
August 6, 1849.

DEAR HAWTHORNE, —. . . I have looked at
a house, which you will probably like . . . and it
commands a fine sea view. If it can be hired, it
is just the place. . . . We are busy in fixing ourselves in our new quarters, where we shall be
most happy to see you. Mrs. Bridge joins me
in kind regards to Mrs. H. and yourself. Love
to Una and the unseen Julian.

Yours ever,   H. B.

A letter from Mrs. Bridge, which does not
mention the year, is a specimen of many similar
ones from other friends : —

PHILADELPHIA, July 1.

MY DEAR MRS. HAWTHORNE, — I heard yesterday by way of *Africa* that you had not received
a note which I left at the Winthrop House for

you last summer. You must have thought me very neglectful. I should have acknowledged the receipt of any book you might have sent me ; but most sincerely did I thank you for that which had given me so much pleasure. I remember very distinctly my past knowledge of Mr. Hawthorne as an author, and the bitter tears I shed over "The Gentle Boy." When I had read it until I thought myself quite hardened to its influence, I offered to read it to our dear old nurse, who had been the patient listener to the whole family for many a year. I prided myself upon my nursery reputation for stoicism, which I should lose if my voice faltered. I was beginning to doubt my ability to get calmly through the next page, when the old lady exclaimed, in such a truly yet ludicrously indignant tone, " *Dretful* creturs ! " that I had a fair right to laugh while she wiped the tears off of her spectacles. The time gained placed me on a firmer footing, and I got safely through thereby. I enjoy Mr. Hawthorne's writings none the less now that I can laugh and cry when I am inclined. Will you give him my kindest regards. He is very often mentioned by Mr. Bridge, who, by the way, goes to the Mediterranean in September. I hope to join him there.

With much regard, truly yours,

C. M. BRIDGE.

Promptly, in their hour of misfortune, arrived a letter from one of Mrs. Hawthorne's dearest friends, which I give here : —

STATEN ISLAND, September 10, 1849.

Thank you, my dear Sophia, for your letter. I have been thinking a great deal of you lately, and was glad to know of your plans. Before I heard from you, I had expended a great amount of indignation upon "General Taylor" and his myrmidons, and politics and parties, and the whole host of public blessings which produce private misfortunes. I am glad you are going to Lenox, because it is such a beautiful place, and you have so many warm friends there. Life is a pretty sad affair, dear Sophia; at least, I find it so. . . . We have felt that Bob [Colonel Robert Shaw] required to be removed from home influences, as he has no brothers; and, being unwilling to send him to a school of the usual order, we chose the Jesuit College at Fordham, near New York, where there are a hundred and fifty boys, and a great many holy fathers to teach and take care of them. I inclose a check from Frank, which he hopes Mr. Hawthorne will accept as it is offered, and as *he* would do if the fate had been reversed. He does not ask you to accept his gift, — so pay it back when you *don't want it*, here or hereafter, or never. I only wish it was a thousand. Dear Sophia, when I think of such men as your husband, Page, and some others, so pinched and cramped for this abominable money, it makes me outrageous. If it were one of those trials that do people good, it would be bearable; but it kills one down so. Shakespeare felt it when he said : —

"Tired with all these, for restful death I cry,
As, to behold desert a beggar born,
And needy nothing trimm'd in jollity."

God bless you, dear Sophia, — as He has, not-withstanding General Taylor. Believe me ever most affectionately your friend,   S. B. S.

Miss Elizabeth Hoar, engaged to Mr. Emerson's brother Charles, who died in youth, writes letters of regret for the departure of the Hawthornes from Concord : —

. . . Remember me to Mr. Hawthorne and beautiful Una. That you three have lived here in Concord for so many fair days is a page of romance which I shall not forget; whatever happens, so much we have and cannot lose.

Affectionately always,

E. HOAR.

. . . I should like very much to see you and Mr. Hawthorne, and your Una and her brother, and have made two unsuccessful efforts to spend a day with you in Salem. I was in New Haven at the time of the publication of the " Mosses," and all my friends were reading them. I found myself quite a lion because I knew Mr. Hawthorne ; and became a sort of author in my turn, by telling stories of the inhabitants of the Old Manse, omitted in the printed books. Father was charmed with them, and wrote to me quite at length about them. Pray remember me to Mr.

Hawthorne, and give him my thanks for writing the book. Mr. Emerson is in Paris from May 6th to 30th, then lectures in London six times, and sees everybody and everything. I am heartily glad. He has letters which are to show him Lamartine.

Affectionately yours,

ELIZABETH HOAR.

The first Mrs. Lowell, who had long been an intimate friend of my mother's, sends beautiful letters, from which I will make selections, too lovely to be set aside : —

"How blessed it is that God sends these 'perpetual messiahs' among us, to lead us back to innocence and free-heartedness and faith. . . . I have seen a picture of the Annunciation in which Mary is reading the prophecy of the Messiah's coming. . . . Mary is a type of all women, and I love the Roman Catholic feeling that enshrines and appeals to her. It has its root in the very deepest principle of life. . . . James is very well, and to say that he is very happy, too, is unnecessary to any one who knows his elastic, joyful nature. . . . When I feel well and strong, I feel *so* well and strong that I could, like Atlas, bear the world about with me. . . . I love to work with my hands ; to nail, to glue, to scour, to dig ; all these satisfy a yearning in my nature for something substantial and honest. My mother often tells me I was born to be a poor man's wife, I have such an aptitude for all trades."

. . . Is not June the crown of the year, the Carnival of Nature, when the very trees pelt each other with blossoms, and are stirring and bending when no wind is near them, because they are so full of inward life, and must shiver for joy to feel how fast the sap is rushing up from the ground? On such days can you sing anything but, " Oh, beautiful Love " ? Does n't it seem as if Nature wore your livery and wished to show the joy of your heart in every possible form? The everlasting hum and seething of myriad life satisfies and soothes me. I feel as if something were going on in the world, else why all this shouting, and bedecking of every weed in its best, this endless strain from every tiny weed or great oaken flute? All that cannot sing, dances ; the gnats in the air and the long-legged spiders on the water. Even the ants and beetles, the workers that are quoted for examples by hoarding men, run about doing nothing, putting their busy antennæ into everything, tumbling over the brown mould for sheer enjoyment, and running home at last without the little white paper parcel in their mouths which gives them so respectable an air. Doubtless the poor things are scolded by their infirm parents, who sit sunning themselves at the door of the house. . . . Beetles seem to me to have a pleasant life, because they, who have fed for two or three years underground upon the roots, come forth at last winged, and find their nourishment in the blooms of the very same tree. It comforts me, because we have ourselves to eat many bitter

roots here, whose perfect flower shall one day
delight us. This, dear Sophia, has been a long
ramble. I promised to copy that sonnet of
James's for you, so I inclose it.

With true sympathy and love,

Affectionately yours,

MARIA WHITE.

From George S. Hillard came the following
letter. On the envelope my father has written
Hillard's name and "The Scarlet Letter," showing with what interest he preserved this friend's
criticism and praise. On the other side of the
envelope is written, "Foi, Foi, Faith." No one
ever was more faithful to, and consequently ever
had more faith in, his friends than my father.

BOSTON, March 28, 1850.

MY DEAR HAWTHORNE, — You have written a
most remarkable book; in point of literary talent,
beyond all your previous efforts; a book full of
tragic power, nice observation, delicate tact, and
rare knowledge of the human heart. I think it
will take a place in our literature among the highest efforts of what may be called the Tragic Muse
of fiction. You are, intellectually speaking, quite
a puzzle to me. How comes it that with so thoroughly healthy an organization as you have, you
have such a taste for the morbid anatomy of the
human heart, and such knowledge of it, too? I
should fancy from your books that you were bur-
dened with secret sorrow; that you had some blue

chamber in your soul, into which you hardly dared to enter yourself; but when I see you, you give me the impression of a man as healthy as Adam was in Paradise. For my own taste, I could wish that you would dwell more in the sun, and converse more with cheerful thoughts and lightsome images, and expand into a story the spirit of the Town Pump. But while waiting for this, let me be thankful for the weird and sad strain which breathes from "The Scarlet Letter," which I read with most absorbing interest.

Yours ever,
GEO. S. HILLARD.

The owner of the cottage which the Hawthornes hired in Lenox sends a welcome : —

DEAR SOPHIA, — Since we came up here, I have examined the little house you think of taking, and cannot but hope you will take the red house in preference; for although that is not so large or convenient as I wish it were for you, it is much more so than the little garden house. You have a rough plan of that, which Mr. Tappan drew for Mr. Hawthorne, and I will give you one of this. There are four good sleeping-rooms upstairs, but without fireplaces, and could only be *ameliorated* in winter by an entry stove. The house is pleasantly situated, having a view of the Lake, as you know. The road passing by the red house is so little traveled that it is no annoyance. Perhaps you and Mr. Hawthorne would like to come and see the houses for yourselves ; if so, we shall be very glad to have you stay with us. I have no time to tell you how lovely it is here, or how glad we are you are coming.

Affectionately yours,

CAROLINE TAPPAN.

The search for a desirable hillside or meadow space where they might make a new home, away from city streets and the hurrying prisoners upon them, was pleasantly ended for the Hawthornes. The transfer of the little family to Lenox soon occurred, and to the " red house," which was in existence until lately. I will quote a description of the cottage and the views about the spot, given in a Stockbridge paper not long after the small dwelling disappeared : —

" On a stand in the curious old hotel in Stock-bridge is a charred chunk of an oaken house-beam that is as carefully treasured as if it were of gold ; and every guest strolling through the par-lor wherein it is shown halts and gazes at it with a singular interest. A placard pinned to the cinder explains in these words why it is treasured and why the people gaze at it : ' Relic from the Hawthorne Cottage.' The Hawthorne Cottage stood half a mile out of Stockbridge on the road to Lenox. It was burned two months ago. It was a little red story-and-a-half house on a lonely farm, and an old farmer, himself somewhat of a bookworm, dwelt in it with his family at the time it mysteriously took fire. The cottage was a landmark, because Nathaniel Hawthorne dwelt therein in 1850 and 1851 for a year and a half. A great many people go out to see the ruins of it.

"Drive along a lonely winding road through a homely New England district several hundred yards west of the pretentious mansions of Stockbridge, pass through a breezy open patch of pines, and one comes to a characteristic hillside New England orchard, the branches of whose trees just now are bright with ripening red apples. On the hillslope in the middle of the orchard and overlooking the famous 'Stockbridge Bowl' — a round deep tarn among the hills — are the brick cellar walls and brick underpinning of what was a very humble dwelling — the Hawthorne Cottage. About the ruins is a quiet, modest, New England neighborhood. There is not much to see at the site of the Hawthorne Cottage, yet every day fashionable folk from New York and Boston and a score of western cities drive thither with fine equipages and jingling harness, halt, and look curiously for a minute or two at the green turf of the dooryard and the crumbling brick walls of the cottage site."

To go from Salem to Lenox was to contrast very forcibly the somewhat oppressed spirits of historical association with the healthy grandeur of nature. The books my father wrote here embrace this joy of untheoried, peaceful, or gloriously perturbed life of sky and land. Theory of plot or principle was as much beneath him as the cobble-stones; from self-righteous harangues he turned as one who had heard a divine voice that alone deserved to declare. He taught as Nature does, always leading to thoughts of something higher than the dictum of men, and nobler than their greatest beauty of action. He said it was difficult for him to write in the presence of such a view as the "little red house" commanded. It certainly must have been a scene that expressed otherwise unutterable sublimity. But if my father struggled to bring his human power forward in the presence of an outlook that so reminded him of God, he did bring it forward there, and we perceive the aroma and the color which his work could not have gained so well in a town or a village covert.

Mrs. Hawthorne's letters, written for the pleasure of her family, in spite of her growing cares, continue to be a source of intelligence to us: —

My dear Lizzie, — I have just received your letter, for which I am very glad. You say that mother may come to-night. I truly hope she will. But as the heavy fog we had here this morning may have been a rain in Boston, I write now, to request father to go to Oak Hall, or to some ready-made linen-store, and buy Mr. Hawthorne two linen sacks, well made, and good linen. He is a perfect bunch of rags, and he will not let me make him anything to wear — absolutely will not. But he consents that something shall be bought. If mother should be delayed beyond Monday, this can be done ; otherwise it cannot.

I am very sorry about the little books ; but I do not see any help. Ticknor & Co. were going to have illustrations drawn for them, and Mr. Hawthorne thinks they are begun, that money has been expended, and that it is too late to change the plan. He says, he is bound by his engagement, and cannot recede ; but that if you can change their purposes independently of him, — if they are willing, he is. Mr. Fields has not said a word about the Fairy Tales, and I do not know whether Mr. H. intends to write them now. I never ask him what he is about. But I know he is not writing seriously this hot weather.

God bless you all,

SOPHIECHEN.

Sunday.

MY DEAR MOTHER, — This has been a dull "heaven's day" for the children, who have not been so merry as on a sunny day. I have read to them, and shown them my drawings of Flaxman's Iliad and Odysse and Hesiod. I wish you could have seen them the other day, acting Giant Despair and Mrs. Diffidence. They were sitting on chairs opposite the doorsteps ; Julian with one little leg over the other, in a nonchalant attitude ; Una also in negligent position. They were discussing their prisoners, Hopeful and Christian, in very gruff and unamiable voices. " Well, what had we better do with them ? " " Oh, beat them

pretty well, every day!" The air of the two figures, and their tones, in comparison with the faces
and forms, were very funny. I heard Una telling Julian that Christian's bundle was a "bunch
of naughtiness." Julian became Columbus all at
once, on Friday, and ran in from out of doors to
get some blocks to build a cross on the island
which he had discovered. He said, "Where is my
sword to hold in my hand when I get out of my
ship?" [He was between four and five years old.]

Sunday, 20th.

A famous snowstorm. I read from Spenser to
the children, in the morning, of St. George and
Una, Una and the Lion, and Prince Arthur.
Then, Cinderella. They made an exquisite picture, with the hobby-horse. Julian was upon the
horse, — as a king; Una at his side, presenting
ambrosia. In the P. M. I read them Andersen's
" Angel and Child," " The Swineherd," and " Little Ida's Flowers ;" and their father read to them
from " The Black Aunt." In the evening my
husband read to me the " Death of Adam and
Eve," by Montgomery, and something of Crabbe's.

Tuesday, 22d. Clear, splendid day. The children took their little straw baskets and went to
find flowers. They were gone a great while, and
came back with a charming bunch — arbutus, anemones, violets, and houstonia.

They went to walk with their father in the
afternoon, to the woods and mountains, and
brought home arbutus ; and Julian, laurel for me

to make a wreath for papa's head, — laurel of last year.

23d. Julian arranged his cabinet of shells and animals, hammered, ran like a wolf, told stories to himself, helped me make beds, and held cotton for me to wind, watched Mr. Tappan at his young trees, and when his father came down [from writing upstairs] played with him. I sewed all the evening while my husband read the " Castle of Indolence," and finished it.

DEAREST LIZZIE, — Mrs. Sedgwick takes the most kind and motherly interest in my affairs. Both she and her husband come quite often, and Mr. Sedgwick sends Mr. Hawthorne a great many papers. I wish you would tell me whether you think Tall Ann is able to do our work ; but from what she said about being deprived of the Church services and Holy Communion, I know she would not do without them. She would be as quiet here as in heaven. There have been a succession of golden days for a long while, and I have thought

" Time had run back, and brought the age of gold,"

it has been so superb. It is now a golden and rose-colored twilight. The most distant mountains are of the palest azure, and the Lake, pale rose. It is haymaking season, and the children roam abroad with the haymakers, — oh, such happy hours ! The air is fragrant with the dying breath of clover and sweet-scented grass. Julian is getting nut-brown. He is a real chestnut. We are all wonderfully happy, and I can conceive of no greater peace and content. Last Sunday afternoon we all went to the Lake, and Una and I wove a laurel wreath, and Una crowned her father. For mountain-laurel grows about us. We have now twelve hens. Twice a day we all go and feed them. We go in single file. Mr. Hawthorne called it to-day the procession of the equinoxes. The hens have some of them been named : Snowdrop, Crown Imperial, Queenie, and Fawn. Snowdrop is very handsome and white.

Mrs. Hawthorne's mother writes to her in this manner : —

June 8, 1850.

MY BELOVED, — Esther Sturgis brought me your letter yesterday. . . . I hope you have time to enjoy this fine weather. I please myself with imagining various enjoyments for you all in the peaceful scenes around you, maugre the household cares that must fall to your lot. May the spirit of inspiration drive all petty cares from your husband, and fill his soul with thoughts that shall bear blessings to ages yet unborn! He must write — therefore you must court the love of the humble, whose destiny it is to lighten the labors of the gifted ones of the earth. I feel ashamed when I detect myself in thinking that a kitchen-maid is lower in the scale of being than I am. What would the learned and the gifted do if there was no humble one to make the bread that supports life? Kiss your precious little ones, and tell them that grandmamma thinks of them daily; that in spirit she joins in their charming walks, in their search for flowers, in their admiration of the woods, mountains, and fields, and in their holy inspirations while gazing at the glories of the starlit heavens, or the rising or setting sun. May God bless and keep you all.

YOUR MOTHER.

August I.

MY DEAREST MOTHER, — I was more troubled at the hindrance Mr. Hawthorne suffered by our being without help a fortnight than by anything else, because he would not let me bear any weight of care or labor, but insisted upon doing everything himself. Yet he says that he cannot write deeply during midsummer, at any rate. He can only seize the skirts of ideas and pin them down for further investigation. Besides, he has not recovered his pristine vigor. The year ending in June was the trying year of his life, as well as of mine [on account of political calumny]. I have not yet found again all my wings; neither is his tread yet again elastic. But the ministrations of nature will have their effect in due time. Mr. Hawthorne thinks it is *Salem* which he is dragging at his ankles still. . . . Yes, we find kindest friends on every side. The truest friendliness is the great characteristic of the Sedgwick family in all its branches. They seem to delight to make happy, and they are as happy as summer days themselves. They really take the *responsibility* of my being comfortable, as if they were mother, father, brother, sister. We have fallen into the arms of loving-kindness, and cannot suffer for any aid or support in emergencies. This I know will give you a reposeful content concerning us. Mr. Tappan is a horn of benefits. He seems to have the sweetest disposition ; and his shy, dark eyes are always gleaming with hospitable smiles for us. We could not be in more agreeable circumstances, very well, — only I feel rather too far from you all. I want you to come, to avoid those terrible prostrations from heat. Here, we will give you a fresh egg every morning, beaten up to a foam with new milk ; and you shall have honey in the comb, and sweetest vegetables out of our garden, and currants to refresh your parched mouth. And you shall have peace, and rest, and quiet walks in stately woods ; and you shall sit in the barn upon clover hay, and see the dear children play about and rejoice in your presence. You shall see us feed the hennipennies, and hear that most quiet sound of their clucking and murmuring.

Last Saturday night who should appear but Mr. O'Sullivan ! The last we had heard of him was that he had the yellow fever at New Orleans, and that he was arrested for some movements with regard to Cuba. He is now on bail, and will return to be tried in December. He returned to Stockbridge that night, and on Monday

came in a double carriage and took us there, to
the house of Mrs. Field, an old friend of his mother's. We were received with the most whole-
hearted hospitality, and Una and I stayed all
night, and Mr. O'Sullivan brought Mr. Hawthorne and Julian back, because Mr.. Hawthorne
did not wish to stay. I stayed ostensibly to go
to a torchlight festival in an ice glen, but I wished
more to see the O'Sullivans than the festival.
We had a charming visit. .Mrs. Field carried me
to the scene of the sacrifice of Everell in "Hope
Leslie," for it is upon her estate, — a superb hill
covered with laurels, — and this sacrifice rock
near the summit, and the council chambers beneath. That was where the noble Magawesca's
arm was stricken off. The children enjoyed
themselves extremely, and behaved so beautifully
that they won all hearts. They thought that
there never was such a superb child as Julian,
nor such a grace as Una. "They are neither too
shy, nor bold," said Mrs. Field, "but just right."
There was a huge black Newfoundland dog,
Hero, which delighted Julian, and he rode on its
back; and a little white silk dog, Fay, very
piquant and intelligent. It was a large, rambling
mansion, with india-rubber rooms that always
stretch to accommodate any number of guests, Mr.
O'Sullivan said, such is Mrs. Field's boundless
hospitality. The house stands in a bower of trees,
and behind it is the richest dell, out of which
rises Laurel Hill, which in its season is one of
perfect bloom. Rustic seats are at hand all

about, and the prettiest winding paths, and glimpses of the Housatonic River gem the plain. It has not the wide scope and proud effect of our picture, but it is the dearest, sweetest, lovingest retreat one can imagine. Mr. O'Sullivan took me to see Mrs. Harry Sedgwick, in the evening ; a noble woman with a gleam in her face. I owed her a call. There I also saw Mrs. Robert Sedgwick, and the Ashburners, who called upon us at Highwood.

We went to a bridge where we could see the torchlight party come out of the Ice Glen, and it looked as if a host of stars had fallen out of the sky, and broken to pieces ; so said the Count O'S. We waited till they arrived to us, and then we saw Mrs. Charles Sedgwick and her pretty schoolgirls embark in an endless open omnibus for Lenox. They were all lighted up by the burning torches, and were dressed in fantastic costumes of brilliant colors, scarlet being predominant. Those girls looked like a bouquet of bright flowers, as they sat waving farewells, and receiving with smiles the cheers of all the young gentlemen, who raised their torches and shouted, " Hurrah ! " Poor, dear Mrs. Charles ! She looked so warm and so flushed — just like a torch, herself ! — and so lovely, kind, and happy, in the midst of her living roses. Above, serenely shone myriads of pale stars in the clear sky ; around the horizon, heat-lightning flashed. The moon was rising in the east ; and in the north, the aurora borealis bloomed like a vast lily. It was really a rare scene. We returned to Mrs. Harry Sedgwick's. There she stood, receiving the greetings of the members of the party ; every gentleman bearing a torch, which lighted up a rosy face at his side. Such happiness as they enjoyed — such spirit and such mirth ! It was worth witnessing. I found that everybody of note in Stockbridge dearly loves our friend, Mr. O'Sullivan. He is the "pet" and "darling" and "the angelic" with them all. And through him we were known to them.

Most affectionately,
SOPHIECHEN.

September 4.

MY DEAREST MOTHER, — To-day, Mr. Hawthorne and Mr. Melville have gone to dine at Pittsfield. Mr. Tappan took them in his carriage. I went to Highwood after breakfast, to ask for the carriage and horses, as you know Mr. Tappan has put them at our disposition, if we will only drive. I found James sitting in state at the gate, in the wagon, and concluded that there was no hope. But behold, Mr. Tappan was just about starting for Pittsfield, himself ; and with the most beautiful cordiality of hospitality he said he would come over to take the gentlemen. This would have been no particular courtesy in some persons, but for this shy dear, who particularly did not wish, for some reason, to be introduced to Mr. Melville, it was very pretty. I have no doubt he will be repaid by finding Mr. Melville a very different man from what he imagines, and very

agreeable and entertaining. We find him so. A
man with a true, warm heart, and a soul and an
intellect, — with life to his finger-tips ; earnest,
sincere, and reverent ; very tender and *modest*.
And I am not sure that he is not a very great
man ; but I have not quite decided upon my own
opinion. I should say, I am not quite sure that *I
do not think him* a very great man ; for my opinion is, of course, as far as possible from settling the
matter. He has very keen perceptive power ; but
what astonishes me is, that his eyes are not large
and deep. He seems to see everything very accu-
rately ; and how he can do so with his small eyes, I
cannot tell. They are not keen eyes, either, but
quite undistinguished in any way. His nose is
straight and rather handsome, his mouth expressive of sensibility and emotion. He is tall and
erect, with an air free, brave, and manly. When
conversing, he is full of gesture and force, and
loses himself in his subject. There is no grace
nor polish. Once in a while, his animation gives
place to a singularly quiet expression, out of these
eyes to which I have objected ; an indrawn, dim
look, but which at the same time makes you feel
that he is at that instant taking deepest note of
what is before him. It is a strange, lazy glance,
but with a power in it quite unique. It does not
seem to penetrate through you, but to take you
into himself. I saw him look at Una so, yesterday, several times. He says it is Mr. Mathews
who is writing in "The Literary World" the visit
to Berkshire. Mr. Mathews calls Mr. Hawthorne

"Mr. Noble Melancholy," in the next number of the paper. You know, what you read was the introduction only. It is singular how many people insist that Mr. Hawthorne is gloomy, since he is *not*. He is pensive, perhaps, as all contemplative persons must be ; especially when, as in him, "a great heart is the household fire of a grand intellect " (to quote his own words), because he sees and sympathizes with all human suffering. He has always seemed to me, in his remote moods, like a stray Seraph, who had experienced in his own life no evil, but by the intention of a divine intellect, saw and sorrowed over all evil.

[Among my mother's early letters to my father, this poem, written in her fine, delicate hand upon old-fashioned fancy note paper, was evidently her expression of this feeling.]

THE SERAPH AND THE DOVE.

A Seraph strayed to earth from upper spheres,
Impelled by inward motion, vague yet strong :
He knew not wherefore he must leave the throng
Of kindred hierarchs for a world of tears :
But, mailed in proof divine, he felt no fears,
Obedient to an impulse clear of wrong :
And so he ceased awhile his heavenly song,
To measure his immortal life by years.
His archèd brow uprose, a throne of light,
Where ordered thought a rule superior held ;
Within his eyes celestial splendors dwell'd,
Ready to glow and bless with subject might,
When he should find why God had sent him here,
Shot like a star from out his native sphere.

He was alone ; he stood apart from men :
His simple nature could not solve their ways ;
For he had lived a life of love and praise,
And they forgot that God their Source had been.
So mused he on the visions of his mind,
Which, wondrous fair, recalled his home above :
He wist not why he was to space confin'd,
But waited, trusting in Omnific love.
Then lo ! came fluttering to his arms a Dove,
Which for her foot had never yet found rest :
The Seraph folded her within his breast,
And as he felt the brooding warmth, he conscious,
    smiled and said,
"Yes, Father ! Heaven can only be where kindred
    spirits wed !"

["My Dove" was one of my father's names for
my mother ; he found her a seal with a dove upon
it. She several times referred to this title with
joy, in talks with me.]

As his life has literally been so pure from the
smallest taint of earthliness, it can only be because he is a Seer, that he knows of crime. Not
Julian's little (no, *great*) angel heart and life are
freer from any intention or act of wrong than his.
And this is best proof to me of the absurdity of
the prevalent idea that it is necessary to go through
the fiery ordeal of sin to become wise and good.
I think such an idea is blasphemy and the unpar-
donable sin. It is really abjuring God's voice
within. We have not received, as we ought to
have done, the last Saturday's number of "The
Literary World." I have a great curiosity to

read about "Mr. Noble Melancholy." Poor aunty! [Her aunt Pickman.] I really do not believe Shakespeare will be injured by being spoken of in the same paper with Mr. Hawthorne. But no *comparison* is made between them, though there is no reason why one great man may not be compared to another. There is no absolute difference in created souls, after all ; and the intuitions of genius are identical, necessarily ; for what is an intuition of genius but God's truth, revealed to a soul in high communion ? I suppose it is not *impossible* for another Shakespeare to culminate. Even I — little bit of a tot of I — have sometimes recognized my own thought in Shakespeare. But do not tell aunt Pickman of this. Not believing in an absolute source of thought, she would pronounce me either irrecoverably insane or infinitely self-conceited.

Here is John. — No more. SOPHIA.

138

CHAPTER VI

LENOX

ONE of the authors in that excellent company congregated at this period in this part of Berkshire — Mr. Mansfield — writes to Mrs. Hawthorne for the pleasure of the thing; and one fairly hears the drone of time as the days hang ripe and sleepy upon his hands. I quote a few paragraphs from his letters: —

HOME, January 15, 1851.

DEAR MADAM, — It was very kind in you to take up my affairs, and I will say here upon the margin of this reply, that I SHOULD have very much liked your opinion of the "Pundison Letters" I sent out; but now — so long ago is it — I have had time to let my whimsical nature find some other occupation; and the "Up-Country Letters" may lie as they are, not unlikely for the next thousand years. I am absorbed and busied with Bishop Butler's Analogy, which is all things to me at this present; and I am not sure that "The House of the Seven Gables" could tempt me away from it until I get my fill. . . . The Bishop is great, and I hope to have him with me until the frost comes out of the ground, and I can busy myself with Nature herself.

I laughed the other day loud and long at a report of the *plot* of " The House of the Seven Gables," in a letter to a lady. . . . The remark was, that "the *plot* of 'The House of the Seven Gables' was — deepening damnably." . . . You speak of "the crimson and violet sunrises, and the green and gold sunsets," etc. ; and I am glad to get so good an authority for the fact of *mixed colors* in sunrising. In my little book, I speak somewhere of " *the silver and rose tint* flame of the morning." . . . My wife, who sends her love, has taken possession of your note, and is to keep it somewhere " with care." That is, it is to be so carefully hidden that no one will ever find it. Perhaps she is a little jealous ; but, in any case, she wants the autograph. Please make my regards to the man in " The House of the Seven Gables," and believe me, with sincere respect,

Yours — obliged —
L. W. MANSFIELD.

HOME, January 22.

DEAR MADAM, — I suppose Mr. Hawthorne will smile at the idea of my writing him a letter of condolence, and such I do not intend ; but I have been a little provoked at an article in "The Church Review ; " and whether Mr. Hawthorne cares for my opinion or not, it will be a relief and satisfaction for me to say my say about it. Nor do I suppose that he can live so exclusively in a world of his own as not to be pleased at knowing that his friends recognize as such any impertinence that may be said about him. In this case also it comes home to the question which I submitted in the "Up-Country Letters," which I sent you. Now I will say (and I venture to say that I am one of twenty thousand respectable people that would say the same) that the little bits of personal description and reference which Mr. Hawthorne has given in two instances have added — I was going to say tenfold to the interest which attaches to all his writings, and so modestly and quietly, and in such exquisite taste were those references made, that it does strike me as the sublime of stupidity that any one could misunderstand them. . . .

Please excuse my long letter, and believe me, with sincere regards, yours,

L. W. MANSFIELD.

My. mother's notes of every-day life proceed : —

January 2. This morning, one cloud in the east looked like a goldfish close to the horizon. I began to build a snow-house with the children, and shoveled paths.

5th. I walked out in the splendid sunset with the children, to meet papa. I told them, on the way, the story of Genevieve.

10th. Walked before dinner with the children along the road, telling them of Mary, Queen of Scots.

11th. My husband read me the preface to the

third edition of the "Twice-Told Tales." It is absolutely perfect, *of course*.

Sunday, 12th. My husband came down from writing at three. It was reviving to see him. I took dear little Julian and walked to Mr. Wilcox's barn. He enjoyed it as much as I did; the soft hues of the mountains, the slumbering sunshine, and the sparkling snow which towards sunset became violet color. He stooped down to lap up snow, and shouted, "Oh, how pretty!" and I found he was admiring the shining globes. "They lie on the air, mamma!" said he. Mr. Hawthorne received a request for an autograph, and an autobiography!

13th. In the evening my husband said he should begin to read his book ["The House of the Seven Gables"]. Oh, joy unspeakable!

14th. When the children had gone to bed, my husband took his manuscript again. I am always so dazzled and bewildered with the richness of beauty in his productions, that I look forward to a second reading during which I can ponder and muse. The reading closed with a legend, so graphic, so powerful, with such a strain of grace and witchery through it, that I seemed to be in a trance. Such a vision as Alice, with so few touches, such a real existence! The sturdy, handsome, and strong Maule; the inevitable fate, "*the innocent suffering for the guilty,*" seemingly so dark, yet so clear a law!

15th. Sewed all day, thinking only of Maule's Well. The sunset was a great, red ball of fire.

In the evening, the manuscript was again read from. How ever more wonderful! How transparent are all events in life to my husband's awful power of insight; and how he perpetually brings up out of the muddied wells the pearl of price!

16th. The sun rose fiery red, like a dog-day sun. Julian is a prisoner, because his india-rubbers are worn out. I looked forward all day to listening to my husband's inspirations in the evening; but behold! he has no more as yet to read. This morning Julian sat down in a little chair and took his father's foot on his lap. "I want to be papa's toadstool!" said Julian, making one of his funniest mistakes. My husband proposed reading "Thalaba." I was glad, though Southey is no favorite of mine. But I like to be familiar with such things, and to hear my husband's voice is the best music. Mrs. Sedgwick called to see us.

18th. In the morning I took the children and went to Luther's. We went to the barn to find him, and there he was, grinding oats. The children were much grieved and very indignant because the horse was in a treadmill, and could not stop if he would.

22d. Mild. In the morning Anna Greene appeared at my door. I was rejoiced to see her. She stayed two hours. In the evening Herman Melville came, and Anna again, also.

23d. Anna Greene came early, and wanted us to walk with her, on this warm, radiant day. We

went to the Lake, with the children, and had a
delightful talk. In the evening Anna and Caroline Tappan came ; and we had champagne and
beaten egg, which they thought ethereal bever-
age. Caroline said she had wanted just this all
winter.

24th. In the evening my husband read De
Quincey.

Sunday, 26th. I read all over to myself "The
House of the Seven Gables," in manuscript.

29th. In the midst of a storm, who should
appear at the door of our shanty but Sarah Shaw!
Anna Greene only began the glories of arrivals. I
cannot tell how glad I was to see her. It was
perfectly delightful to talk with her again, after
a separation of four years.

February 1. In the evening my husband read
"David Copperfield." I cannot express how
much I enjoy it, made vocal by him. He reads
so wonderfully. Each person is so distinct; his
tones are so various, apt, and rich. I believe that
in his breast is Gabriel's harp. It is better than
any acting I ever saw on the stage.

5th. My husband answered a letter from Robert Adair, of Kentucky, which was to appoint
him an honorary member of the Prescott Literary
Society there. I took a walk with the children
to the brook.

9th. Two proofs came of "The House of the
Seven Gables," which I read with fresh interest.
There never was such perfection of style.

12th. We all walked out, papa and Una to

the Lake, and across it, and Julian and I on the sunny side of the house. There was a golden sunset.

19th. My husband took the children out on the ice-bound lake. He read aloud "Samson Agonistes" in the evening.

March 3. Una's birthday. She is seven years old. My husband began "Wallenstein."

5th. Mr. Ticknor sent five engraved heads of Mr. Hawthorne. The face is very melancholy.

8th. Mr. Tappan thinks Mr. Hawthorne's portrait looks like Tennyson.

10th. Mrs. Sedgwick brought me a letter from Elizabeth Bartol. My husband read me Pope's "Epistles."

12th. At dusk arrived Herman Melville from Pittsfield. He was entertained with champagne foam, manufactured of beaten eggs, loaf sugar, and champagne. He invited us all to go and spend to-morrow with him. My husband decided to go, with Una.

13th. Snowstorm. My husband has gone to Pittsfield. As soon as he and Una drove off in the wagon, dear little Julian for the first time thought of himself, and burst into a heart-breaking cry. To comfort him, I told him I would read him "The Bear and the Skrattel," and "Sam, the Cockerel," which made him laugh through floods of tears. Then he relapsed, and said he would do nothing without Una. So I told him he should have the Swiss cottage, the pearls, and the velvet furniture. This was enchantment.

During his dinner he discoursed all the time about Giant Despair and Christian. He improvised, while playing ball, a sad tragedy, and among other things said, "I wept, and pitied myself." Now he has stopped playing, for the lambs have come to graze before the windows, and he is talking incessantly about having one for his own pet lamb. It is now snowing thickly. I cannot see the Lake ; no farther than the fringe of trees upon the banks. The lambs look anything but *snow-white*, half covered with snowflakes. Julian ran for his slate, and drew one pretty well. Then Midnight came [dog, man, or cat is not known] and frightened them away, and Julian reminded me of my promise to read "The Bear." This I did, squeaking as sharply as occasion required. "I feel very lonely without papa or Una," said Julian. After dinner he asked me to read to him the story of Sir William Phips. When I put him to bed, he said, as he jumped into it, that the angels were lying down beside him.

14th. What a superb day ! But Julian and I are worn out with waiting. Prince Rose-Red talked without one second's intermission the whole time I was dressing him ; and I allowed it, as papa and Una were not here to be disturbed by the clishmaclaver. At breakfast we were dismal. Julian mourned for his father most touchingly, and more than for Una. "Oh, dear," said he, "I feel as if I were alone on a great mountain, without papa !" I have clipped off the ends of his long curls ; and all of these he has tenderly

146

shut up in a domino-box, to distribute among his friends hereafter. After his dinner, I dressed him to go out. He hopes to meet his father, and get into the wagon. But before he went out I took down the "Twice-Told Tales" from the shelf, to look at the engraving. We enjoyed it very much. Blessed be Phillebrown, blessed be Ticknor, Reed & Fields, blessed be Thompson, C. G. Julian was struck with its life. "It is not a drawn papa," said he, "for it smiles at me, though he does not speak. It is a real papa!" Now that he has gone out, I have put it up before me, so that I can see it every time I lift my eyes. Was ever one so loved?

George W. Curtis sends a letter, once more: —

BOSTON, March 19, 1851.

MY DEAR MR. HAWTHORNE, — You will see by the book which I send you with this note ["Nile Notes of a Howadji"] that I break our long silence by a speech of some length; and I should not have waited until now to tell you that I had returned, had I not wished to tell you at the same time something of the delights that kept me so long away. For, like a young lover, I think, of course, that no one had ever so good a time as I. In this book I have aimed to convey the character of the satisfaction that I experienced, and that, I am sure, every man like me must needs experience upon the Nile.

But you will believe — if you still believe in

147

me — that I have seized this small paper, only that I may not send you preserved in cold ink those fruits of travel that I hope one day to shake upon you, warm from the tongue.

I am passing a brace of days only in Boston, having as yet seen no one, and in despair and disgust at the storm. You, I think of in Lenox — which is a summer spot only to my memory; alas! with nothing summery now, I fancy, but your rage at the equinoctial. Does Mrs. Hawthorne yet remember that she sent me a golden key to the studio of Crawford, in Rome? I have neither forgotten that, nor any smallest token of her frequent courtesy in the Concord days. Such be our days forever! Yours truly,

GEORGE W. CURTIS.

Among many messages from friends there was a welcome note from Cambridge: —

MY DEAR HAWTHORNE, — Mr. Duyckinck and his friend Mr. Beekman, of New York, having read your "Twice-Told Tales" with great wonderment and delight, "desire you of more acquaintance." I therefore am happy to make you known to each other. Yours truly,

LONGFELLOW.

June 30.

Mr. G. P. R. James, the novelist, lived somewhat near, but writes to Hawthorne between calls: —

MY DEAR MR. HAWTHORNE, — The night before last I received the two portentous bundles
[essays by Miss Sedgwick's scholars]. Last
night — though to give up reading " The House
of the Seven Gables " for the purpose of reading
a packet of seventy gabbles was like tearing the
flesh from my bones — I set to, and got through
ten of the compositions — six of the minors and
four of the majors. . . . Of what I have read, I
am inclined to say, " the devil a barrel a better
herring." All contain great inaccuracies of style
and grammar ; and few display a trace of original
thought. As far as I have gone, it is all desk-
fancy and " *book larning* " — parrotism, in short.
. . . I was exceedingly sorry to find, from my
son and daughter, that you could not bring your
young people to our haymaking on Wednesday.
But they consoled me with a promise, in your
name, of bringing them another day to spend the
whole of it with us. I hold you to it ; and if
you fail, or fail of prompt performance, I shall
look upon you as faithless and mansworn to

> Yours ever,   G. P. R. JAMES.

Mrs. Hawthorne writes on : —

MY DEAREST LIZZIE, — What a sumptuous
present, or budget of presents, you are making
me ! I am affronted, if they come in the way
of return for the pitiful hospitality you received.
You not only had no bed to sleep on, and no room

to sleep in, but nothing to eat, besides sewing all the time, and washing your own clothes! I was very unhappy about it all, but thought I would not add to the trouble by complaining, as I did not see how I could remedy the matter. I never intend to have a guest again for so long as father stayed, on Mr. Hawthorne's account. It fairly destroys both his artistic and his domestic life. He has no other life — never visiting, and having nothing to do with the public. I do not know as any one but myself can estimate the cost to him of having a stranger in our courts; especially in these narrow ones. A week or so does very well; but months will not do at all. . . . You know that he has but just stepped over the threshold of a hermitage. He is but just *not* a hermit still.

Hawthorne responds to the substantial friendship of a lifelong comrade : —

LENOX, July 24, 1851.

DEAR PIKE, — I should have written to you long since, acknowledging the receipt of your gin, and in answer to your letter, but I have been very busy with my pen. As to the gin, I cannot speak of its quality, for the bottle has not yet been opened, and will probably remain corked until cold weather, when I mean to take an occasional sip. I really thank you for it, however; nor could I help shedding a few quiet tears over that which was so uselessly spilt by the expressman.

The most important news I have to tell you (if

you have not already heard it) is, that we have another daughter, now about two months old. She is a very bright and healthy child, and neither more nor less handsome than babies generally are. I think I feel more interest in her than I did in the other children at the same age, from the consideration that she is to be the daughter of my age — the comfort (at least, so it is to be hoped) of my declining years — the last child whom I expect or intend to have. What a sad account you give of your solitude, in your letter! I am not likely ever to have the feeling of loneliness which you express; and I most heartily wish that you would take measures to remedy it in your own case, by marrying Miss Brookhouse or somebody else as soon as possible. If I were at all in the habit of shedding tears, I should have felt inclined to do so at your description of your present situation; without family, and estranged from your former friends.

Whenever you feel it quite intolerable (and I can hardly help wishing that it may become so soon), do come to me. By the way, if I continue to prosper as heretofore in the literary line, I shall soon be in a condition to buy a place; and if you should hear of one, say, worth from $1500 to $2000, I wish you would keep your eye on it for me. I should wish it to be on the seacoast, or at all events with easy access to the sea. Very little land would suit my purpose, but I want a good house, with space enough inside, and which will not need any considerable repairs. I find that I do not feel at home among these hills, and should not like to consider myself permanently settled here. I do not get acclimated to the peculiar state of the atmosphere, and, except in mid-winter, I am continually catching cold, and am none so vigorous as I used to be on the seacoast. The same is the case with my wife; and though the children seem perfectly well, yet I rather think they would flourish better near the sea. Say nothing about my wishes, but if you see a place likely to suit me, let me know. I shall be in Salem probably as soon as October, and possibly you will have something in view by that time.

Why did you not express your opinion of The House of the Seven Gables, which I sent you? I suppose you were afraid of hurting my feelings by disapproval; but you need not have been. I should receive friendly censure with just as much equanimity as if it were praise; though certainly I had rather you would like the book than not. At any rate, it has sold finely, and seems to have pleased a good many people better than the others, and I must confess that I myself am among the number. It is more characteristic of the author, and a more natural book for me to write, than The Scarlet Letter was. When I write another romance, I shall take the Community for a subject, and shall give some of my experiences and observations at Brook Farm. Since the publication of the Seven Gables I have written a book for children, which is to be put to press immediately.

My wife, with the baby and Una, is going southward in two or three weeks to see her mother, who, I think, will not survive another winter. I shall remain here with Julian. If you can be spared from that miserable Custom House, I wish you would pay me a visit, although my wife would hardly forgive you for coming while she was away. But I do long to see you, and to talk about a thousand things relating to this world and the next. I am very glad of your testimony in favor of spiritual intercourse. I have heard and read much on the subject, and it appears to me to be the strangest and most bewildering affair I ever heard of. I should be very glad to believe that these rappers are, in any one instance, the spirits of the persons whom they profess themselves to be; but though I have talked with those who have had the freest communication, there has always been something that makes me doubt. So you must allow me to withhold my full and entire belief, until I have heard some of the details of your own spiritual intercourse.

On receiving your letter, I wrote to Longfellow, requesting him to forward you any books that might facilitate your progress, in the Swedish language. He has not told me whether or no he did so. I asked him to send them to the Mansion House in Salem. I wish you had rather undertaken Latin, or French, or German, or indeed, almost any other language, in which there would have been a more extensive and attainable literature than in the Swedish. But if it turns out to be a pleasure and improvement to yourself, the end is attained. You will never, I fear (you see that I take a friend's privilege to speak plainly), make the impression on the world that, in years gone by, I used to hope you would. It will not be your fault, however, but the fault of circumstances. Your flower was not destined to bloom in this world. I hope to see its glory in the next.

I had much more to say, but it has escaped my memory just now, and it is of no use trying to say any real thing in a letter. Hoping to see you sooner or later,

Your friend ever,

NATHANIEL HAWTHORNE.

Excuse this illegible scrawl; but I have contracted such a habit of scrawling that I cannot possibly help it.

Mr. Pike was one of the half-earthy intelligences which are capable of bloom, like a granite-strewn hill, revealing upon a closer glance unexpected imagination. I once saw him coming through a little pine grove near The Wayside with my father; it was after our return from England. He was so short, sturdy, phlegmatic of exterior, and plebeian, that I was astonished at my father's pleasure in his company, until I noticed a certain gentleness in his manner of stepping, and heard the modulations of his voice, and caught the fragrance of his humility. One or two letters of his already printed are delightfully straightforward,

—even more so in their unabridged state than as they now stand ; showing unconsciousness of the methods of a devious subtlety of penetration, though ·sensitiveness to its influence, as an ox slowly turns his great eye about at the sound of a bee, but never catches a glimpse of him ; showing a restful stupidity that nevertheless had enough intellectual fire to take a kind, eager delight in telling, as it were, the sculptor that his clay was gray and his marble white. To a mind whose subtlety could never bewilder itself by no matter what intricacies of sudden turning, the solid stare before his nose of Mr. Pike must have been agreeable, since it was joined to a capital vision of whatever actually crossed that patient gaze, and to a tenderness which sprang like purest refreshment from a hard promise. Anything that can restfully attract a thinker is, of course, at a premium with him. Mr. Pike might be as plebeian as he pleased, the more the better, since he was one of the people who could apprehend truth, talk of love like a troubadour for sincere belief in it, and say a good thing when one least expected him to do so, which is the nick of time for brilliancy.

Herman Melville writes, the date being recorded by my father, " Received July 24, 1851," one of the frolicsome letters which it requires second-sight to decipher, the handwriting being, apparently, " writ in water : " —

155

Tuesday afternoon.

MY DEAR HAWTHORNE, — This is not a letter, or even a note, but only a passing word said to you over your garden gate. I thank you for your easy - flowing long letter (received yesterday), which flowed through me, and refreshed all my meadows, as the Housatonic — opposite me — does in reality. I am now busy with various things, not incessantly though ; but enough to require my frequent tinkerings ; and this is the height of the haying season, and my nag is dragging home his winter's dinners all the time. And so, one way and another, I am not a disengaged man, but shall be very soon. Meantime, the earliest good chance I get, I shall roll down to you, my good fellow, seeing we — that is, you and I — must hit upon some little bit of vagabondism before autumn comes. Graylock — we must go and vagabondize there. But ere we start, we must dig a deep hole, and bury all Blue Devils, there to abide till the Last Day. . . . Good-by.

HIS X MARK.

And again : —

PITTSFIELD, Monday afternoon.

MY DEAR HAWTHORNE, — People think that if a man has undergone any hardship, he should have a reward ; but for my part, if I have done the hardest possible day's work, and then come to sit down in a corner and eat my supper comfortably — why, then I don't think I deserve any reward for my hard day's work — for am I not now at peace? Is not my supper good? My peace and my supper are my reward, my dear Hawthorne. So your joy-giving and exultation-breeding letter is not my reward for my ditcher's work with that book, but is the good goddess's bonus over and above what was stipulated for — for not one man in five cycles, who is wise, will expect appreciative recognition from his fellows, or any one of them. Appreciation! Recognition! Is love appreciated? Why, ever since Adam, who has got to the meaning of his great allegory — the world? Then we pygmies must be content to have our paper allegories but ill comprehended. I say your appreciation is my glorious gratuity. In my proud, humble way, — a shepherd-king, — I was lord of a little vale in the solitary Crimea; but you have now given me the crown of India. But on trying it on my head, I found it fell down on my ears, notwithstanding their asinine length — for it 's only such ears that sustain such crowns.

Your letter was handed me last night on the road going to Mr. Morewood's, and I read it there. Had I been at home, I would have sat down at once and answered it. In me divine magnanimities are spontaneous and instantaneous — catch them while you can. The world goes round, and the other side comes up. So now I can't write what I felt. But I felt pantheistic then — your heart beat in my ribs and mine in yours, and both in God's. A sense of unspeakable security is in me this moment, on account of your having understood the book. I have written a wicked book, and feel spotless as the lamb. Ineffable socialities are in me. I would sit down and dine with you and all the gods in old Rome's Pantheon. It is a strange feeling — no hopefulness is in it, no despair. Content — that is it; and irresponsibility; but without licentious inclination. I speak now of my profoundest sense of being, not of an incidental feeling.

Whence come you, Hawthorne? By what right do you drink from my flagon of life? And when I put it to my lips — lo, they are yours and not mine. I feel that the Godhead is broken up like the bread at the Supper, and that we are the pieces. Hence this infinite fraternity of feeling. Now, sympathizing with the paper, my angel turns over another page. You did not care a penny for the book. But, now and then as you read, you understood the pervading thought that impelled the book — and that you praised. Was it not so? You were archangel enough to despise the imperfect body, and embrace the soul. Once you hugged the ugly Socrates because you saw the flame in the mouth, and heard the rushing of the demon, — the familiar, — and recognized the sound; for you have heard it in your own solitudes.

My dear Hawthorne, the atmospheric skepticisms steal into me now, and make me doubtful of my sanity in writing you thus. But, believe me, I am not mad, most noble Festus! But truth is ever incoherent, and when the big hearts strike

together, the concussion is a little stunning. Farewell. Don't write a word about the book. That
would be robbing me of my miserly delight. I
am heartily sorry I ever wrote anything about you
— it was paltry. Lord, when shall we be done
growing? As long as we have anything more to
do, we have done nothing. So, now, let us add
Moby Dick to our blessing, and step from that.
Leviathan is not the biggest fish; — I have heard
of Krakens.

This is a long letter, but you are not at all
bound to answer it. Possibly, if you do answer it,
and direct it to Herman Melville, you will missend
it — for the very fingers that now guide this pen
are not precisely the same that just took it up
and put it on this paper. Lord, when shall we be
done changing? Ah! it's a long stage, and no
inn in sight, and night coming, and the body cold.
But with you for a passenger, I am content and
can be happy. I shall leave the world, I feel,
with more satisfaction for having come to know
you. Knowing you persuades me more than the
Bible of our immortality.

What a pity, that, for your plain, bluff letter,
you should get such gibberish! Mention me to
Mrs. Hawthorne and to the children, and so,
good-by to you, with my blessing.

HERMAN.

P. S. I can't stop yet. If the world was entirely
made up of Magians, I'll tell you what I should
do. I should have a paper-mill established at one
end of the house, and so have an endless riband

of foolscap rolling in upon my desk ; and upon that endless riband I should write a thousand — a million — billion thoughts, all under the form of a letter to you. The divine magnet is on you, and my magnet responds. Which is the biggest ? A foolish question — they are *One*. H.

P. P. S. Don't think that by writing me a letter, you shall always be bored with an immediate reply to it — and so keep both of us delving over a writing-desk eternally. No such thing ! I sha'n't always answer your letters, and you may do just as you please.

Hawthorne is left alone for a few days, while his wife visits her mother, which causes the following notes to be written : —

LENOX, August 8, 1851.

OWNEST PHŒBE, — I wrote thee a note yesterday, and sent it to the village by Cornelius ; but as he may have neglected to put it in, I write again. If thou wilt start from West Newton on *Thursday* next, I will meet thee at Pittsfield, which will answer the same purpose as if I came all the way. . . .

Julian is very well, and keeps himself happy from morning till night. I hope Una does the same. Give my love to her. . . .

Thine, N. H.

August 9, Saturday.

I received yesterday thy note, in which thou speakest of deferring thy return some days longer. Stay by all means as long as may be needful. Julian gets along perfectly well ; and I am eager for thy coming only because it is unpleasant to remain torn asunder. Thou wilt write to tell me finally what day thou decidest upon ; but unless I hear further, I shall go to Pittsfield on *Saturday*, a week from to-day. But if thou seest reason for staying longer do so, that nothing may be left at loose ends.

Julian and I had a fine ride yesterday with Herman Melville and two other gentlemen.

Mrs. Peters is perfectly angelic.

Thinest,   N. H.

Mrs. Peters, a negress of the dignified type, was the general house-servant, an aged, forbidding, harmlessly morose soul, often recalled by my mother in her references to Lenox, when talking, as she did most easily and fascinatingly, to us children of the past. The picturing of Mrs. Peters always impressed me very much, and she no doubt stood for a suggestion of Aunt Keziah in "Septimius Felton." She was an invaluable tyrant, an unloaded weapon, a creature who seemed to say, "Forget my qualities if you dare — there is one of them which is fatal ! " As my parents possessed the capacity to pay respect where it could be earned, the qualities of Mrs.

Peters were respected, and she found herself in a sort of heaven of courteous tolerance.

Mrs. Hawthorne writes to her mother : —

On Sunday Mr. Samuel G. Ward came to see us. He gave me an excellent drawing of Highwood Porch, for " The Wonder-Book," which he said he had asked Burrill Curtis to draw. We have sent it to Mr. Fields. On Monday Mr. Curtis called. He is taking sketches all about, and is going back to Europe this autumn. Just now, Dr. Holmes and Mr. Upham's son Charles drove up. They came in, a few moments. First came Dr. Holmes, to peep at the Lake through the boudoir window, — for he was afraid to leave the horse, even tied ; then he went out for Charles to come in ; and Mr. Hawthorne insisted upon holding the horse, and having them both come in. When Dr. Holmes went back, he laughed to see Mr. Hawthorne at his horse's head, and exclaimed, " Is there another man in all America who ever had so great an honor, as to have the author of ' The Scarlet Letter ' hold his horse ? " My love to your lovely household. Your most

Affectionate child,   SOPHIA.

CHAPTER VII

The following letters were evoked by one of those entanglements concerning the petty matters of existence which will sometimes occur in the most enchanting web and woof of good feeling and high thought. A luxuriant fruit garden, attached to the "red house," seems to have suddenly cast a spell over its original mistress, and around this humorous tragedy my father throws some gleams of mirth and sense, as follows : —

September 5.

Dear Mrs. Tappan, — As questions of disputed boundary are very ticklish ones, whether between nations or individuals, I think it best to take the diplomatic correspondence, on our part, into my own hands ; and I do it the more readily as I am quite an idle man nowadays, and shall find it rather agreeable than otherwise ; whereas Sophia is exceedingly busy, and moreover is averse to any kind of a dispute. You will be kind enough to give me credit for writing in a spirit of undisturbed good humor and friendly courtesy ; and this being the case, I shall feel myself safe in writing with likewise the most perfect frankness.

In the first place permit me to notice the question which you put to Sophia, whether she would not prefer to receive kindness rather than assume rights. I do not know what would be her reply; but, for myself, in view of the infirmities of human nature in general and my especial infirmities, and how few people are fit even to receive kindnesses, and how far fewer are worthy to do them, I infinitely prefer a small right to a great favor. It was this feeling that made me see the necessity of a sum stipulated in the way of rent, between Mr. Tappan and myself. The little difficulty, in which we now find ourselves, merely serves to confirm me in my principle, and will instruct me in all future cases, to have my rights more sharply defined than they are now.

Undoubtedly, by consenting to receive money from me, Mr. Tappan did invest me with certain rights, and among the most evident of them, I consider the property in the fruit. What is a garden without its currant bushes and fruit trees? Last year, no question of this nature was raised: our right seemed to be tacitly conceded, and if you claimed or exercised any manorial privileges, it never came to my knowledge. This season when Mr. Tappan inquired what part of the garden I wanted to cultivate, I supposed that he wished to know in order that he might send Cornelius to plough it — as he very kindly did. It never came into my mind that I should lose the most valuable part of the demesne by failing to plant it. If the fruit trees have suffered by my neglect, this was reasonable ground for remonstrance on Mr. Tappan's part, but would hardly justify him in so summary a measure as that of taking the property out of my hands, at once, and without a word of explanation, or even informing me of the fact. Nor do I conceive that he had any purpose of doing so.

At all events, Sophia and I supposed ourselves to be in full possession of that part of the garden, and in having a right of property over its products, more extensive than that of Adam and Eve in Eden, inasmuch as it excluded not a single tree. Such being our view of the matter, you meet Mary Beekman, carrying a basket of fruit. You stop her, look at the contents of the basket, and inquire as to its destination. You ask her (at least so she averred to Mrs. Peters, although she has since qualified her statement) whether it had been given away or *sold*. You conduct this examination in such a mode, as to make it evident to our servant-girl that you consider Sophia and Mrs. Peters as combining in a depredation on your property.

You follow this up with a note of remonstrance to Sophia, in which you take her to task not merely for giving away some of the fruit, but for presuming to choose her own time to gather it for our own use. Now let us suppose the perfectly parallel case, that Mrs. Ward should take upon herself to pursue the same course in regard to the fruit of Highwood. Would Mrs. Tappan have responded to Mrs. Ward by a gentler assertion of right than Sophia's to yourself? I think

not. I do not see how you could. And if you
did so, it would be purely out of your own abundant grace and good nature, and would by no
means be due to any propriety in the supposed
behavior of Mrs. Ward.

Finally in your note of last evening, you give
us very clearly to understand that you look upon
us as having no rights here whatever. Allow me
to say that this is precisely the crisis which I
contemplated when I felt it essential to be understood that I had *bought* my rights, even from
persons so generously disposed as yourself and
Mr. Tappan. The right of purchase is the only
safe one. This is a world of bargain and sale;
and no absurdity is more certain to be exposed
than the attempt to make it anything else.

As regards the apples of discord (meaning
thereby the plums, pears, peaches, and whatever
besides) we sincerely hope you will take as many
of them as you please, and on such grounds as
may cause them to taste most agreeably. If you
choose to make a raid, and to seize the fruit with
the strong hand, so far from offering any armed
resistance, we shall not so much as remonstrate.
But would it not be wiser to drop the question of
right, and receive it as a free-will offering from
us? We have not shrunk from the word "gift,"
although we happen to be so much the poorer of
two parties, that it is rather a suspicious word
from you to us. Or, if this do not suit you, you
can take the fruit in humble requital of some
of the many favors bestowed in times past and

which we may perhaps remember more faithfully than you do.

And then the recollection of this slight acidity of sentiment, between friends of some years' standing, may impart a pleasant and spirited flavor to the preserves and jams, when they come upon your table. At any rate, take what you want and that speedily, or there will be little else than a parcel of rotten plums to dispute about.

With kind regards to Mr. Tappan,

Very truly yours, N. H.

Mrs. Hawthorne writes to her sister, Miss E. P. Peabody : —

I send you Mr. Tappan's answer, so noble and beautiful. Mr. Hawthorne wrote him a beautiful note in reply, in which he said : " My dear sir, I trust you will not put more weight than it deserves upon a letter which I wrote rather to relieve Sophia of what might have disturbed her, than because I look upon the affair in a serious light. Your own letter is of a character to make one ashamed of any narrower or ignobler sentiment than those of universal beneficence and good will ; and I freely confess that the world will not deserve to be called a world of bargain and sale so long as it shall include men like yourself. With much regard truly yours, N. H."

Two letters to Mrs. Peabody describe the Lenox scene : —

MY DEAREST MOTHER, — It is heaven's day, to-day, and the Lord's day, and now baby sleeps and Una is at Highwood and Julian at play, and I will begin at least to answer your sweet, patient, wise, and tender letters. Yesterday and to-day have been tropical in heat and richness and expansiveness, and I feel as if it is on such days only that we really live and know how good is GOD. I wish I knew that you enjoy such warmth and are not made languid by it. You will perhaps remember that I am always strongest at 98° Fahrenheit. I delight to think that you also can look forth as I do now upon a broad valley and a fine amphitheatre of hills, and are about to watch the stately ceremony of sunset from your piazza. But you have not this lovely Lake, nor I suppose the delicate purple mist which folds these slumbering mountains in airy veils.

Mr. Hawthorne has been lying down in the sunshine, slightly fleckered with the shadows of a tree, and Una and Julian have been making him look like the mighty Pan by covering his chin and breast with long grass-blades, that looked like a verdant and venerable beard. I walked down to them a moment, leaving baby asleep, and while there Una exclaimed, "Oh, how I wish Georgie was here!" [George C. Mann, her cousin.] Thus the dear little boy harmonizes with the large and dreamy landscape, so that his presence would only help the beauty of this peerless day. I never heard Una wish for any one before, when

enjoying Elemental life, *and her father.* Baby
Rose has had a carriage for a week or more, and
we took her one day down to the Lake. I wish
you could have seen her in the wood, when I held
her in my arms. She smiled and smiled and
smiled, at the trees and the Lake and the woodland sounds, till she transported mamma almost
out of the proprieties. "To kiss her all to pieces,"
"to hug her to death," "to devour her," were
processes to which she rendered herself fearfully
liable. How wonderful is this love for which
there is no mortal expression, but which we can
only shadow forth by death and destruction. Julian has begun to speak to the baby now. He
exclaims, "Oh, you darling!" and holds her on his
lap, with such a look of bountiful and boundless
tenderness and care as would charm you to see.
I should as soon expect an angel from the sky to
descend to a rough scuffle with a desperado as
for Julian to disturb or annoy the little Rosebud.
Sometimes we go down to the wood near, and
baby sleeps in the carriage to the music of pine-
tree murmurs and cricket-chirpings, and once in
a while of birds, while Una and Julian build piles
of tiny sticks for the fairies' winter fuel, and papa
and mamma sit and muse in the breathless noon.
But it is seldom warm enough. These last two
days *are* warm enough, and my soul seems to
"expand and grow like corn and melons," and I
remember all beautiful behavior and noble deeds
and grand thoughts and high endeavors ; and the
whole vast Universe seems to blend in one sin-

gle, unbroken recognition of the " Higher Law."
Can there be wrong, hate, fraud, injustice, cruelty,
war, in such a lovely, fair world as this before my
eyes ? Cannot cities be abolished, so that men
may realize the beauty of love and peace by contemplating the broad and genial spaces where
there is no strife ? In the country they would
see that sunbeams do not wrangle, that forests
of trees agree together, that no flower disturbs
another flower. I have written and the sun has
set ; and the moon has risen, and reveals the fine
sculpture of nature. Una and Julian and Baby
Rose are all in profound repose. Not a sound
can be heard but my pen-strokes, and the ever
welcome voice of the cricket, which seems expressly created to announce silence and peace. . . .
It is very singular how much more we are in
the centre of society in Lenox than we were in
Salem, and all literary persons seem settling
around us. But when they get established here
I dare say we shall take flight. . . . Our present
picture is Julian, lying on an ottoman in the boudoir, looking at drawings of Grecian gems ; and
just now he is filled with indignation at the man
who sent Hercules the poisoned shirt, because
he is contemplating that superb head of the " Suffering Hercules." He says he hopes that man
is dead ; and I assure him that he *is* dead, dead,
dead, and can send no more poisoned shirts to
anybody. It happened to be a woman, however,
sad to tell, but I thought I would not reveal to
him the terrible story of Dejanira and the wicked

Nessus. Una is whittling, but at this instant runs off to help Mary Beekman to do something. Mr. Hawthorne has retired to his Study. Baby sleeps. Good-by, dear mother. Love to your household. Your loving child, SOPHIA.

DEAREST MOTHER, — To-day I took Julian for a walk. He waited to speak to his beloved Mr. Tappan, who was in his field. Julian picked up one sheaf after another, and carried them to him, calling, " Mr. Tappan ! Mr. Tappan ! Here are your oats ! " Mr. Tappan turned at last, smiling, and thanked him for his help. The afternoon was so beautiful that every incident seemed like a perfect jewel on a golden crown. The load of yellow sheaves, the rainbow child, the Castilian with his curls and dark smiling eyes [Mr. Tappan] — every object was a picture which Murillo *could not* paint. I waited for Julian till he ran to me ; and when we came into our yard, there was lady baby in her carriage, in a little azure robe, looking like a pale star on a blue sky. We came into the dining-room, and out of the window there was this grand and also exquisite picture — lake, meadow, mountains ; forever new, forever changing ; now so rich with this peculiar autumn sunshine, like which my husband says there is nothing in the world. The children enjoy, very much, this landscape, while they eat their supper. Una ate hers, and went upstairs to see grandmamma ; and Julian sat on my lap, very tired with play, eating a cold buckwheat cake, and gazing out. "Mamma! *Mountain! Lake!*" he kept ejaculating. Wise child! What could be added, in the way of adjective, that would enhance? "Thou eye among the blind!" thought his mother. At last he was so weary with sport that he slipped down upon the floor, and lay upon his back, till he finished eating his buckwheat cake. Then I put him to bed. He clasped his blessed little arms so tightly around my neck, with such an energetic kiss, that we both nearly lost breath. One merry gleam from his eyes was succeeded by a cloud of sleepiness, and he was soon with the angels. For he says the angels take him, when he goes to sleep, and bring him back in the morning. Then I began this letter. Dear little harp-souled Una — whose love for her father grows more profound every day, as her comprehending intellect and heart perceive more and more fully what he is — was made quite unhappy because he did not go at the same time with her to the Lake. His absence darkened all the sunshine to her ; and when I asked her why she could not enjoy the walk as Julian did, she replied, "Ah, *he* does not love papa as *I* do!" But when we arrived, there sat papa on a rock, and her face and figure were transfigured from a Niobe's to an Allegra's instantly. After I put Julian to bed, I went out to the barn to see about the chickens, and she wished to go. There sat papa on the hay, and like a needle to a magnet she was drawn, and begged to see papa a little longer, and stay with him. Now she has come, weary

enough ; and after steeping her spirit in this rose
and gold of twilight, she has gone to bed. With
such a father, and such a scene before her eyes,
and *with eyes to see*, what may we not hope of
her ? I heard her and Julian talking together
about their father's smile, the other day. They
had been speaking of some other person's smile
— Mr. Tappan's, I believe ; and presently Una
said, " But you know, Julian, that there is no
smile like papa's ! " " Oh no," replied Julian.
" Not like *papa's !* " Una has such an intuitive
perception of spheres, that I do not wonder at
her feeling about her father. She can as yet
hardly tell why she is so powerfully attracted ;
but her mother can sympathize, — and knows
very well.

Do not wait an hour to procure the two last
numbers of " The Literary World," and read a
new criticism on Mr. Hawthorne. At last some
one speaks the right word of him. I have not
before heard it. I have been wearied and annoyed hitherto with hearing him compared to
Washington Irving and other American writers,
and put, generally, *second.* At last some one
dares to say what in my secret mind I have
often thought — that he is only to be mentioned
with the Swan of Avon ; the great heart and the
grand intellect combined. I know you will enjoy
the words of this ardent Virginian as I do. But
it is funny to see how he does not know how this
heart and this intellect are enshrined.

It was decided to return to the neighborhood of Boston, and for a short time the family remained in West Newton : —

November 28.

MY DEAR ELIZABETH, — Here we are, in possession of Mary Mann's house and effects. I took baby on a sledge to see her grandmother Peabody on Thanksgiving Day, who was charmed with my smiling, fair baby. Una reads her grandmother "The Wonder-Book," very sweetly, when she is there. Mother says she could never tire of listening to her.

Your affectionate sister,

SOPHIA.

WEST NEWTON, December 25, 1851.

MY DEAR LOUISA [HAWTHORNE], — This very morning I intended to write to you again, to inquire why you neither came nor responded to my letter, and then I received yours. The children watched for you many days, and finally gave you up. They will be delighted at your coming. Pray come as soon as the second week of January. Grace Greenwood spent two or three days, and was very pleasant. Mr. Fields writes from Paris that Mr. Hawthorne's books are printed there as much as in England ; that his fame is great there [in England], and that Browning says he is the finest genius that has appeared in English literature for many years.

Your affectionate sister,

SOPHIA.

P. S. [By Hawthorne.] I have published a new collection of tales ; but you shall not have a copy till you come for it.   N. H.

P. S. [By Mrs. Hawthorne.] This new volume of "Twice-Told Tales" was published on Thursday ; and yesterday Mr. Ticknor told Nathaniel that he had already sold a thousand copies, and had not enough bound to supply the demand.

I give a letter which must have come like the song of a wood-thrush to the author, its diction being as pure as his own, and yet as strong.

BROOKLYN, July 7, 1852.

MR. HAWTHORNE, — You have expressed the kind hope that your writings might interest those who claim the same birthplace with yourself. And as we need but slight apology for doing what inclination suggests, I easily persuade myself that it will not be very inappropriate for me to assure you that in one heart, at least, pride in your genius and gratitude for high enjoyment owed to you have added to, and made still more sacred, the strong love otherwise felt for the spot where the precious gift of life was received.

In earlier days, with your "Twice-Told Tales," you played upon my spirit-harp a sweet melody, the notes of which have never died away — and years after, when my heart was just uplifting itself from a deep sorrow, I read the introduction to your "Mosses from an Old Manse ;" and I rejoiced in your words, as a tree, borne down by the wind and storm, rejoices in the first gentle breeze or ray of kindly sunshine.

And now, as after repeated griefs and lengthened anxieties I think I am come to that period of second youth of which you speak, I am permitted to delight in the marvelous beauty and infinite delicacy of the narration of "The Scarlet Letter," and the deep insight into human hearts and minds shown in that and the later production. When I am tempted to lay down the burden which, of one kind or another, mortals must daily bear, and forget that "all human liberty is but a restraint self-imposed or consented to," I shall call to mind the touching moment when Hester Prynne sadly bound up her flowing tresses, but just released, and meekly reassumed the badge of her shame. And the little Phœbe, — with her genial sympathies and cheerful tones, — I am not altogether without hope that she may aid me to throw off some of the morbid tendencies which have ever clung to my life (if, perchance, this last moral lesson should not destroy the first) ; and these sorrows once overcome, existence would not lose its corresponding exquisiteness of enjoyment.

I once lived in the "Old Hawthorne house;" whether or not you, sir, ever crossed the threshold tradition hath not deigned to inform me. Possibly you lived there when a child. And if the spirit renew itself once in seven years, as the body is said to do, the soul of those younger hours may have remained, may have shared with us our more ethereal pleasures, while it frowned on our prosaic sports. At least, to some such fancy as this, united with the idea of second childhood before alluded to, must be referred the folly of which I have been guilty in addressing a person, who, so far as bodily presence is concerned, is to me an entire stranger, and to whom I am utterly unknown.

However, sir, humbly begging your pardon for this same folly, and entreating that by no accident may the shades of the Salem witches become aware of it,

I am yours with much esteem,

MARY A. PORTER.

Upon the envelope Hawthorne has written, "Answered, July 18th." The letter has been preserved out of many thrown aside, and Mrs. Hawthorne has spoken to me of Mary Porter as of a real friend. Her delicacy and good sense of expression contrast well with the over-fanciful, unliterary quality of the letters of persons who came prominently forward as teachers of thought and literature, and who no doubt jarred miserably in their letters, if not in their conversation, upon the refined skill of Hawthorne and his wife. At any rate (and though the intercourse with these persons to whom I refer with daring comment was received most gratefully and cordially as generally the best to be found) Mary Porter was never forgotten.

That my mother and father enjoyed their next

177

home at The Wayside there are immediate letters to prove ; but if they had not feasted their eyes upon a vision of beautiful spaces, it might have been less delightful to return to the haunts of friends, and a hollow among hills. One grandeur of the distance they did not leave behind at Lenox : the sunsets to be seen over the meadows between The Wayside and the west are spaciously revealed and splendidly rich. Economy had a restless manner of drifting them from place to place. Now, however, a home was to be bought (the title-deed exists, with Mr. Emerson's name, and that of his wife, attached) ; so that the drifting appeared to be at an end. I have reserved until now several letters from Concord friends, of an earlier date, in order to show to what the Hawthornes looked forward in the matter of personalities, when reestablishing themselves in the distinguished village.

Mr. Alcott was prominent. In her girlhood, Mrs. Hawthorne, hearing from Miss Peabody that Mr. James Freeman Clarke had talked with some amusement of the school prophet's ideas, etc., had written : —

" Mr. Alcott's sublime simplicity and depth of soul would make it impossible for me to make jest of him. I cannot imagine why persons should not do themselves justice and yet be humble as a little child. I do not believe he is in the least self-elated. I should think it impossible, in the nature of things, for him to arrive at the kind of truths he does without entire simplicity of soul. I should think they could not be accessible to one of a contrary character."

But, nevertheless, Mr. Alcott's official post seems to have been that of visionary plenipotentiary, and one which was a source of most excellent entertainment. He writes in 1836 : —

August 23.

DEAR FRIEND, — I have just returned, and find your two letters waiting for me. I have read them with a double sentiment. The interest which you express in my thoughts, and their influence over you, I can explain in no other way than as arising from similarity of temperament and of taste, heightened exceedingly by an instinctive tendency — almost preternatural — to reverence whatever approaches, either in Spirit or Form, your standard of the Ideal. Of minds of this class it is impious to ask for tempered expressions. They admire, they marvel, they love. These are the law of their being, and to refuse them the homage of this spiritual oneness with the object of their regard, is death ! Their words have a significance borrowed from their inmost being, and are to be interpreted, not by ordinary and popular acceptation, but by the genius of the individual that utters them. These have a significance of their own. They commune not with words, but in spite of them. Ordinary minds mistake them. . . . You inquire whether portions of "Psyche" are to be copied for the press. Mr. Emerson has not returned the manuscript. But

179

should I find anything left (after his revisions) worthy of attention, I will send it to you. . . . I send you some numbers of the "Reformer," among others is the one containing Mr. [Orestes] Brownson's notice of the "Story Without An End." The allegories which you copied while with us are also among them. I read your allegory to Mr. Brownson, who was interested in it, and took it for the "Reformer." It is a beautiful thing, and will be useful. . . . Write me as often as you feel inclined. I would write often, were I at all given to the practice. My mind flows not freely and simply in an epistle.

Very truly yours,

A. BRONSON ALCOTT.

P. S. I have read Carlyle's "Schiller." You re-utter my conceptions at the time. You are very kind to propose copying the Young Christ [for Mr. Alcott's schoolroom]. The original is a borrowed one, and a copy would be useful.

September 12, 1836.

DEAR FRIEND, — I was glad to hear from you again, for I find my thoughts often dwelling on you. The sympathy of spirits is the heart's *undersong*, and its warblings are heard in the quiet hours of solitude, as if they were from the soft voices of celestial choirs. Music reaches us from the distance, amid the discordant noises of the External. Your remarks on de Maistre have interested me in the book. Mr. Brownson [afterwards famous as a Catholic writer] takes it to-day, and I shall have the interesting passages from him. If you have a copy of the "Valley of Solitude" [one of my mother's original allegories] will you send it? I am under the impression that you preserved portions of the "Valley," and intended to recall and write out the remainder at your leisure. Now, don't attempt this, because Mr. Thacher wants it for his "Boston Book," but simply tell me how much is preserved. . . . Have you seen Mr. Emerson's "Nature"? If you have not, let me send you a copy. It is a divine poem on the External. It is just to your taste. . . . It reminds me more of Sampson Reid's "Growth of the Mind" than any work of modern date. But it is unlike any other work. I send you Mr. Brownson's notice of it. Mr. Brownson gave us two splendid discourses lately. Surely this man is a terror to pseudo-ministers and would-be philosophers. He is one of the most eloquent preachers. He grapples with the highest truths and deepest wants of our being, and spreads these before the reason as with a light from heaven. He will write to you soon. With great regard,

A. BRONSON ALCOTT.

Emerson in the same year responded to a gift of some drawings which my mother had made for him, in these kind and thoughtful sentences : —

MY DEAR MISS SOPHIA, — I beg you to accept my thanks for the beautiful drawings you have sent me. . . . I shall keep them as a treasure to be shown to all my friends who have good or capable eyes, that they may rejoice with me in the power of the artist. From these fair forms I hope to receive many a wise suggestion, many a silent reproof. . . .

Your obliged friend and servant,

R. WALDO EMERSON.

And later : —

CONCORD, January 20, 1838.

You make me heartily ashamed, my kind friend, by the excess of your praise of two such little books. I could not possibly recognize anything of me in your glowing and pictorial words. So I take it for granted that as a true artist you have the beauty-making eye, which transfigures the landscape and the heads it looks upon, and can read poetry out of dull prose. I am not the less glad to have been the occasion to you of pleasant thoughts, and I delight in the genuine admiration you express of that ideal beauty which haunts us ever and makes actual life look sometimes like the coarsest caricature. I like very well what you say of Flaxman, and shall give him the greater heed. And indeed who can see the works of a great artist without feeling that not so much the private as the common wealth is by him indicated. I think the true soul — humble, rapt, conspiring with all, regards all souls as its lieutenants and proxies — itself in another place — and saith of the Parthenon, of the picture, of the poem, — It is also my work. I can never quarrel with your state of mind concerning original attempts in your own art. I admire it rather. And I am pained to think of the grievous resistance which your genius has been so long tasked to overcome, of bodily suffering.

You ask for my lectures. I wish they were fit to send. They should go immediately to Salem if they were. I have not allowed one of them to go in manuscript out of my family. The first one of the course, which is the most presentable, I will cheerfully lend you whenever I can get time to patch his coat a little. It is, however, already promised to two persons.

I thank you for the beautiful little drawing you sent me of Perseus. It is admired of all beholders. Tell your sister Elizabeth that her account of Mr. Very interested me much, and I have already begged Mr. Whiting to bring him to our Lyceum, and he promised his good offices to get him here.

R. W. EMERSON.

A letter mentions a medallion which Mrs. Hawthorne had made of Charles Emerson, after his death : —

CONCORD, May 18, 1840.

MY DEAR MISS SOPHIA, — I have begged Mr. Garey to call on you to-day for the medallion to go to Waterford, and the one for New York, if ready . . . one of which I wish to send to Mr. Abel Adams.

Elizabeth [Hoar] is very well content with the

cast, though she thinks it has lost some of the precision, as well as the agreeable tint, of the clay. All our friends find the likeness — some of them slowly — but all at last. We all count it a beautiful possession ; the gift of a Muse, and not the less valuable that it was so unexpected. You must now gratify us all by fixing a time when you will come to Concord and hear what we have to say of it.

Will you not come hither the last week of this month, or the second week in June ? If neither of these dates suits you, you shall choose any day thereafter, only do not fail us.

Your friend and servant,

R. W. EMERSON.

When arranging to escort the young artist to Concord for the proposed visit, he proceeds : —

. . . In regard to certain expressions in your letter, I ought to say, you will presently be undeceived. Though I am fond of writing, and of public speaking, I am a very poor talker and for the most part very much prefer silence. Of Charles's beautiful talent in that art I have had no share ; but our common friend, Mr. Alcott, the prince of conversers, lives little more than a mile from our house, and we will call in his aid, as we often do, to make amends for our deficiency, when you come. . . . Will you say to your sister Elizabeth that I received her kind letter relating to certain high matters, which I have not yet

184

been in the vein to answer, — indeed, I dream that she knows all my answer to that question, — has it ready in her rich suggestion, and only waits for mine to see how well they will tally. I have laid the letter by, shall. presently read it again, and if I have anything material, I will write.

With great regard, yours,
R. W. EMERSON.

CONCORD, April 20, 1841.

MY DEAR MISS SOPHIA, — Will you accept from my sister Elizabeth Hoar and me the few accompanying prints ?

A word of apology must go with them. Elizabeth and I sent, last summer, by a gentleman who was going to Europe, an order for a few prints of pictures of Raffaelle and Michel Angelo (specifying particularly the Prophets and Sibyls of Michel), with the hope that we might receive something fit to send you. Our agent was less acquainted with these matters than we supposed ; still, we hope they will not be quite without value in your studio, as we have both of us found something to admire in these stern drawings. The Transfiguration is a more spirited copy than most that I have seen, though the principal figure seems never to be quite well copied. Here is a Virgin of Leonardo da Vinci and one from Correggio.

Will you have the goodness to thank your sister Elizabeth for the fine statement she has given the Englishwoman [Miss Martineau] of the enterprise we are all so proud of ; and I can easily suppose the colonists were content with the portrait. She has in a note propounded to me certain questions which and the like of which I always fancy one can answer with a word, as they arise ; — but to answer them with the pen, one must sit like Simmides from month to month, from year to year.

With great regard,

Your friend and servant,

R. WALDO EMERSON.

Elizabeth Hoar wishes to keep the Martineau letter a day or two longer. I am also to thank your sister Elizabeth for the summons to the torchlight exhibition, which however I could not easily obey.

A fragment, of most informal import, but exemplifying Emerson's quaint agility of expression, written about 1843, runs : —

Do not be chagrined, and excellent lady, if I should demand interest in advance for my loan ; but if possibly I can get my errands ready, I shall stop the passing coach, and load you with freight and commissions ; not compliments and congratulations, merely. Do not misconceive me — but messages relative to merest chores. And so with thanks,

Yours, R. W. E.

Margaret Fuller d'Ossoli expresses herself, at the time of my parents' marriage, as thoughtfully

as the rest. Her personality never ceased to
hover about Concord, even after her death. She
is a part of its fascination : —

My dear Sophia, — After reading your letter
I wanted to write a few lines, as are not in such a
hasty, interrupted fashion. Yet not much have
I to say, for great occasions of bliss, of bane, —
tell their own story, and we would not by unnecessary words come limping after the true sense.
If ever mortal was secure of a pure and rational
happiness which shall grow and extend into immortal life, I think it is you, for the love that
binds you to him you love is wise and pure and
religious ; it is a love given not chosen, and the
growth not of wants and wishes, but of the demands of character. Its whole scope and promise
is very fair in my eyes ; and in daily life as well
as in the long account I think there will be great
happiness ; for if ever I saw a man who combined
delicate tenderness to understand the heart of a
woman, with quiet depth and manliness enough
to satisfy her, it is Mr. Hawthorne. . . . To one
who cannot think of love merely in the heart, or
even in the common destiny of two souls, but as
necessarily comprehending intellectual friendship
too, it seems the happiest lot imaginable that lies
before you. . . . The whole earth is decked for a
bridal. I see not a spot upon her full and gold-
bespangled drapery. All her perfumes breathe,
and her eye glows with joy. . . . My affectionate
remembrances to your friend. You rightly felt

how glad I should be to be thought of in the happy hour. As far as bearing an intelligent heart, I think I deserve to be esteemed a friend. And thus in affection and prayer, dear Sophia,

Yours,   MARGARET F.

A year or two later my father received the following letter from her : —

DEAR MR. HAWTHORNE, — You must not think I have any black design against your domestic peace. Neither am I the agent of any secret tribunal of the dagger and cord ; nor am I commissioned by the malice of some baffled lover to make you wretched. Yet it may look so, when you find me once again, in defiance of my failure last summer, despite your letter of full exposition, once more attempting to mix a foreign element in your well compounded cup. But indeed, oh severest and most resolute man, these propositions are none of mine. How can I help it, if gentle souls, ill at ease elsewhere, wish to rest with you upon the margin of that sleepy stream ? How can I help it if they choose me for an interpreter ? [A suggestion is then made, for the second time, that my parents should admit a friend into the Old Manse as a boarder. The notion was sometimes alluded to by my mother in after-years with unfading horror.] I should like much to hear something about yourselves ; what the *genius loci* says, whether through voice of ghost, or rat, or winter wind, or kettle-singing symphony to the happy duet ; and whether by any chance you sometimes give a thought to your friend

MARGARET.

And again : —

NEW YORK, May 22, evening.

DEAR SOPHIA AND MR. HAWTHORNE, — I received your letter and read it with attention ; then laid it aside, and thought I would not reply, for so much had been said and written about my pamphlet that I was weary of it, and had turned to other things. When my interest revives, I shall probably make reply, but I hope *vivâ voce*.

Yes ! I hope to see you once more at the dear old house, with the green fields and lazy river ; and have, perhaps, sweet hours [fragment torn away] and if all works well, I hope to come. Una alone will be changed ; yet still, I think, the same. Farewell, dear friends, now ; for this is only meant as a hasty sign of affection from   M.

Mrs. Hawthorne writes, at the threshold of The Wayside residence : —

June 6, 1852, Sunday.

MY DEAREST MOTHER, — Your beautiful little note was very grateful to me. . . . We arrived at the Middlesex Hotel after one o'clock. At four o'clock I was driven to The Wayside. The cartman had tumbled all the wet mattresses in a heap in the farthest corner of the barn, and I had them all pulled out to dry. It was very hot weather.

189

A good deal was accomplished, when the man and woman who were working for me went to supper, and left me and Una in quiet possession of our home.

We set forth slowly village-ward, and met Mr. Emerson and Mr. Thoreau. Mr. Emerson was most cordial, and his beautiful smile added to the wonderful beauty of the sunset. He turned back and walked with us till we met the carriage. The next morning, Una actually nailed down the brown paper upon the dining-room and Study, and was very helpful and charming, and perfectly enchanted with her home. It is really astonishing what magical changes have been wrought inside the horrible old house by painters, paperers, and carpenters, and a little upholstery. The carpet on the Study looks like rich velvet. It has a ground of *lapis lazuli* blue, and upon that is an acanthus figure of fine woodcolor ; and then, once in a while is a lovely rose and rosebud and green leaf. I like it even better than when I bought it. The woodwork downstairs is all painted in oak, and it has an admirable effect, and is quite in keeping with the antiquity of the dwelling. The dining-room is quite elegant, with a handsome paper having a silvery sheen, and the brown and green Brussels carpet. When Mr. Hawthorne arrived, he had quite a civilized impression of the house at first glance, and was delighted with it, not having seen it since his first visit in snow-time, when it seemed fit only for a menagerie of cattle. You will be glad to know that I have done nothing myself, having so many assistants. But it is no sinecure to keep people at work. Una was impatient of waiting for papa and Julian, and walked off to meet them. At last I heard the rumble of the carriage, and took baby out on the piazza. When Julian passed, he was at the open window of the carriage ; and baby saw him and screamed for joy ; and Julian shouted to see me ; and the echoes were fairly roused by the ecstasy of meeting, all round.

The other morning, at the Middlesex Hotel, Una remarked that she was going to see Mr. Emerson. I supposed she was jesting ; but I missed her soon after, and in about an hour she returned, and said she had been to see him. She had rung at the door, and a servant came, and she inquired for Mr. Emerson! He came out and greeted her very kindly, and said, " I suppose you have come to see Mrs. Emerson." " No," replied Una, " I have come to see *you*." So he politely put aside his studies, and accompanied his young lady visitor over the gardens and into the Gothic summer-house [constructed of twisted branches by Mr. Alcott]. I called there on my way here, and Mr. Emerson told me that he would like Una to go in and out, just as if it were her own home. I said that he was Una's friend ever since she had heard " The Humble Bee " and " The Rhodora."

Una likes her native place prodigiously, and everybody near and far seems quite "angelic," as Julian would say. . . . Last Sunday Mrs. Emer-

son and her three children came to make a call.
The Study is the pet room, the temple of the
Muses and the Delphic Shrine. The beautiful
carpet lays the foundation of its charms, and the
oak woodwork harmonizes with the tint in which
Endymion is painted. At last I have Endymion
where I always wanted it — in my husband's Study,
and it occupies one whole division of the wall.
In the corner on that side stands the pedestal
with Apollo on it, and there is a fountain-shaped
vase of damask and yellow roses. Between the
windows is the Transfiguration [given by Mr.
Emerson]. (The drawing-room is to be redeemed
with one picture only, — Correggio's Madonna and
Christ.) On another side of the Study are the two
Lake Comos. On another, that agreeable picture
of Luther and his family around the Christmas-
tree, which Mr. George Bradford gave to Mr.
Hawthorne. Mr. Emerson took Julian to walk
in the woods, the other afternoon. I have no
time to think what to say, for there is a dear little mob around me. Baby looks fairest of fair
to-day. She walks miles about the house.

Ever and ever your most loving child,

SOPHIA.

July 4.

MY DEAREST MOTHER, — Here is another Sunday again, with seemingly no time between, so
fast does the old Father hasten on. Last week
was memorable in the children's life by the occur-
rence of a party. Mrs. Emerson, with magnifi-

cent hospitality, invited all the children in town, from babyhood upwards (and their mothers), for a great festival. Rose and I were prevented from going by the arrival of three gentlemen from Boston, who stayed to tea, one being the brilliant Mr. Whipple. On that day we had five gentlemen, among them another Whipple, a man of genius and a colonel of brave renown, whose hair stands up straight upon his brow, over fine eyes and a swarthy face. He invited us to go to his beautiful home on the borders of Winnipiseogee Lake. A great many gentlemen come to see Mr. Hawthorne all the time from foreign parts. That morning the first arrival was General Solomon McNeil, a veteran of nearly seven feet in height, whose head was amazingly near the ceiling of our low dining-room, and who stooped low to go out of the door. He had an extraordinary face. His gray hair stood up straight, as well as Colonel Whipple's, and was full of demonic energy ; and his gray eyes flashed beneath overhanging brows. As he entered the room, I advanced to meet him. He said, "Mrs. Hawthorne, I presume. I have scarcely seen your husband ; but I have known him well for fifteen years." (At this, he raised his hand and arm as if he were wielding a sword, with intent to do battle.) "And I told his friend, when I read his book, — his friend who said that he was perfect, except for a want of confidence in his power, — I told him, Never fear; he will go it !" (Another sweep with the sword.) "*He will go it !* I found ideas there — *ideas !*" I vanished, to call my husband. Mr. Hawthorne then came in, and we found the old gentleman intently gazing at my husband's portrait, — so intently that he did not observe our entrance, till Mr. Hawthorne spoke. He turned, and placed his hand with such force upon my husband's shoulder that you would have supposed he had dubbed him knight. They left the room to go to the Study, the General brandishing the sword tremendously at every sentence he uttered on the way. It was really good to see such a man; so mighty in physique, with such a strong character, such resolute will, and such a gleam of loving-kindness in his eyes, to temper the force.

I have wandered off from the party. The children had a charming time, and brought back word that each had behaved perfectly. The next day I went to tell Mrs. Emerson why Rose and I did not appear. I found Mr. Emerson, sitting on the side doorstep, with Edith on his knee and Edward riding about the lawn on his pony. Mr. Emerson said that "the show of children was very pretty. But Julian! *He* makes his mark everywhere; there is no child so fine as Julian!" Was not that pleasant to hear from him? I told him how singular it was that Julian should find in Concord the desire of his imagination for two years — a pony [Mr. Emerson had already superintended the little boy's mounting, and falling off from, Edward's pony]; and he smiled like Sirius. "Well, that is good. Send him this afternoon." He then called Edward, and bade him go home with me, mount

Julian, and bring him back ; and this was accordingly done. But first, Mr. Emerson invited me to go up with him to the hilltop, opposite his house, where there is a fine view. His house is in a thick bower of evergreen and horse-chestnut trees. The grove is Academe, and could not have been more musical or deep ; and Plato's disciple walks there.

Last week I drew The Wayside for George Putnam, who is going to have it engraved. I must also make sketches of Mr. Emerson's and the Old Manse. To-morrow Una goes to a picnic at Mrs. Pratt's [mother-in-law of a daughter of Mr. Alcott's] with Ellen and Edith Emerson. We expect Louisa Hawthorne this week. She has been coming for a good while, but was delayed by the severe illness of Mrs. Robert Manning.

Yesterday Mr. Hawthorne went to Boston to meet Mr. Atherton. A daguerreotypist seized him, and took three pictures of him, from which the man politely asks me to choose. They are somewhat good. Julian had a tooth out the other day, and laughed instead of crying. Edward was so unfortunate a day or two since as to have four teeth drop out at once ; and Mr. Emerson says he must be put under a barrel until the others grow.

Monday P. M. Mr. Hawthorne, Una, and Julian have gone to the picnic. This morning I went to the post-office, for I did not like to send Una when boys were firing crackers in every direction. Julian always is my shadow — so he went with me. I stopped at Mrs. Emerson's, to ask her when and how her children were going. I found a superb George Washington in the dining-room, nearly as large as life, engraved from Stuart's painting. We saw no one of the family, but finally a door opened, and the rich music of Mr. Emerson's voice filled the entry. Julian ran out at the sound, and Ellen and her father came into the room. Mr. Emerson asked me if that head (pointing to Washington) were not a fine celebration of the Fourth of July. " He would seem to have absorbed into that face all the serenity of these United States, and left none elsewhere, excepting" (and he laid his hand on Julian) — "excepting what is in Julian. Washington is the Great Repose, and Julian is the Little Repose — hereafter to become also the Great Repose ! " He asked if Julian were going to the picnic ; and I told him "no," as I was not going. "Oh, but if Una is going, that would be a divided cherry, would it not ? " Finding that Mrs. Emerson was to go, and that they were all to ride, I of course had no objection. And then Mr. Emerson wanted Mr. Hawthorne to go with him, at five o'clock. My lord consented, and so they are all gone. Last evening, Mrs. Emerson came to see us with her sister, loaded with roses, and she was delighted with our house. Rosebud walked all round with us, in perfect sobriety, listening to our conversation. Is not this hot weather delightful ? It is to me luxury and strength. Mr.

Hawthorne has sold the grass for thirty dollars. He has cut his bean-poles in his own woods. We find The Wayside prettier and prettier. Baby keeps pulling my arm.

Your child,   SOPHY.

CHAPTER VIII

THE LIVERPOOL CONSULATE

THE letters to Mrs. Peabody sketch on : —

DEAREST MOTHER, — We have had an Englishman here, an artist, whom George Putnam [a cousin] sent to take sketches. He came here with his carpet-bag, and there seemed nothing to be done but to ask him to stay with us while in town. I was the more glad to do so, hoping thereby to save George some pennies, as I was obliged to disappoint him about making the drawings myself. This artist is from the North of England. He seems very good and simplehearted, and he talks like the Cataract of Lodore. He has the magnetic influence upon Mr. Hawthorne which produces sleepiness.

He is enchanted with The Wayside.

You know Mr. Hawthorne is a sort of loadstone, which attracts all men's confidences without a word of question, and scarcely any answer; and so Mr. Miller tells his whole life and thoughts. If he has the national reservedness generally, it certainly vanishes in my husband's presence, for it seems as if he could not tell enough. On Monday and Tuesday we expected to have Mr. Ticknor here, whom Mr. Hawthorne wished to see about his book, but he did not come.

Mr. Hawthorne feels better now, and looks natural, with living color. [He had been terribly shocked and overcome by the death, by drowning from a burning vessel, of his sister Louisa.] Poor, dear Louisa! It is harder and harder for me to realize that I shall not see her again. And she had such a genuine joy in the children. But it is a positive bliss to me to contemplate Louisa and her mother together. If there is anything immortal in life it is the home relations, and heaven would be no heaven without them. God never has knit my soul with my husband's soul for such a paltry moment as this human life! I have not loved my mother for one short day! My children do not thrill my heartstrings with less than an eternal melody. We know that God cannot trifle! This is all more real to me than what my human eye rests on. I heard one of the truly second-sighted say once, that in a trance he saw the spiritual world; and while gazing enraptured on its green pastures, a spirit whispered to him, "Out of this greenness your earthly pastures are green."

Yesterday afternoon Mr. Miller left us. Oh, dear, how the little man talked! I do not know as the Cataract of Lodore is an adequate exemplification, for that has some airy, fairy jets and overfalls. But the good faith and earnestness with which Mr. Miller coined the air into words were more like the noise and pertinacity of a manufactory. He was certainly a new phase of man to me. When he finally vanished, with his portfolio under his arm, my wings sprang up as if an iron band had been holding them down. It was with a truly divine patience that my husband gave ear to this personated Paper-Mill, because he saw that he was good and true and honest. (I might have only said "good.") Into those depths of misty gray light which stand for eyes under my husband's brow, the little man was drawn as by a line. Miss Bremer said to me of Mr. Hawthorne's eyes, "Wonderful, wonderful eyes! They give, but receive not." But they do *draw in.* Mr. Miller kept his face turned to him, as the sunflower to the sun; and when I spoke, and he tried to turn to me, his head whirled back again. It really is marvelous, how the mighty heart, with its charities, and comprehending humanity, which glows and burns beneath the grand intellect, as if to keep warm and fused the otherwise cold abstractions of thought, — it is marvelous how it opens the bosoms of men. I have seen it so often, in persons who have come to him. So Mr. Melville, generally silent and incommunicative, pours out the rich floods of his mind and experience to him, so sure of apprehension, so sure of a large and generous interpretation, and of the most delicate and fine judgment. Thus only could the poetic insight and far-searching analytic power be safely intrusted to him. To him only who can tenderly sympathize must be given the highest and profoundest insight.

How wonderfully it is arranged, that in the very person who most imperiously demands absolute beauty and perfection (for so does Mr. Hawthorne), in this very person is found the subtlest and widest appreciation of human shortcomings, and the pleadings of weakness and failure. In "Blithedale" I think one feels this tender humanity. It will come out more and more.

Shall I tell you where I am? I am sitting in our acacia grove, on the hill, with a few pines near enough for me to hear their oceanic murmur. It is only necessary for me to shut my eyes, to hear every variety of water sounds. The pine gives me the long, majestic swell and retreat of the sea waves; the birch, the silvery tinkle of a pebbly brook; the acacia, the soft fall of a cascade; and all mingled together, a sound of many waters most refreshing to the sense. I thank heaven that we possess a *hilltop*. No amount of plains could compete with the value of this. To look down on the world actually is typical of looking down spiritually, and so it is good. Una and Julian are wandering around; Una having been reading to Julian. Rosebud is asleep. Oh, she enjoys a summer day so much! This morning I set her down on the green grass. Without looking at me, the happiest smile began to dawn over her face; and then she suddenly waved her hands like wings, and set forth. To fall down seemed a new joy. Julian undertook to be her escort. It was a charming picture — the two figures grouped together; the fair little blue-eyed face turned up to the great brown, loving eyes, and all sorts of dulcet sounds responding to one another. I could not help smiling to read in your letter that you would have a rug spread for her. I should as soon think of keeping an untamed bird on a rug as baby. I assure you that since she has had the use of her·feet she does not pause in the race of life. . . . It is good to see such an expression of immense satisfaction as dwells upon her face.

Most lovingly your child,

SOPHIECHEN.

September 19.

MY DEAR MOTHER, — On Friday Mr. Hawthorne returned from nearly a three weeks' visit to the Isles of Shoals. I did not tell you about it while he was there, because your heart is so tender I knew you would have no peace, and you would all the time be thinking that he was separated from us by *water*. But here he is, looking in splendid health, all safe and sound. General Pierce, and some other dignitaries with their wives, met Mr. Hawthorne for a day or two ; and the rest of the time he had all to himself. I must tell you a story, by which you will be enabled to see into political slander. An officer of the army, resident at Baltimore, told the editor of a paper friendly to General Pierce, that while in Mexico General Pierce was at a gambling-table with another officer ; and, a squabble ensuing, this officer struck General Pierce in the face, and that the General took it without a word. He told the editor also that the officer who offered this insult was in California, making it difficult to have a word from him upon the subject. The editor, in perplexity, sent the paragraph to General Pierce, who was at a loss how to prove the utter falsity of the whole story. But, behold, the next thing which he laid his hand upon, on his table, was a letter postmarked "California." He opened it, and it was from the very officer who was said to have insulted him so foully, and was an expression of the highest admiration and respect, and congratulations upon his present position. This was an unanswerable denial ; and so he sent the letter to Baltimore. This story, fabricated out of nothing but malice, was meant to injure in two ways, by proving him a gambler, and also pusillanimous. The slanderous officer will probably cease to be one, as I believe falsehood is not considered a military grace.

Mr. Hawthorne went to Brunswick, having been cordially invited by the President of the College. He met his classmates there. On account of the heavy rains he was detained so many hours on his way thither that he did not arrive till noon of the day, and thus providentially escaped hearing himself orated and poetized about in the morning. Brunswick was so full that he had to go to Bath to sleep ; and there he had funny adventures, some old sea-captains insisting upon considering him a brother, and calling him all the time "Cap'n Hathorne." At the Isles of Shoals he had the ocean all to himself ; but when he wished to see human beings, he found Mr. and Mrs. Thaxter very pleasant. Mrs. Thaxter sent Una a necklace of native shells with a gold and coral clasp, Julian a plume made of white owl feathers, and Rosebud a most exquisite wreath of sea-moss upon a card. I kept a journal for my husband, according to his express injunction. The children missed papa miserably, and I could not bear the trial very well. I could not eat, sitting opposite his empty chair at table, and I lost several pounds of flesh.

To-day, when baby waked from a nap of four hours and a half, she called for the first time, "Mamma!" I ran up, and she was smiling like a constellation of stars. She mourned after papa a great deal, and sometimes would hold a long discourse about him, pointing all the while at the portrait. One day a neighbor sent me, to cheer my loneliness, the most superb bouquet of rare and costly rosebuds that I ever saw. I put them in the Study, in a pretty champagne-glass [the tall, old-fashioned kind], and they filled the room with fragrance. I tended them very carefully; but they bloomed too fully at last. Yet just at that moment, the lady gave me a fresh supply — the very day before Mr. Hawthorne's return; and on that bright Friday afternoon I put the vase of delicious rosebuds, and a beautiful China plate of peaches and grapes, and a basket of splendid golden Porter apples on his table; and we opened the western door [leading from the Study to the lawn] and let in a flood of sunsetting. Apollo's "beautiful disdain" seemed kindled anew. Endymion smiled richly in his dream of Diana. Lake Como was wrapped in golden mist. The divine form in the Transfiguration floated in light. I thought it would be a pity if Mr. Hawthorne did not come that moment. As I thought this, I heard the railroad-coach — and he was here. He looked, to be sure, as he wrote in one of his letters, "twice the man he was." Dear little Una went to the village with the mail-bag, just before it was time to expect her father, and I told her I hoped she would drive home with him. She met him, caught a glance, and he was gone. It surprised me that her sense of duty prevented her from turning back at once. I asked her why she did not, as the letters were not of so much importance, since papa had come. "Oh," said she, "I did not know but it would be wrong to go back *only because I wanted to.*" At last she came. She entered the Study in a very quiet way (apparently), received his loving greeting, and then, taking off her hat, sat down at my feet to look at him, and hear him. When she went to bed, she said, "Oh, mamma, my head has tingled so, ever since I saw papa, that I could hardly bear the pain! Do not tell him, for it might trouble him." Was it not sweet and heroic in her to keep so quiet for two hours? This is a good specimen of Una's powers of self-sacrifice. It has sometimes made me wish to weep over her delicious tears.

Sunday, October 24, 1852.

MY DEAREST MOTHER, — To-day we all went into the woods above and behind our house, and sat down and wove wreaths of red and russet leaves, and dreamed and mused with a far-off sound of booming waves and plash of sea on smooth beach in the pine-trees about us. It was beautiful to see the serene gleam of Una's face, fleckered with sunlight; and Julian, with his coronet of curls, sitting quiet in the great peace. My husband, at full length on the carpet of withered pine, presented no hindrance to the tides of divine life that are ready to flow through us, if we will. There are no words to describe such enjoyment; but you can understand it well. It is the highest wisdom, I think, to sometimes *do nothing;* but only keep still, and reverently be happy, and receptive of the great omnipresence. How studiously we mortals keep it out of our eternal *business.* There should be no business at least once a week. I rather think it is the best proof that Moses was inspired that he instituted a Sabbath of rest from labor. God needs not, but man needs, rest.

Sunset. I left you to go out again and join my husband on the hilltop, while the children's voices kept us advised of their welfare somewhere about the place. My husband and I sat on a terrace on the side of the hill, both looking off upon the tranquil horizon, beginning to be veiled with a dim blue haze. Una ran up, calling out that Mr. Hosmer wished to see papa and mamma. So we descended, and met the old gentleman on a lower terrace, where I invited him to sit on the green sofa ; and we grouped about him. Julian at first went rushing through our ranks like a young Olympian exercising heroic games, and finally extended himself on the grass to listen to the palaver. Mr. Hosmer began with the Great Daniel [Webster], who died at three o'clock this morning. He expressed admiration of him, as we all did ; and I thought his death an immense loss. Mr. Hosmer was very glad that he died in the fullness of his power of mind, and not sunken in the socket. He discoursed upon the massive grandeur of his speeches, his wonderful letters, and of all that was mighty in him. Also of his shortcomings and their retribution. You would have liked to have heard Mr. Hosmer glorify John Adams — even his appearance. He said that at eighty-three (when he sat near him every Sunday at church) he was a "perfect beauty ;" that his cheeks were as unwrinkled as a girl's, and as fair and white, and his head was a noble crown ; and that any woman would fall in love with him. So we talked of great men, till I came in to watch baby's sleep. She soon waked, all smiles and love; and then Mr. Hawthorne and Mr. Hosmer came in, still upon the theme of great men. Mr. Hosmer thought Oliver Cromwell greatest of all, I believe. Una and I made you a wreath of richly tinted oak leaves to-day, and when I go to Newton I will take it. I wish you could hear her repeat poetry in her dulcet, touching tones. I never heard any one repeat poetry so much to my mind.

Evening. Mr. Hawthorne is drawn forcibly out of doors by the moon's rays, they are so clear and superb to-night. He looked out and sighed, for he did not really want to go ; but he felt under a moral necessity. I walk out *in him*, being mamma and nurse [Rosebud was still up]. When you write to Mr. Plumly, bless him for me for the mantle [his gift to Mrs. Peabody] and his beautiful, refreshing letter about it. I had a great mind to write to him myself of his appreciation of you and of my husband. What a noble, lovely person he is!

Your child,   SOPHY.

April 14, 1853.

My husband went off in a dark rain this morning, on his way to Washington. Mary Herne called to baby to come and take care of her dolly, who was upon the floor in the kitchen. Rose rushed in a breakneck manner across the parlor, exclaiming as if in the utmost maternal distress, " Oh, mershy, mershy ! " and rescued Dolly from her peril. She was quite happy and still in the kitchen ; and then I heard her shout, " I like it — I like it motch ! " I asked Mary what it was that baby liked so "motch." When Mary got up to investigate, she found baby in the closet at the molasses jug, still crying, " I like it — I like it motch ! " She was very much diverted by our consternation ; and when, at tea-time, I was speaking of it, she burst into inextinguishable laughter; and as soon as she could speak, said, "I glad! Was ever such a mischief?" Twice to-day she began to go into the Study for "papa take her." I sent Julian to the village at five, and he returned in a pouring rain. His sack kept him dry, but he thought he was soaked to the skin because his nose was wet. He brought a letter from Charlotte Bridge, inclosing two notes to my husband from Mr. Bridge. To-day I found nothing in the post-office but Mr. Emerson. He walked along with me and said he had a letter from Mr. Synge [whom Hawthorne met, later, in England], an attaché of the British Legation, asking for an autograph of Mr. Hawthorne. Grandpapa, baby, and I sat in the parlor in the afternoon, and baby was in the highest spirits, and conversed for the first time in the most facetious manner, casting side glances, and laughing with a great pretense of being vastly amused, and of superior insight into the bearing of things.

April 19. The great day of the Concord fight. I was awakened by cannon and the ringing of bells. The cannon thundered all around the welkin, in a very grand, stately, and leisurely manner. I read the history of the day to the children. What made the morning beautiful and springlike to me was a letter which Julian brought from my husband.

April 21. A day like a dulcimer. It was so charming to rake and plant and prune that I remained out a long time, and tore my hands nicely.

Julian requested to go and take a quiet walk in the woods, and returned just as I was becoming anxious about him, shouting, with a sweet-brier bush which he had pulled up by the roots in the wood. I took a spade, and dug a great cave, and planted it beneath his western window; and I am sure it must grow for him, for he sent sunshine down into the earth from his eyes upon the roots while I was setting it out.

The stage-coach drove up and brought me Mrs. S. G. Ward and Sarah Clarke. Mrs. Ward was cruelly disappointed not to see Mr. Hawthorne; and I told her that he would probably tear his hair when he came back and found what he had lost. "Tell him," said she, "that I tore out all mine." She was splendid and radiant beyond my power to tell; dressed in rich green and a rose-colored bonnet, and her beautiful hair curling round her wonderful face. I do not believe there is another such woman in the world. When she had stepped from the house, Julian begged me to run after her, and tell her she *must* go to England [whither the family now expected to journey]; and with the most enchanting grace she laughed, and said, "Tell him I certainly shall!"

Sunday. At ten, my little flock gathered [Mrs. Hawthorne taught reading, geography, drawing, etc., to several children besides her own, for love, and gave them Sunday-school lessons also]; and I read them the story of Balaam's ass, and about the death of Moses. They were much afflicted that Moses was not allowed to go to the Promised

Land. I read that he looked down from Mount Pisgah and saw Canaan and the City of Palms, and showed them my Cuban sketch of a palm, describing exactly how they looked and grew; and the vision of the City of Palms became very beautiful to them. Poor little Mary Ellen felt ill, but she was so interested that I could not persuade her to go home.

April 26. I met Mr. Rockwood Hoar, who congratulated us upon our expected residence in England, which he said was "the only place fit to live in out of America."

April 29. A neighbor came yesterday with an English white rose, and set out the tree for me. He said it was for Rosebud. We are getting to look quite nice, but all will look black and bare to my husband, after being at the South. Baby is filled with joy to be out in such lovely weather, and makes no hesitation to take the heaviest tools, and dig and rake and hoe. She will not come in even to drink her milk. Some documents came this morning from the State Department, relating to the Consulate at Liverpool. The peach-trees are all in bloom, and the cherry-trees also. I looked about, as I sat down in our pine grove, and tried to bear my husband's absence but it is desolation without him. This is the sweetest place — I really cannot bear to leave it. My scholars drew flowers, this morning. Mr. Emerson and Ellery Channing passed along ; and Mr. Emerson asked Julian to go with the children to Fairy Land [in Walden woods]. He went, in a state of ecstatic bliss. He brought me home, in a basket, cowslips, anemones, and violets.

In June the voyage to England, as Hawthorne was appointed Consul at Liverpool by President Pierce, was undertaken, and pleasantly accomplished.

Hawthorne's "English Note-Books," as well as the elaborated papers that make up "Our Old Home," disclose something of his daily life in England during his consulship ; but it was in the rapid, familiar letters of my mother to her family that his life was most freely narrated. I have preserved these letters, and shall give extracts from them in the pages that follow, prefacing and interpolating a few girlish memories of my father and of the places in which I saw him, although they are trivial and meagre in incident. He died the day before my thirteenth birthday, and as my existence had begun at a time when his quiet life was invaded (if we may use that term in connection with a welcome guest) by fame, with its attendant activity in the outside world, my intercourse with him was both juvenile and brief. In England, he mingled more than ever before with the members of literary and fashionable society. I, who in 1853 was but two years old, had to be satisfied with a glance and a smile, which were so much less than he had been able to give to my brother and sister in their happier childhood days, for they had enjoyed hours of his companionship as a constant pastime. I was, moreover, much

younger than the others, and was never allowed
to grow, as I wished, out of the appellations of
Rosebud, Baby, and Bab (as my father always
called me), and all the infantine thought which
those pet names imply. I longed myself to hear
the splendidly grotesque fairy tales, sprung from
his delicious jollity of imagination, which Una and
Julian had reveled in when our father had been at
leisure in Lenox and Concord; and the various
frolics about which I received appetizing hints as
I grew into girlhood made me seem to myself a
stranger who had come too late. But a stranger
at Hawthorne's side could be very happy, and,
whatever my losses, I knew myself to be rich.

In the early years of our stay in England his
personality was most radiant. His face was sunny,
his aspect that of shining elegance. There was
the perpetual gleam of a glad smile on his mouth
and in his eyes. His eyes were either a light
gray or a violet blue, according to his mood. His
hair was brown and waved loosely (I take it very
hard when people ask me if it was at all red!),
and his complexion was as clear and luminous as
his mother's, who was the most beautiful woman
some people have ever seen. He was tall, and
with as little superfluous flesh and as much sturdy
vigor as a young athlete; for his mode of life
was always athletic, simple, and abstemious. He
leaned his head a little to one side, often, in a
position indicating alert rest, such as we find in
many Greek statues, — so different from the
straight, dogged pose of a Roman emperor. He

was very apt to make an assent with an upward movement of the head, a comfortable h'm-m, and a half-smile. Sympathetic he was, indeed, and warm with the fire that never goes out in great natures. He had much dignity; so much that persons in his own country sometimes thought him shy and reticent to the verge of morbidness. But it was merely the gentlemanliness of the man, who was jocund· with no one but his intimate friends, and never fierce except with rascals, as I observed on one or two occasions. Those who thought him too silent were bores whom he desired not to attract. Those who thought him unphilosophical (and some philosophers thought that) were not artists, and could not analyze his work. Those who knew him for a man and a friend were manly and salubrious of soul themselves. They have given plenty of testimony as to the good-fellowship of a nature which could be so silent at will.

He was usually reserved, but he was ready for action all the time. His full, smooth lips, sensitive as a child's, would tell a student of facial lines how vivid was his life, though absolutely under his cool command. He was a delightful companion even when little was said, because his eyes spoke with a sort of apprehension of your thought, so that you felt that your expression of face was a clear record for him, and that words would have been a sort of anticlimax. His companionship was exquisitely restful, since it was instinctively sympathetic. He did not need to

exert himself to know you deeply, and he saw all
the good in you there was to know; and the weakness and the wrong of any heart he weighed as
nicely in the balance of tender mercy as we could
do in pity for ourselves. I always felt a great
awe of him, a tremendous sense of his power.
His large eyes, liquid with blue and white light
and deep with dark shadows, told me even when
I was very young that he was in some respects
different from other people. He could be most
tender in outward action, but he never threw
such action away. He knew swine under the
cleverest disguise. I speak of outward acts of
tenderness. As for his spirit, it was always arous-
ing mine, or any one's, and acting towards one's
spiritual being invisibly and silently, but with
gentle earnestness. He evinced by it either a
sternly sweet dignity of tolerance, or an approbation generous as a broad meadow, or a sadly
glanced, adverse comment that lashed one's inner
consciousness with remorse. He was meditative,
as all those are who care that the world is full
of sorrow and sin, but cheerful, as those are who
have the character and genius to see the finite
beauty and perfection in the world, which are
sent to the true-hearted as indications of heaven.
He could be full of cheer, and at the same time
never lose the solemnity of a perception of the
Infinite, — that familiar fact which we, so many
of us, have ceased to fear, but which the greatest
men so remember and reverence. He never
became wholly merged in fun, however gay the

games in which he joined with us children; just as a man of refinement who has been in war never quite throws aside the dignity of the sorrow which he has seen. He might seem, at a superficial glance, to be the merriest of us all, but on second thoughts he was not. Of course, there were times when it was very evident to me that my father was as comfortable and happy as he cared to be. When he stood upon the hearth-rug, before the snapping, blushing English fire (always poked into a blaze towards evening, as he was about to enter the parlor), — when he stood there with his hands clasped behind him, swaying from side to side in a way peculiar to him, and which recalled the many sea-swayed ancestors of his who had kept their feet on rolling decks, then he was a picture of benevolent pleasure. Perhaps, for this moment, the soldier from the battlefields of the soul ceased to remember scenes of cruelty and agony. He swayed from side to side, and raised himself on his toes, and creaked his slippered heels jocosely, and smiled upon me, and lost himself in agreeable musings. He was very courteous, entirely sincere, and quiet with fixed principles as a great machine with consistent movement. He treated children handsomely; harshness was not in him to be subdued, and scorn of anything that was honestly developing would have seemed to him blasphemy. He stooped to my intelligence, and rejoiced it. We were usually a silent couple when off for a walk together, or when we met by chance in the household. I suppose that we were seeing which could outdo the other at "holding the tongue." But still, our intercourse, as I remarked before, might be complete. I knew him very well indeed, — his power, his supremacy of honesty, his wealth of refinement. And he, I was fully aware, could see through me as easily as if I were a soul in one of his own books.

Even as a child, knowing that he could not think me a remunerative companion, I realized how remarkable it was that in all his being there was not an atom of the poison of contempt. If he did not love stupidity, he forgave it. If he was strong with analysis and the rejection of all sham and wrong, his hand was ready to grasp any hand, because it was a human creature's, whose destiny was a part of every destiny — even Christ's. This sympathy, which caused the choice he had made of his character-studies, and brought many confessions to his judgment from bewildered men and women, was with him so entire that it showed itself in the little things of existence, as a whole garden-path is noble with the nature of the rose that stands blooming there.

His aspect avoided, as did that of his art, which exactly reproduced his character, anything like self-conscious picturesqueness. It is pleasant to have the object of our regard unconscious of himself. He had a way of ignoring, while observing automatically, all accessories, which reminded us that his soul was ever awake, and waiting to be made free of earthly things and common ideas.

During our European life he frequently wore a soft brown felt hat and a brown talma of finest broadcloth, whose Greek-like folds and double-decked effect were artistic, but did not tempt him to pose or remember his material self. He was as forgetful of his appearance as an Irishman of the true quality, who may have heard something about his coat or his hair, but has let slip from his mind what it was, and cares not, so long as the song of his comrades is tender and the laughter generous. In some such downright way, I was convinced, my father regarded the beauty and stateliness which were his, and for which he had been praised all through his existence. He forgot himself in high aims, which are greater than things seen, no matter how fine soever.

We made a very happy family group as we gladly followed and looked upon him when he took ship to start for the Liverpool Consulate; and of this journey and the new experiences which ensued my mother writes to Dr. Peabody as follows : —

STEAMER NIAGARA, ATLANTIC OCEAN,
July 7, 1853.

MY DEAREST FATHER, — It is early morning. Wrapped in furs and blanket shawl, in the sun and close against the vast scarlet cylinder of scalding hot steam, I have seated myself to greet you from Halifax, where we shall arrive to-night. I was glad to leave the sight of you while you were talking with Mr. Fields, whose cheerful face (and words, no doubt) caused you to smile. I was so glad to leave you smiling happily. Then came the cannonade, which was very long. And why do you suppose it was so long? Mr. Ticknor says that always they give a salute of two guns ; but that yesterday so many were thundered off because Mr. Hawthorne, the distinguished United States Consul and author, was leaving the shore, and honoring her Majesty's steamship with his presence. While they were stabbing me with their noise I was ignorant of this. Perhaps my wifely pride would have enabled me to bear it better if I had known that the steamer were trembling with honor rendered to my husband. After this we were quiet enough, for we were moving magically over a sea like a vast pearl, almost white with peace. I never saw anything so fair and lovely as the whole aspect of the mighty ocean. Off on the horizon a celestial blue seemed to meet the sky. Julian sat absorbed. He did not turn his head, but gazed and gazed on this, to him, new and wondrous picture. Seeing a point of land running out, he said, " That, I suppose, is the end of America! I do not think America reaches very far! " I managed to change his beaver and plume for his great straw Fayal hat, but he would not turn his head for it. It was excessively hot. An awning was spread at the stern, and then it was very comfortable. I heard that the British minister was on board, and I searched round to find him out. I decided upon a fine-looking elderly gentleman who was asleep near the helm-house. Afterwards the mail-agent came to Mr. Hawthorne and said the minister wished to make his acquaintance; and behold, here was my minister, a stately, handsome person, with an air noble and of great simplicity and charm of manner. Mr. Hawthorne introduced me, but I had no conversation then. Later, I had a very delightful interview. . . . Near by stood a gentleman whom I supposed his attaché; and with him I had a very long and interesting conversation. We had a nice talk about art and Rome, and America and England, and architecture. I do not yet know his name, but only that his brother was joint executor with Sir Robert Peel on the estate of Hadley, the artist. This unknown told me that the minister was an exquisite amateur artist, and his portfolio was full of the finest sketches. This accounted for the serene expression of his eyes, that rest contemplatively upon all objects. Mr. Silsbee looks so thin and pale that I fear for him; but I will take good care of him. At table, Mr. and Mrs. Hawthorne have the seats of honor, on either hand of the captain. He is a very remarkable man. The minister told me that he sailed with him five years ago, when the captain was very young, and he was then astonished at his skill and power of command; that the captains of these great English steamers are picked men, trained in the navy, and eminent for ability and accomplishment, and that Captain Leitch is remarkable among the best. It was good to see his assured military air, as he walked back and forth while we moved out of the beautiful harbor. He made motions with his hand with such an air of majesty and conscious power. His smile is charming, and his voice fine. The enunciation of Mr. Crampton, the minister, is also wonderfully fine. Mr. Crampton says that these steamers have run for seventeen years, and that not one accident has happened, and not a man been lost, except that *once* a steamer was lost in a fog, but all the passengers and crew were safely got off. Una enjoys herself very much, and reads the "Tanglewood Tales," and walks and races on the upper deck with Julian, this fine cold morning. It is glorious, glorious, — this blue surrounding sea, and no land.

Your affectionate daughter,
SOPHIA.

WATERLOO HOUSE, LIVERPOOL,
July 17, Sunday morning.

Here we are, dear father, in England; and I cannot realize it, because a moment ago we were in Boston Harbor, and how can I be three thousand miles afar? If we had had more difficulty, storms, and danger, I could realize it better; but it seems like a pleasure excursion on a lake. I sit in a parlor, with one great, broad window from ceiling to floor, a casement opening upon a balcony, which commands a handsome street. It does not look like Boston, and, Mr. Hawthorne says, not like New York, but — like Liverpool. People are going to church, and the bells are chiming in a pleasant jangle. Every gentleman has an umbrella under his arm; for it is bright sunshine one moment, and a merry little shower the next.

I spoke in my note from Halifax of Mr. Crampton, and a gentleman whom I thought his attaché. Mr. Crampton we lost at Halifax, but the supposed attaché remained; and I was glad, for he was the most interesting person in the steamer. We in vain tried to discover his name, but at last found it to be Field Talfourd, brother of Sir Thomas Talfourd, author of "Ion." I had very charming conversations with him. He was a perfect gentleman, with an ease of manner so fascinating and rare, showing high breeding, and a voice rich and full. Whenever he spoke, his words came out clear from the surrounding babble and all the noise of the ship, so that I could always tell where he was. He is one of the primitive men, in contradistinction to the derivative (as Sarah Clarke once divided people). He seemed never at a loss on any subject soever; and when the passengers were trying feats of skill and physical prowess to pass the time, I saw Mr. Talfourd exhibit marvelous power as a gymnast in performing a feat which no one else would even attempt. His education was all-sided, body and mind, apparently; and, with all, this charm of gentlemanliness, — not *very* often met with in America. It seems to require more leisure and a deeper culture than we Americans have yet, to produce such a lovely flower. . . .

July 19. We all have colds now, except Mr.

Hawthorne, with whom earth's maladies have nothing to do. Julian and Una are homesick for broad fields and hilltops. Julian, in this narrow, high room, is very much like an eagle crowded into a canary-bird's cage! They shall go to Prince's Park as soon as I can find the way; and there they will see water and green grass and trees. They think of the dear Wayside with despair. As soon as possible we shall go into the country. Yesterday the waning consul, Mr. Crittendon, called. Mr. Hawthorne likes him much. Mr. Silsbee and Mr. Wight called. The latter talked a great deal of transcendental philosophy to me, on the Niagara; and I was sometimes tempted to fling him to the fishes, to baptize him in realities.

July 21. An Oxford graduate, who went to see Mr. Hawthorne in Concord, called to see him, and brought his father, a fine-looking gentleman. Their name is Bright. Mary Herne thought the son was Eustace Bright himself! To-day the father came to invite us all out to West Derby to tea on Saturday, and the son is coming for us. There the children will see swans and gardens and green grass, and they are in raptures. Young Henry Bright is a very enthusiastic young gentleman, full of life and emotion; and he very politely brought me from his gardens a radiant bouquet of flowers, among which the heliotrope and moss-roses and all other roses and mignonette make delicious fragrance. Yesterday Miss Lynch sent me a bunch of moss-rose buds — *nine!* Just think of seeing together *nine* moss-rose buds! Henry Bright brought the "Westminster Review" to Mr. Hawthorne, and said he should bring him all the new books. Mrs. Train called to see me before she went *to town* [London], and Mr. Hawthorne and I went back with her to the Adelphi, and walked on to see a very magnificent stone building, called St. George's Hall. It is not quite finished; and as far as the mist would allow me to see, it was sumptuous. . . . We have strawberries as large as small peaches, one being quite a feast, and fine raspberries. The head of the Waterloo House, Mr. Lynn, is a venerable-looking person, resembling one's idea of an ancient duke, — dressing with elaborate elegance, and with the finest ruffled bosoms. Out of peculiar respect to the Consul of the United States, he comes in at the serving of the soup, and holds each plate while I pour the soup, and then, with great state, presents it to the waiter to place before each person. After this ceremony he retires with a respectful obeisance. This homage diverts Mr. Hawthorne so much that I am afraid he will smile some day. The gravity of the servants is imperturbable. One, Mr. Hawthorne calls our Methodist preacher. The service is absolutely perfect.   Your affectionate child,

SOPHIA.

The Brights, especially Henry Bright, appear frequently in the "Note-Books," and their names occur very often in my mother's letters. The young Oxford graduate I remember most distinctly. He was thin, and so tall that he waved like a reed, and so shining-eyed that his eyes seemed like icebergs ; they were very prominent. His nose was one of your English masterpieces, — a mountainous range of aristocratic formation ; and his far-sweeping eyebrows of delicate brown, his red, red lips and white doglike teeth, and his deeply cleft British chin were a source of fathomless study. In England a man can be extraordinarily ordinary and material ; but the men of culture are, as a rule, remarkably forcible in unique and deep-cut characteristics, both of face and of mind, with a prevailing freedom from self-analysis — except privately, no doubt.

The strong features of Henry Bright, at any rate, made a total of ravishing refinement. He and my father would sit on opposite sides of the fire ; Mr. Bright with a staring, frosty gaze directed unmeltingly at the sunny glow of the coals as he talked, his slender long fingers propping up his charming head (over which his delicately brown hair fell in close-gliding waves) as he leaned on the arm of his easy-chair. Sometimes he held a book of Tennyson's poetry to his near-sighted, prominent eyes, as closely as two materials could remain and not blend into one. He recited "The Brook" in a fine fury of appreciation, and with a sure movement that suggested well the down-tumbling of the frolicking element, with its undercurrent of sympathizing pathos, the life-blood of the stream. "For men may come, and men may

go, but I go on for *ever!*" rang in my empty little head for years, and summed up, as I guessed,
all of Egyptian wisdom and spiritual perpetuity
in a single suggestive fact. Mr. Bright had a way
of laughing that I could never cease to enjoy,
even in the faint echo of retrospect. It always
ended in a whispered snort from the great mountain range of his nose. He laughed often, at his
own and my father's remarks, and at the close of
the tumbling diction of "The Brook;" and he
therefore frequently snorted in this sweeping-of-
the-wind fashion. I listened, spellbound. He
also very gently and breezily expressed his touched
sensibility, after some recitation of his of rare lines
from other poems, but in the same odd manner.
My father stirred this beloved friend with judicious, thought-developing opposition of opinion
concerning all sorts of polite subjects, but principally, when I overheard, concerning the respec-
tive worth of writers. The small volume of
Tennyson which Mr. Bright held in his two hands
caressingly, with that Anglo-literary filliping of
the leaves which is so great a compliment to any
book, contained for him a large share of Great
Britain's greatness. His brave heart beat for
Tennyson ; I think my father's did not, though his
head applauded. My mother, for her part, was
entranced by the goldsmith's work of the noble
poet, and by the gems enclasped in its perfection
of formative art, — perfections within the pale of
convention and fashion and romantic beauty which
make lovely Tennyson's baronial domain. Henry

Bright wrote verses, too; and he was beginning to be successful in a certain profound interest which customarily absorbs young men of genuine feeling who are not yet married; and therefore it was worth while to stir the young lover up, and hear what he could say for "The Princess" and "The Lord of Burleigh." My mother, in a letter written six months after we had reached England, and when he was established as a household friend, draws a graphic picture of his lively personality : —

ROCK PARK, December 8.

. . . We had a charming visit from Henry Bright a fortnight ago. He stayed all night, and he talks — I was going to say, like a storm ; but it is more like a breeze, for he is very gentle. He is extremely interesting, sincere, earnest, independent, warm and generous hearted; not at all dogmatic ; full of questions, and with ready answers. He is highly cultivated, and writes for the "Westminster." . . . Eustace Bright, as described in "The Wonder-Book," is so much like him in certain things that it is really curious : " Slender, pale, yet of a healthy aspect, and as light and active as if he had wings to his shoes." He is also near-sighted, though he does not wear spectacles. His eyes are large, bright, and prominent, rather, indicating great facility of language, which he has. He is an Oxford scholar, and has decided literary tastes. He is delicately strung, and is as transparent-minded and pure-hearted as a child, with great enthusiasm and earnestness of character ;

and, though a Liberal, very loyal to his Queen and very admiring of the aristocracy. This comes partly by blood, as his mother has noble blood in her veins from various directions, even the Percys and Stanleys, and is therefore a native aristocrat. He enjoyed his visit to America extremely, and says Boston is the Mecca of English Unitarians, and Dr. Channing is their patron saint. I like to talk with him : he can really converse. He goes to the Consulate a good deal, for he evidently loves Mr. Hawthorne dearly. I wish my husband could always have visitors so agreeable. The other day a woman went to him about a case in Chancery. Mr. Hawthorne thought she was crazy ; and I believe all people are who have a suit in Chancery.

A few weeks after the date of the last letters, a visit was paid to the Brights at their family home, and my mother thus writes of it : —

ROCK PARK, February 16, 1854.

I returned yesterday from a visit to Sandheys, the domain of Mr. Bright. He has been urging all winter that we should go and dine and stay all night, and I have refused, till last week Mrs. Bright wrote a cordial note and invited Mr. Hawthorne and Una and me to go and meet Mr. and Mrs. James Martineau, and stay two nights. It seemed not possible to refuse without being uncivil, though I did not like to leave Julian and baby so long. Mr. Hawthorne, however, intended

to stay but one night, and the next morning
would come home and see Julian and Rose, and
take Julian to spend the day at the Consulate
with him ; and we left King, that excellent butler,
in the house. It was really safe enough ; only,
you know, mothers have, perhaps, unfounded
alarms. We took a carriage at Pier-head (Una
and I) and drove to the Consulate, where we
took up Mr. Hawthorne and Mr. Bright. . . . We
arrived at about six o'clock, and Una and I had to
dress for dinner after our arrival. It was a party
of twelve. . . . Mrs. H. [aunt of Henry Bright]
is a fashionable lady, who resides in London in
season, and out of season at Norris Green. She
was dressed in crimson velvet, with pearls and
diamonds, and her neck and arms were very fair
and pretty.

She was resolved to tease Mr. Hawthorne into
consenting to go to her ball. Just imagine him
in the clutches of a lady of fashion ! But he
always behaves so superbly under the most trying
circumstances, that I was exceedingly proud of
him while I pitied him. . . . Finally she could
not tell whether he would accept or not, and said
she would leave the matter to me, with confidence
that I would prevail. . . . Just after luncheon on
Tuesday, Mrs. Bright's brother came to tell her
that the Great Britain had come, and she would
not believe it, because her husband had not tele-
graphed her about it, . . . that largest ship in
the world, belonging to Mr. Bright. It had come
back from Australia. . . . Mr. Martineau has a

kind of apostolic dignity about him. . . . But the full dress of the gentlemen now requiring a white cravat and tie, they all looked ministerial to me, except the United States Consul, who *will* hold on to black satin, let the etiquette be what it may. He does not choose to do as the Romans do while in Rome. At least, he is not yet broken in. I suppose it is useless for me to say that he was by far the handsomest person present, and might have been taken for the king of them all. The chandelier that poured floods of light down on the heads beneath was very becoming to him ; for the more light there is, the better he looks always. The dinner was exceedingly elegant, and the service as beautiful as silver, finest porcelain, and crystal could make it. And one of the attendants, the coachman, diverted me very much by the air with which he carried off his black satin breeches, white silk long hose, scarlet vest buttoned up with gold, and the antique-cut coat embroidered with silver. Not the autocrat of all the Russias feels grander than these livery servants. The butler, who is really above the livery servants in position, looked meek in his black suit and white vest and cravat, though he had a right to look down on the varlet in small-clothes. This last, however, was much the most imposing in figure, and fair round red cheeks, and splendid shining black hair. Dear me, what is man ! At the sound of a bell, when the dessert was put upon the table, the children came in. They never dine with mamma and papa, . . . and all troop in at dessert, looking so pretty, in full dress, . . . thin white muslin or tulle, with short sleeves and low necks, and long streaming sashes. I found the next day that it was just the same when there was no great party at dinner. Little S. looked funny in his white vest and muslin cravat, — like a picture of the old régime. In the evening we had music, weaving itself into the conversation.

Mrs. Bright is . . . a person of delicate and fine taste ; . . . she has eight children, but in her face one does not find wearing care. . . . It is a face of great sensibility. . . . Her smile breaks out like real sunshine, revealing a happy and satisfied spirit, a fresh and unworn nature. Her children seem to regard her as a precious treasure. Her husband, with a white head and perfectly Eastern face, is exceedingly pleasant ; and when he comes home to dinner he goes to his wife and takes her hand, as if he had been gone many months, and asks her particularly how it is with her, in a tender and at the same time playful way, which causes a great deal of sunshine. Then he runs upstairs to dress, and comes back in an incredibly short time, as nice as a new pin, and overflowing with the kindest hospitality. It is such a pretty scene : the elegant drawing-room, the recess a bow window of great size, filled with such large and clear plate glass that it seems wide open, looking out upon the verdant lawn and rich green — evergreen — shrubbery ; two superb cranes, with stately crests, walking about with proud steps, or with outspread wings half flying, and uttering a short, sharp cry ; oval and circular plots of ground surrounded now with snowdrops, about twice as large as those we have in America. Everything is lovely outside. Inside, innumerable gems of art and mechanism cover the tables. . . . In the evening . . . the group of airily dressed children ; the tender mother in her rich brocade and lace mantle ; the happy father ; the agreeable governess (Miss Cumberland is a remarkably accomplished person, and has been with the family fifteen years) ; the music, talk, and æsthetic tea, — it is a charming picture. . . . The grave butler brings in a tray with cups and saucers and an urn, and leaves the room. H. makes tea, pours it out, and takes it to each person, with a little morsel of spread bread. S. and A. look about for empty cups, and return them to the tray. There is no fuss ; it is all *en famille ;* and the tray is borne off again by the butler, stepping with noiseless feet. There is no noise at any time anywhere in the house, except the angry squall of the cockatoo, who gets into a violent rage once in a while with some invisible foe, and tears his cage, and erects the long feathers on his head like so many swords drawn out of their scabbards. . . . The Brights treated me in the sweetest way, as if they had always known me, and I felt quite at home. H. is to go to her aunt's fancy ball as a mermaid ; and on Tuesday I helped sprinkle her sea-green veil with pearls.

This family is very charming. Mrs. Bright is the lady of ladies ; her children are all clever (in

an English sense), and one son a prodigy. . . .
They are all good as well as clever; well edu-
cated, accomplished, and most entirely united. It
is all peace and love and happiness there, and I
cannot discover ·where the shadow is. Health,
wealth, cultivation, and all the Christian graces
and virtues — I cannot see the trail of the serpent anywhere in that Paradise.

. . . Mrs. Bright and I had some nice little
talks. She told me elaborately how she admired
and loved Mr. Hawthorne's books; how she had
found expressed in them what she had found nowhere else; with what rapture one of her sisters
read, re-read, and read again "The Wonder-Book;"
. . . how Mrs. H. thought him peerless; and so
on. There is not the least extravagance about
Mrs. Bright, but remarkable sobriety; and so
what she said had double force. We talked . . .
while we sprinkled pearls over the mermaid's sea-
green veil. On Wednesday the sun shone! If
you lived here [in or near Liverpool] you would
hardly credit such a phenomenon.

CHAPTER IX

ENGLISH DAYS: I

In order to give a full idea of Henry Bright and his home, I have anticipated dates somewhat, but at this point will go back a little to the summer of our arrival in England, since the atmosphere which surrounded Hawthorne and the aspect of typical personalities which he enjoyed are thus easily caught.

August 5, 1853.

. . . We have been so hospitably received that very little clear leisure has been left for my own private use. . . . The children have suffered very much from confinement within doors and bad air without, and almost "everduring" rain. We find it will not do to remain in the city any longer, and to-morrow we go across the Mersey to Rock-ferry, a fine watering-place, twenty minutes off by steam, where the air is pure and healthy.

We had a call from a certain Mrs. R. S. Ely and her mamma. She said she herself was an American. On the afternoon of the same day we received a formal invitation from this lady for a dinner-party. But Mr. Hawthorne was engaged for that day to dine with Mr. Crittendon. As she was a very fine lady, and resides in a very aristocratic street, I was glad to be obliged to refuse, because my brocade was not yet appointed, and I could wear nothing less in state. At the Waterloo we received a call from Mrs. William Rathbone and her daughter, Mrs. Thom. It was a sister-in-law, Mrs. Richard Rathbone, who wrote that exquisite book, " The Diary of Lady Willoughby." She resides in London. Mr. William Rathbone is a millionaire. His wife is a cordial and excellent lady, who seemed to take us right into her heart, just as the Brights did. . . . We have been to make our promised call at Sandheys. Before we drove there, Mr. Bright took us to Norris Green, the estate of his uncle. How can I convey to you an adequate idea of it? I do not know what we are to do with the regal paradises of England if I cannot cope with this. . . . Here in all directions spread out actual velvet lawns, upon which when I trod I seemed to sink into a downy enchantment ; and these lawns were of such a tint, of the most delicate pea-green, with a *lustre* upon it ! . . .

Evening. I have been interrupted all day, receiving and making calls. Mr. Hawthorne has made his maiden speech, and followed it by another to-day, when he received the Chamber of Commerce in Mrs. Blodget's great drawing-room.

Mrs. William Rathbone sent her carriage to take us to Green Bank. The floors of the halls are almost invariably pavements of stone, sometimes in colored mosaic. . . . By and by came Mr. Rathbone, — a very animated, upright, facetious old gentleman, who seems to enjoy life and his millions quite serenely. He is a person of great energy, and full of benevolence, and the fountain of many of the great charities of Liverpool. Then came his son, and then a pretty lady, Miss Stuart; remarkably pretty she was. We were summoned to tea by what I at first thought was a distant band of music; but I believe it was an East Indian gong, merely stirred into a delicate melody. Tea was at one end of the table, and coffee at the other; and old Mr. Rathbone presided at the coffee, and Mrs. Thom at the tea. The house was hung with pictures from ceiling to floor, every room I entered. In walking all round the grounds before tea, we came upon a fine view of the Welsh mountains over the sunny slopes; for it proved the loveliest afternoon, though in the morning it rained straight down. Mrs. Thom spoke to me with great fervor of "The Scarlet Letter." She said that no book ever produced so powerful an effect upon her. She was obliged to put it away when half through, to quiet the tumultuous excitement it caused in her. She said she felt as if each word in it was the only word that ought to be used, and the wholeness, the unity, the perfection of art amazed her. . . .

The Chamber of Commerce wished to pay their respects to Mr. Hawthorne; but Mr. Hawthorne could not receive a cloud of gentlemen at our parlor there, unless they had *all* "stood upon their dignity," as the witty Miss Lynch suggested that

Mr. Hawthorne should. The President of the Chamber was a Mr. Barber, and, behold, when we came out to Rockferry he called again, and invited us to dine at Poulton Hall, his country-seat at Bebbington, on this side of the Mersey, where he resides with his two maiden sisters. He came for us in his beautiful carriage, — a chariot it was, with a coachman as straight as a lightning-rod, — and off we bowled to Poulton Hall. [My mother's inexperience concerning splendid effects in luxurious life led her to look upon them in a naïve, though perfectly composed manner. One is reminded of the New Adam and Eve, and one is glad that the patient objects of time-honored beauty had found surprise at last.] It is four hundred years old; and there we came upon unspoiled nature, as well as elaborate art. It is an enchanting spot, with a lawn shaded by ancient oaks and other forest trees; but green fields beyond and around that had never been trimmed and repressed into thick velvet. The Hall had belonged to the Greens, and the history of it is full of ghost stories and awful tragedies. We entered a hall, and by the ancient oaken staircase reposed upon the carpet a fox, in a fine attitude, with erect head and brilliant eyes, — really a splendid specimen of a creature. I was surprised at the quiet manner in which he reposed, undisturbed by our entrance; but I was much more astonished to find it was a dead fox stuffed. I could scarcely believe it after I was told. Mr. Barber is a lover of sport, and is going with his family to-morrow to Scotland to hunt grouse. He says that at this season the hills of Scotland are gorgeous with heath flowers, like a carpet of rich dyes. We were ushered into the drawing-room, which looked more like a brilliant apartment in Versailles than what I had expected to see. The panels were richly gilt, with mirrors in the centre, and hangings of gilded paper; and the broad windows were hung with golden-colored damask; the furniture was all of the same hue; with a carpet of superb flowers; and vases of living flowers standing everywhere; and a chandelier of diamonds (as to indefatigable and vivid shining), and candlesticks of the same, — not the long prisms, like those on Mary's astral, but a network of crystals diamond-cut. The two ladies were in embroidered white muslin dresses over rose-colored silk, and black velvet jackets, basque-shaped, with a dozen bracelets on their arms, which were bare, with flowing sleeves. They received us with that whole-hearted cordiality we meet everywhere. They told us some terrible stories about the haunted house, and about a lady who was imprisoned and tortured in one of the attic chambers on account of her faith, and how she resisted to the end, and was starved to death. The room bore the name of the "Martyr's Chamber." ["Dr. Grimshawe's Secret" refers to this mansion.] We went up there, and saw the window in the roof, — so high that the wretched lady could not look out; and the door of solid oak, which was ruthlessly barred. We saw the spot where one of the gentlemen of the former family cut his throat, and was found dead; and Miss Marianne said children had been murdered in the house, and uneasy spirits revisited the " glimpses of the moon." We went all over the house, in which are twenty-five sleeping apartments. One room contains a library in black letter, but that we could only peep at through a great keyhole, because it was barred and padlocked. I think Mr. Hawthorne would like to examine that. The ladies said that, if we wished to go to church, we could tell the beadle of the old Bebbington church to guide us to their pew. We passed this venerable church on our way. Its tower is very fine, and has ivy and golden flowers far up near its summit, and is built of reddish stone. Both ladies spoke of "The Scarlet Letter" with admiration and wonder. They said it had the loftiest moral of any book they had ever read. . . . On Friday, Mr. Hawthorne dined with his worship the Mayor, the Judges, the Grand Jury, the leading members of the bar, and some other gentlemen, at the Town Hall. Mr. Hawthorne said the room was the most stately and handsomest he ever saw. The city plate was superb, and the city livery of the footmen was very splendid, and the footmen themselves very handsome. His worship wore his robes of state, as did the worshipful Judges, with their wigs. Speeches were made, and Mr. Hawthorne made his *third* speech! Oh, how I wish I could have heard it! . . . This morning the ferry steamers brought over two or three thou-

sand children — boys and girls of the Industrial
School — to have a good time. I hope they are
kindly treated ; but it makes me shudder, and
actually weep, to look upon the assemblage of
young creatures, not one of them able to call upon
a mother ; each with a distinct character, each
with a human heart. Poor little motherless children !

On Sunday afternoon we took a delightful
walk. I think we made a circuit of five miles, if
not more. We went over Dacre Hill, from which
a sweet, tranquil landscape is seen ; and onwards,
down a lovely lane. These lanes are all bordered
with hedges of hawthorn, ivy, and holly ; and one
of them abounded in lovely harebells, with stems
so delicate that I found it very difficult to see and
seize them, so as to pluck them. These hedges
had not walls before them, and were not too high,
so that we could look over into the fields. A
well-worn path led from the harebell lane along
the edge of a field ; and very convenient stone
steps led over the walls. When we got to the
street, it seemed a very ancient place. This region was once the kingdom of Mercia. The road
seemed hewn out of stone. I cannot tell you how
much the cottages seemed like the first dwellings
that ever were made. . . . When I called on Mrs.
Squarey, we found her a pleasant lady, and Una
thought she looked like Miss Maria Mitchell, and
therefore Una liked her. Our call was extremely
agreeable. Mr. Hawthorne insists upon calling
her Mrs. Roundey. When Mr. Hawthorne came

home this afternoon, he said he met on the othe side the children of the Industrial School just landed. He saw them face to face, and he said their faces were uncomely to the last degree. He said he never imagined such faces, — so irredeemably stupid and homely. I do not think I have realized the sin of the Old World in any way so much as in a few faces I saw in Liverpool. It made me shiver and contract to look at them, — so haggard, so without hope or faith, or any sign of humanity. . . . Mr. Hawthorne had a letter from Kossuth to-day.

August 26.

MY DEAR FATHER, — I am just as stupid as an owl at noonday, but it is a shame that a steamer should go without a letter from me to you, and it shall not. Mr. Hawthorne wishes to escape from too constant invitations to dinner in Liverpool, and by living in Rockferry will always have a good excuse for refusing when there is really no reason or rhyme in accepting, for the last steamer leaves Liverpool at ten in the evening ; and I shall have a fair cause for keeping out of all company which I do not very much covet. I have no particular fancy for Liverpool society, except the Rathbones' and Brights'.

Mr. Hawthorne was obliged the other day to bury an American captain who died at his boarding-house. He paid for the funeral out of his private purse, though I believe he expects some brother captains will subscribe a part of the amount. Mr. Hawthorne was the whole funeral, and in one of those plumed carriages he followed the friendless captain. The children are delighted with the aspect of things, and with the house, which they think very stately and elegant. I have been racing round the lawn and shrubberies with them. The flowers rejoice. The scarlet geraniums, the crimson and rose-colored fuchsias, the deep garnet carnations, the roses, and the enormous variously colored pansies (pensées) look radiantly in the sun. There are many other kinds of flowers besides; and the beautiful light green, smooth-shaven lawn is a rest to the eyes.

There is a vast amount of latent force and energy here, but it takes a cannon to put it in action. Of course there are exceptions enough. Our friend Henry Bright is a slender, diaphanous young gentleman, of a nervous temperament, with no beer or roast beef apparent in his mind or person; and there are doubtless many like him. The English are unfortunate in noses. Their noses are unspiritual, thick at the end; and there is an expression about the mouth of enormous self-complacency. The specimens of this amount to superb sometimes, when the curves of the mouth are Apollo-like. Unfortunately there is too often a deep stain of wine in the cheeks, or a general suffusion; and unless the face is quite pale, one can find no other hue, — no healthy bloom either in man or woman.

A young American was found in a deranged state, and taken before a magistrate. There was one of two things to do, — either to put him in the workhouse, or pay his board at the insane hospital. Mr. Hawthorne, of course, chose the latter. It was just like him to choose it. The young man's mother had lately married a second time, and was in Naples. When Mrs. Blodget came to see me, a day or two since, she exclaimed that she knew his mother, and that she was a lady of fortune. . . .

September 30. Mr. Hawthorne and Mr. Ticknor had a fine excursion to Old Chester, and were so occupied with it that no time was left for Eaton Hall. Julian has been parading round the garden this morning, blowing a trumpet which papa brought him from Chester, and dragging after him a portentous wooden cannon, which would not help to gain the smallest battle. It is actually a sunny day ! . . . A very great joy it is to Rosebud to see the lovely little English robins come to pick up crumbs. They excite a peculiar love. They have great faith in man, and come close to the window without fear. They have told the linnets and thrushes of our hospitality, and the linnets actually come, though with dread and trembling ; and they carry off the largest crumbs for their families and neighbors. The English robin is very dear. . . .

Mr. Ticknor has been to see De Quincey, and says he is a noble old man and eloquent, and wins hearts in personal intercourse. His three daughters, Margaret, Florence, and Emily, are also very attractive and cultivated, and they are all most impatient to see Mr. Hawthorne. . . .

We are all going to Chester first on a Sunday,
to attend the Cathedral service with the children.
How very singular that this dream of mine, like
so many other dreams, is coming true! For I
always wished earnestly that the children might
go to church first in a grand old cathedral, so
that their impression of social worship might be
commensurate with its real sublimity. And, behold, it will be so, — for they never yet have
been to church. The echoes of those lofty vaults
are scarcely ever silent, for an anthem is sung
there every day. Afterwards we shall go on a
week-day to examine the old town, said to be
older than Rome itself!

October 5. On Saturday, the 1st, Mr. Hawthorne went to dine at Mr. Aikens's with the two
sons of Burns, Colonel and Major Burns. He
says they were gentlemanly persons, and agreeable, but not resembling their father. After
dinner, one of them sang one of Burns's songs,
and again another in the drawing-room. . . . Mr.
Fields says, "'Tanglewood' is going finely. Three
thousand were sold at once on its appearance, and
it is still moving rapidly. The notices have been
glorious everywhere; and they ought to be, for
the book is one of the most delightful which your
pen has let slip."

October 21. We are going to dine out this
evening, at Mr. and Mrs. Charles Holland's, Liscard Vale. These persons Mr. Hawthorne met
a little while ago at the house of Mr. Aikens,
where he saw the sons of Burns. For the benefit

of cousin Mary Loring [the very beautiful and spirited Mrs. George B. Loring, *née* Pickman], I will say now that my wreath is just from Paris, and consists of very exquisite flowers that grow in wreaths. Part of it is the blackberry - vine (strange to say), of such cunning workmanship that Julian says he *knows* the berries are good to eat. The blossoms, and the black and red and green fruit and leaves, are all equally perfect. Then there are little golden balls, to imitate a plant that grows in Ireland, — fretted gold. Small flowers are woven closely in, over the top of the head, and behind the ears the long, streaming vines hang in a cluster.

October 23. At sunset the clouds cleared off and the sun shone, so that our drive of six miles to Liscard Vale was much more pleasant than we expected. It was rather dreary ; uncultivated moors and sea-nipped foliage. Finally we began to hasten, at a greatly accelerated pace, down, down, and then entered a gate. It was too dark to see distinctly ; but, as far as I could discover, the land seemed formed of low hills and vales, with trees in thin groves ; and the mouth of the Mersey, and Liverpool glittering with a thousand lights, were visible through the vistas. Mrs. Holland is ladylike, and therefore simple in her manners. Mr. Holland has the figure and air of an American gentleman, rather thin and pale. The drawing-room was beautiful. It was of very great size, and at one end was a window in semicircular form, larger than any but a church window. Depending from the lofty ceiling were several chains, in different parts of the room, holding vases filled with richly colored flowers with long vines streaming. Mr. Hawthorne as chief guest — there were twelve — took Mrs. Holland, and sat at her right hand. The table was very handsome ; two enormous silver dish-covers, with the gleam of Damascus blades, putting out all the rest of the light. After the soup, these covers were removed, revealing a boiled turbot under one, and fried fish under the other. The fish was replaced by two other enormous dishes with shining covers ; and then the whole table was immediately covered with silver dishes ; and in the centre was a tall silver stand holding a silver bowl of celery. It would be useless to try to tell you all the various dishes. A boiled turkey was before Mrs. Holland, and a roasted goose before Mr. Holland ; and in the intermediate spaces, cutlets, fricassees, ragoûts, tongue, chicken - pies, and many things whose names I did not know, and on a side-table a boiled round of beef as large as the dome of St. Peter's. The pastry of the chicken-pie was of very elaborate sculpture. It was laid in a silver plate, an oak vine being precisely cut all round, and flowers and fruits moulded on the top. It really was a shame to spoil it. All these were then swept off in a very noiseless manner. Grouse and pheasants are always served with the sweets in England, and they appeared at either end of the table. There were napkins under the finger-bowls, upon each of which a castle or palace was traced in indelible ink, and its name written beneath. The wines were port, sherry, madeira, claret, hock, and champagne. I refused the five first, but the champagne was poured into my glass without any question. So now you have the material elements of the dinner-party. Perhaps I cannot give the spiritual so well. Mr. Littledale was a gentleman with a face in full bloom, a very white cravat coming out even with his chin; and within it he bridled with the unmistakable English sense of superiority to the rest of mankind. He is a specimen of the independent, rich country gentleman of England. His conservatories were the best in the world, . . . and so on through all things appertaining to him. One could see directly that any attempt to convince him to the contrary would be utterly futile. His ears were not made to admit any such remarks. . . . He declared that the weather of the last twelve months was unprecedented. I meekly suggested Bulwer's testimony, but he scoffed at it. . . . He discussed with Mrs. Holland the probable merits of a pudding before her, and concluded he would not try it. There was something peremptory, petulant, and whimsical about him. . . . He was precisely a character such as I have read about in English novels, and entertained me very much. He was evidently of the war party of Britain, and thought Kossuth's last letter to the people of Straffan " exceedingly clever." In speaking of contested elections, he referred to one which cost £100,000; and some one asked Mr. Hawthorne if an election ever cost so much as that in America. Upon this question, a young gentleman, a fair-haired Egbert, with an aristocratic face and head, observed that he supposed £100,000 would purchase all America! Was not that impertinent? Mr. Hawthorne gravely replied that from the number of elections it was impossible that any such purchasing could be made. Opposite me sat a Mrs. Mann; — an old lady with an extraordinary cap, trimmed with pink ribbon, and a magnificent necklace of rubies round her neck, and bracelets of the same. She had a very intelligent face. There was a Mrs. Miller, who floated in fine, white, embroidered muslin, with a long scarlet sash, and a scarlet net upon the back of her head, confining her dark hair in a heavy clump, very low. She was a very romantic, graceful-looking person, slender and pale and elegant; and I had a good deal of conversation with her. She is one of Mr. Hawthorne's profound admirers. . . . She smiled very brightly; but a look of unspeakable sadness alternated with her smile that expressed great suffering of some kind. She spoke of having been ill once, when her friends called her the White Lady of Avenel; and that is just her picture now. Her dress made her fairness so apparent, — the gossamer tissue, the bright scarlet, and raven hair and dark eyes and lashes. The tones of her voice were very airy and distant, so that I could scarcely catch her words; and this I have observed in several English ladies. "Where could Zenobia have found her ever-fresh, rich flower?" asked Mrs. Holland. It is singular to observe how familiar and like a household word Mr. Hawthorne is to all cultivated English people. People who have not heard of Thackeray here, know Mr. Hawthorne. Is not that funny? We ladies had a very good time together in the drawing-room. Coffee was served in exquisite little china cups all flowers and gold. . . . Mr. Holland asked me whether Mr. Hawthorne was mobbed in "the States," and said that if he should go to London it would be hard work for him, for he would inevitably be mobbed. He then remarked that he did not like "Blithedale" so well as the other books. He spoke of Bulwer, and said that when he saw him he concluded it was better never to see an author, for he generally disappointed us; that Bulwer was an entirely made-up man in appearance, effeminate and finical, — flowing curls and curling mustachios, and elaborate and formal manners. I told him I should expect just such a looking person in Bulwer, from reading all his first novels, so very inferior to "The Caxtons" and "My Novel."

November 6.

MY DEAREST FATHER, — Last Sunday was a day that seemed to be dropped from heaven. I immediately thought that this was the Sunday for Chester. . . . So we sent to Mr. Squarey, who returned word that he would meet us at the depot at nine. We did not pick him out from all others for a companion to the Cathedral, but his wife first requested us to go with them, and so we were, in a certain way, bound not to go without them. It was very affecting to me when I came suddenly upon the Cathedral. . . . Every "Amen" was slow, solemn, full music, which had a wonderful effect. It was like the melodious assent of all nature and mankind to the preceding prayer, — "*So be it!*" . . . Una and Julian, especially Julian, suffered much *ennui* during the sermon ; and Una wrote the other day in one of her letters that " it was very *tegeuse*" (her first attempt at spelling "tedious ") "for there was hardly anything in it." Julian inadvertently gaped aloud, which so startled Mr. Hawthorne that he exclaimed, "*Good God!*" thus making the matter much worse ; but as even I, who sat next him, did not hear him, I presume that the same great spaces which took up the canon's voice disposed of Mr. Hawthorne's exclamation. I am sorry the children were obliged to stay through the sermon, as it rather spoiled the effect of the preceding service. It would have been far better to have had another of David's Psalms chanted. While listening to those of the morning lesson, I thought how marvelous it was that these Psalms, sung by the Jewish king and poet to his harp three thousand years ago, should now be a portion of the religious service of nearly all Christendom ; so many organs grandly accompanying thousands of voices in praising God in his very words, as the worthiest which man has yet uttered. And they are indeed worthy; and in this stately old Cathedral with its manifold associations they sounded grander, more touching, more eloquent than ever, borne up from the points of the flaming pinnacles, on solemn organ-tones, to God. This united worship affected me very deeply, it is so long since I have been to church, — hardly once since Una was born! You know I always loved to go to church, always supplying by my imagination what I did not find. . . . I think that the English Church is the merest petrifaction now. It has not the fervor and unction of the Roman Catholic even (that is dead enough, and will be dead soon). The English Church is fat, lazy, cold, timid, and selfish. How natural that some strong souls, with warm hearts and the fire of genius in them, should go back to Romanism from its icy presence!

November 8. Yesterday afternoon was beautiful, and we (Una, Julian, and I) were quite rejoiced to find Mr. Hawthorne in the ferry-boat when we returned from Liverpool. It was beautiful, — up in the sky, I mean; for there never was anything so nasty as Liverpool. Thousands of footsteps had stirred up the wetness and earth into such a mud-slush as one can have no idea of in America. It was necessary to look aloft into the clean heavens to believe any longer that mud was not eternal, infinite, omnipresent. . . . I left you introduced into the Cathedral cloisters in Chester, but I suppose you do not wish to stay there any longer. We went upon the walls afterwards, as we had

three hours upon our hands. I had a great desire
to plant my foot in Wales, and so we crossed the
river Dee. I stopped to look at the river Dee.
It is a mere brook in comparison to our great
rivers, though the Concord is no wider in some
places. It was flowing peacefully along; and I
remembered that Edgar the Peaceable was rowed
in triumph by eight kings from his palace on the
south bank to the monastery in 973. It was
too late to walk far into the immense grounds
of Eaton Hall, the seat of the Marquis of Westminster. He is a Norman noble. I told Mr.
Squarey that my father was of Welsh descent,
and he asked me why I did not fall down and
kiss my fatherland.

November.

Mr. Hawthorne's speeches are never "reported,"
dear father, or I would send them to you. They
remain only in the ear of him who hears them,
happy man that he is.

Oh, these fogs! If you have read "Bleak
House," you have read a description of a London
fog; but still you could scarcely have a true image of it. Out of doors one feels *hooded* with
fog, and cannot see his own hand. It is just as if
one should jump into a great bag of cotton-wool,
— not lamb's wool, for that is a little pervious.
Our fogs here are impervious. Mr. Ogden (the
large-hearted western gentleman whom Elizabeth
knows) called at the Consulate upon Mr. Hawthorne, and Mr. Hawthorne invited him to make
us a visit. He is overflowing with life, and seems

to have the broad prairies in him. He entertained me very much with an account of the Lord
Mayor's dinner in London, and other wonders
he had seen. At the dinner he had a peculiarly
pleasant, clever, and amiable group immediately
around him of baronets. He told us about going
with Miss Bacon to the old city of Verulam to see
Lord Bacon's estate and his tomb. They went
into the vault of the church where the family is
buried, but they could not prevail upon the beadle
to open the brick sepulchre where Lord Bacon
himself is supposed to be interred. The ruins of
the castle in which Lord Bacon lived show that it
was very rich and sumptuous ; and the very grove
in which he used to walk and meditate and study
stands unmolested, — a grand old grove of stately
trees planted by man, for they are in regular rows.
When Mr. Hawthorne came home the next evening, he brought me a superb bouquet of flowers,
which he said was a parting gift to me from Mr.
Ogden, who actually followed him to the boat with
them. They are a bright and fragrant memory
of that agreeable and excellent gentleman.

From the "Westminster Review" which lies
on the table I will extract for you one passage :
"Few have observed mankind closely enough to
be able to trace through all its windings the tor-
tuous course of a man who, having made one false
step, finds himself thereby compelled to leave the
path of truth and uprightness, and seldom regains
it. We can, however, refer to at least one living
author who has done so ; and in 'The Scarlet

Letter' by Hawthorne, the greatest of American novelists, Mr. [Wilkie] Collins might see the mode in which the moral lesson from examples of error and crime ought to be drawn. *There* is a tale of sin, and its inevitable consequences, from which the most pure need not turn away." In another paper in the same number the reviewer speaks of some one who "writes with the pure poetry of Nathaniel Hawthorne." As I have entered upon the subject of glorification, I will continue a little. From London an American traveler writes to Mr. Hawthorne: "A great day I spent with Sir William Hamilton, and two blessed evenings with De Quincey and his daughters. In De Quincey's house yours is the only portrait. They spoke of you with the greatest enthusiasm, and I was loved for even having seen you. Sir William Hamilton has read you with admiration, and says your 'House of the Seven Gables' is more powerful in description than 'The Scarlet Letter.'" Did I tell you once of an English lady who went to the Consulate to see Mr. Hawthorne, and introduced herself as a literary sister, and who had never been in Liverpool before, and desired Mr. Hawthorne to show her the lions, and he actually escorted her about? An American lady, who knows this Englishwoman, sent the other day a bit of a note, torn off, to Mr. Hawthorne, and on this scrap the English lady says, " I admire Mr. Hawthorne, *as a man* and *as an author*, more than any other human being."

I have diligently taken cold these four months,

and now have a hard cough. It is very noisy
and wearying. Mr. Hawthorne does not mind
fog, chill, or rain. He has no colds, feels perfectly
well, and is the only Phœbus that shines in England.

I told you in my last of Lord Dufferin's urgent
invitation to Mr. Hawthorne to go to his seat of
Clandeboye, in Ireland, four or five hours from
Liverpool. Mr. Hawthorne declined, and then
came another note. The first was quite formal,
but this begins : —

"MY DEAR MR. HAWTHORNE, — . . . Mrs.
Norton [his aunt, the Honorable Mrs. Norton]
hopes . . . that you will allow her to have the
pleasure of receiving you at her house in Ches-
terfield Street ; and I trust you will always remember that I shall esteem it an honor to be
allowed to receive you *here* whenever you may
be disposed to pay this country a visit. Believe
me, my dear Mr. Hawthorne,

"Yours very truly,

"DUFFERIN."

"CLANDEBOYE, HOLYWOOD."

Now have I not given you a fine feast of
homage, — "flummery" Mr. Hawthorne calls it ?

To-morrow is Thanksgiving Day. We are going
to observe it in memory of the fatherland. Mr.
Bright will dine with us by his own invitation,
not knowing it was a festival day with us. He
has long been projecting a visit, and finally
proposed coming this week. He will remain all
night, as Sandheys is on the other side of Liver-

pool, and his mamma does not wish him to cross the river [usually foggy] in the dark.

The English people, the ladies and gentlemen with whom we have become acquainted, are very lovely and affectionate and friendly. They seem lifelong acquaintances. I suppose there is no society in the world that can quite compare to this. It is all stereotyped, crystallized, with the repose and quiet in it of an immovable condition of caste. There is such a simplicity, such an ease, such an entire cordiality, such sweetness, that it is really beautiful to see. It is only when looking at the matter outside — or rather *out of it* — that one can see any disadvantage or unloveliness. It is a deep and great question, — this about rank. Birth and wealth often are causes of the superior cultivation and refinement that are found with them. In this old civilization there seems to be no jealousy, no effort to alter position. . . . Provided that the lowest orders could be redeemed from the brutal misery in which they are plunged, there could be a little more enjoyment in contemplating and mingling with the higher. But it seems as if everything must be turned upside down rather than for one moment more to tolerate such suffering, such bestiality. There have been one or two individual cases that went before the courts that really make it almost wicked ever to smile again. . . . As Mr. Hawthorne delays to go to London, London is beginning to come to him, for Mr. Holland says he must inevitably be mobbed in England. Two Londoners called lately, — one a Mr. William Jerdan, about seventy years old, a literary man, who for fifty years has been familiar with the best society in London, and knows everybody for whom one cares to ask. He is a perfect mine of rich memories. He pleased me mightily, and made me think of Dr. Johnson. Rose sat on his knee, and gazed with unwinking, earnest eyes into his face. He said he never saw anything like it except the gaze of Talleyrand (whom he knew very well). He said that Talleyrand undertook to look at a man and not allow a man to look into him, — he always fixed such a glance as that upon one. Imperturbably, baby continued to gaze, without any smile ; and he kept dodging from her and making funny contortions, but she was not in the least moved. "Why," he exclaimed, "you would be an admirable judge, and I should not like to be the fellow who would take sentence from your Lordship when you get on your black cap !" At last she smiled confidingly at him. "There," he said, "now I have it ! She loves me, she loves me !" At eight they left us for London, intending not to shoot through that night, but sleep at Birmingham, halfway. "Oh," said Mr. Jerdan, "I make nothing of going out to dine an hundred miles and returning !" The gentleman with him was Mr. Bennoch, a patron of poets and artists, and as pleasant, merry, and genial as possible. He told Julian that, if he would go to London with him, he should have a pony as low as the table and a dog as high as the pony ; but Julian would not, even in prospect of possessing what his heart desireth most.

December 8.

Yesterday who should come to see me but Mr. James Martineau and his wife! I have the greatest admiration for him as a divine, and I do not know what I expected to see in the outward man. But I was well pleased with his aspect as I found it. He is not tall, and he is pale, though not thin, with the most perfectly simple manners and beautiful expression. It seemed as if he had always been *my brother;* as if I could find in him counselor, friend, saint, and sage; and I have no doubt it is so, so potent is the aroma of character, without a word or sign. How worse than folly it is to imagine that character can either be cried up or cried down! No veil can conceal, no blazonry exalt, either the good or the evil. A man has only to come in and sit down, and there he is, for better, for worse. I, at least, am always, as it were, *hit* by a person's sphere; and either the music of the spheres or the contrary supervenes, and sometimes also nothing at all, if there is not much strength of character. Mr. Martineau did not say much; but his voice was very pleasant and sympathetic, and he won regard merely by his manner of being. Mrs. Martineau sat with her back to the only dim light there was, and I could receive no impression from her face; but she seemed pleasant and friendly. Mrs. Martineau said she wished very much that we would go to her party on the 19th, which was their silver

wedding day. She said we should meet Mrs. Gaskell, the author of "Mary Barton," "Ruth," and
"Cranford," and several other friends. It is the
greatest pity that we cannot go; but it would be
madness to think of going out at night in these
solid fogs with my cough. They live beyond
Liverpool, in Prince's Park. Mrs. Martineau
showed herself perfectly well-bred by not being
importunate. It was a delightful call; and I feel
as if I had friends indeed and in need just from
that one interview. Mr. Martineau said Una would
be homesick until she had some friends of her
own age, and that he had a daughter a little older,
who might do for one of them. They wished to
see Mr. Hawthorne, and came pretty near it, for
they could not have got out of the lodge gate
before he came home! Was not that a shame?

I must tell you that there is a splendid show
which Mr. Jerdan wants us to see at Lord Warre-
more de Tabley's; it is a vast salt mine of twenty
acres, cut into a symmetrical columned gallery!
He says it shall be lighted up, so that we shall
walk in a diamond corridor. Mr. Jerdan said that
salt used to be the medium of traffic in those dis-
tricts; and I think Lord de Tabley [1] is a beauty
for having his mines cut in the form of art, instead of hewed and hacked as a Vandal would
have done. Mr. Jerdan said that on account of
some circumstance he was called Lord de *Ta-
bleau* for a pseudonym, and in the sense I have

---

[1] Mr. Hawthorne's severe taste is annoyed by that expression,
but I must let it go for the sake of what follows.

heard people exclaim to a good child, " Oh, you picture ! "

In the "North British Review" this week is a review of Mr. Hawthorne's three last romances. It gives very high praise.

December 18.

I went to Liverpool yesterday for a Christmas present for you, and got a silver pen in a pearl handle, which you will use for Una's sake. While I was gone, Mr. Martineau and Mrs. Gaskell called ! I was very sorry to lose the visit. They left a note from the Misses Yates inviting us to dine to-day and stay all night, and go to Mrs. Martineau's evening party to-morrow ! It would be a charming visitation, if it were possible. Mr. Bright cannot find language to express the Misses Yates' delightsomeness, and was wishing that we knew them.

By this steamer Mr. Ticknor has sent us a Christmas present of a barrel of apples. I wish you could see Rosebud with her bright cheeks and laughing eyes. A lady thought her four years old, the other day ! Julian has to-day gone with his father to the Consulate. Una is in the drawing-room reading Miss Edgeworth. Rose is on the back of my chair.

On Christmas night the bells chimed in the dawn, beginning at twelve and continuing till daybreak. I wish you could hear this chiming of bells. It is the most joyful sound you can imagine, — the most hopeful, the most enlivening. I waked before light, and thought I heard some ineffable music. I thought of the song of the angels on that blessed morn; but while listening, through a sudden opening in the air, or breeze blowing towards us, I found it was not the angels, but the bells of Liverpool. One day when I was driving through Liverpool with Una and Julian, these bells suddenly broke forth on the occasion of a marriage, and I could scarcely keep the children in the carriage. They leaped up and down, and Una declared she would be married in England, if only to hear the chime of the bells. The mummers stood at our gate on Christmas morning and sang in the dawn, acting the part of the heavenly host. The Old Year was tolled out and the New Year chimed in also, and again the mummers sang at the gate.

Perhaps you have heard of Miss Charlotte Cushman, the actress? The summer before we left America, she sent a note to Mr. Hawthorne, requesting him to sit to a lady for his miniature, which she wished to take to England. Mr. Hawthorne could not refuse, though you can imagine his repugnance on every account. He went and did penance, and was then introduced to Miss Cushman. He liked her for a very sensible person with perfectly simple manners. The other day he met her in Liverpool, and she told him she 'had been intending to call on me ever since she had been at her sister's at Rose Hill Hall, Woolton, seven miles from Liverpool. Mr. Hawthorne wished me to invite her to dine and pass the night. I invited her to dine on the 29th of December. She accepted and came. I found her tall as her famous character, Meg Merrilies, with a face of peculiar, square form, most amiable in expression, and so very untheatrical in manner and bearing that I should never suspect her to be an actress. She has left the stage now two years, and retires upon the fortune she has made; for she was a very great favorite on the English stage, and retired in the height of her fame. The children liked her prodigiously, and Rose was never weary of the treasures attached to her watch-chain. I could not recount to you the gems clustered there, — such as a fairy tiny gold palette, with all the colors arranged; a tiny easel with a colored landscape, quarter of an inch wide; a tragic and comic mask, just big enough for a gnome; a cross of the Legion of Honor; a wallet, opening with a spring, and disclosing compartments just of a size for the Keeper of the Privy Purse of the Fairy Queen; a dagger for a pygmy; two minute daguerreotypes of friends, each as large as a small pea, in a gold case; an opera-glass; Faith, Hope, and Charity represented by a golden heart and anchor, and I forget what, — a little harp; I cannot remember any more. These were all, I think, memorials of friends. In the morning she sat down to Una's beautifully toned piano, and sang one of Lockhart's Spanish ballads, with eloquent expression, so as to make my blood tingle.

Hospitality was quite frequent now in our first

English home, as many letters affirm. The delightful novelty to my small self of a peep at the glitter of little dinner-parties was as surprising to me as if I could have had a real consciousness of its contrast to all the former simplicity of my parents' life. Down the damask trooped the splendid silver covers, entrancingly catching a hundred reflections from candle-flame and cut-glass, and my own face as I hovered for a moment upon the scene while the butler was gliding hither and thither to complete his artistic arrangements. On my father's side of the family there had been a distinct trait of material elegance, appearing in such evidences as an exquisite tea-service, brought from China by my grandfather, with the intricate monogram and dainty shapes and decoration of a hundred years ago ; and in a few chairs and tables that could not be surpassed for graceful design and finish ; and so on. As for my mother's traits of inborn refinement, they were marked enough, but she writes of herself to her sister at this time, "You cannot think how I cannot be in the least tonish, such is my indomitable simplicity of style." Her opinion of herself was always humble ; and I can testify to the distinguished figure she made as she wore the first ball-dress I ever detected her in. I was supposed to be fast asleep, and she had come to look at me before going out to some social function, as she has told me she never failed to do when leaving the house for a party. Her superb brocade, pale-tinted, low-necked, and short-sleeved, her happy, airy manner, her glowing though pale face, her dancing eyes, her ever-hovering smile of perfect kindness, all flashed upon me in the sudden light as I roused myself. I insisted upon gazing and admiring, yet I ended by indignantly weeping to find that my gentle little mother could be so splendid and wear so triumphant an expression. "She is frightened at my fine gown!" my mother exclaimed, with a changed look of self-forgetting concern; and I never lost the lesson of how much more beautiful her noble glance was than her triumphant one. A faded bill has been preserved, for the humor of it, from Salem days, in which it is recorded that for the year 1841 she ordered ten pairs of number two kid slippers, — which was not precisely economical for a young lady who needed to earn money by painting, and who denied herself a multitude of pleasures and comforts which were enjoyed by relatives and friends.

In our early experience of English society, my mother's suppressed fondness for the superb burst into fruition, and the remnants of such indulgence have turned up among severest humdrum for many years; but soon she refused to permit herself even momentary extravagances. To those who will remember duty, hosts of duties appeal, and it was not long before my father and mother began to save for their children's future the money which flowed in. Miss Cushman's vagary of an amusing watch-chain was exactly the sort of thing which they never imitated; they smiled at it as the saucy tyranny over a great character of great wealth. My father's rigid economy was perhaps more un

broken than my mother's. Still, she has written,
"I never knew what charity meant till I knew my
husband." There are many records of his having
heard clearly the teaching that home duties are
not so necessary or loving as duty towards the
homeless.

Julian came home from Liverpool with papa one
afternoon with four masks, with which we made
merry for several days. One was the face of a
simpleton, and that was very funny upon papa, —
such a transformation! A spectacled old beldame,
looking exactly like a terrific auld wife at Lenox,
was very diverting upon Julian, turning him into a
gnome ; and Una was irresistible beneath the mask
of a meaningless young miss, resembling a silly-
looking doll. Julian put on another with a portentous nose, and then danced the schottische with
Una in her doll's mask. Hearing this morning
that a gentleman had sent to some regiments £50
worth of postage stamps, he said he thought it
would be better to have an arrangement for all
the soldiers letters to go and come free. I do not
know but he had better send this suggestion to
the "London Times."

March 12.

Mr. Hawthorne dined at Aigburth, one of the
suburbs of Liverpool, with Mr. Bramley Moore,
an M. P. Mr. Moore took an effectual way to
secure Mr. Hawthorne, for he went one day
himself to his office, and asked him for the very
same evening, thus bearding the lion in his den

and clutching him. And Mrs. H., the aunt of Henry Bright, would not be discouraged. She could not get Mr. Hawthorne to go to her splendid fancy ball, to meet Lord and Lady Sefton and all the aristocracy of the county . . . but wrote him a note telling him that if he wished for her forgiveness he must agree with me upon a day when we would go and dine with her. Mr. Hawthorne delayed, and then she wrote me a note, appointing the 16th of March for us to go and meet the Martineaus and Brights and remain all night. There was no evading this, so he is going; but I refused. Her husband is a mighty banker, and she is sister of the present Chancellor of the Exchequer, W. E. Gladstone, and they are nobly connected all round. . . . Mr. Hawthorne does not want to go, and especially curses the hour when white muslin cravats became the *sine qua non* of a gentleman's full dress. Just think how reverend he must look ! I believe he would even rather wear a sword and cocked hat, for he declares a white muslin cravat the last abomination, the chief enormity of fashion, and that all the natural feelings of a man cry out against it ; and that it is alike abhorrent to taste and to sentiment. To all this I reply that he looks a great deal handsomer with white about his throat than with a stiff old black satin stock, which always to me looks like the stocks, and that it is habit only which makes him prefer it. . . .

March 16.

Mr. Hawthorne has gone to West Derby to dine . . . and stay all night. He left me with a powerful anathema against all dinner-parties, declaring he did not believe anybody liked them, and therefore they were a malicious invention for destroying human comfort. Mr. Bramley Moore again seized Mr. Hawthorne in the Consulate, the other day, and dragged him to Aigburth to dine with Mr. Warren, the author of " Ten Thousand a Year " and " The Diary of a Physician." Mr. Hawthorne liked him very well. Mr. Warren commenced to say something very complimentary to Mr. Hawthorne in a low tone, across an intermediate gentleman, when Mr. Bramley Moore requested that the company might have the benefit of it, so Mr. Warren spoke aloud ; and then Mr. Hawthorne had to make a speech in return ! We expected Mr. Warren here to dine afterwards, but he has gone home to Hull.

Mrs. Sanders again sent a peremptory summons for us all to go to London and make her a visit. I wish Mr. Hawthorne could leave his affairs and go, for she lives in Portman Square, and Mr. Buchanan would get us admitted everywhere. Mr. Sanders has been rejected by the Senate ; but I do not suppose he cares much, since he is worth a half million of dollars.

Sir Thomas Talfourd, the author of " Ion," suddenly died the other day, universally mourned. I believe his brother Field, who came to England with us, is again in America, now. I trust the rest of the notable men of England will live till I have seen them. This gentleman wished very much to meet Mr. Hawthorne.

March 30.

Mr. Hawthorne went to Norris Green and dined with the H——s, Martineaus, and Brights, and others, and stayed all night, as appointed. He declared that, when he looked in the glass before going down to dinner, he presented the appearance of a respectable butler, with his white cravat — and thought of hiring himself out. He liked Mr. H. . . . He gives away £7000 a year in charity! Mrs. H. is good, too, for she goes herself and sees into the condition of a whole district in Liverpool, though a dainty lady of fashion. She showed Mr. Hawthorne a miniature of the famous Sir Kenelm Digby, who was her ancestor; and so through his family she is connected with the Percys and the Stanleys, Earls of Derby. Everything was in sumptuous fashion, served by gorgeous footmen. Mr. Hawthorne was chief guest. . . . Mrs. H. has sense, and is rather sentimental, too. She has no children, and had the assurance to tell Mr. Hawthorne she preferred chickens to children.

The next day Mr. Bright invited Mr. Hawthorne to drive. Mr. Bright wanted to call on his cousin, Sir Thomas Birch. And as he was the nearest neighbor of the Earl of Derby, he took them to Knowsley, Lord Derby's seat. At Sir Thomas's, Mr. Hawthorne saw a rookery for the first time; and a picture of Lady Birch, his mother, painted by Sir Thomas Lawrence, but not quite finished. It is said to be one of his best pictures. Mr. Hawthorne was disappointed in the house at Knowsley. It was lower than he had imagined, and of various eras, but so large as to be able to entertain an hundred guests.

April 14, Good Friday.

MY DEAR FATHER, — This is a day of great and solemn fast in England ; when all business is suspended, and no work is done in house or street ; when there is really a mighty pause in worldly affairs, and all people remind themselves that Christ was crucified, and died for us. From early morning till late evening, all churches are open and service is performed.

I wish you could be undeceived about the income of this Consulate. Mr. Hawthorne now knows actually everything about it. . . . He goes from us at nine, and we do not see him again till five!!! I only wish we could be pelted within an inch of our lives with a hailstorm of sovereigns, so as to satisfy every one's most gorgeous hopes ; but I am afraid we shall have but a gentle shower, after all. . . . I am sorry I have had the expectation of so much, because I am rather disappointed to be so circumscribed. With my husband's present constant devotion to the duties of his office, he could no more write a syllable than he could build a cathedral. . . . He never writes by candle-light. . . . Mr. Crittenden tells Mr. Hawthorne that he thinks he may save $5000 a year by *economy*. He himself, living in a very quiet manner, not going into society, has spent $4000 a year. He thinks we must spend more. People will not let Mr. Hawthorne alone, as they have Mr. Crittenden, because they feel as if they had a right to him, and he cannot well forego their claim. " The Scarlet Letter " seems to have placed him on a pinnacle of fame and love here. . . . It will give you pleasure, I think, to hear that Mr. Cecil read a volume of "The Scarlet Letter" the other day which was one of the thirty-fifth thousand of *one* publisher. Is it not provoking that the author should not have even *one* penny a volume?

I have only room to put in the truest, warmest sympathy with all your efforts and trials, and the wish that I could lift you up out of all, and sorrow that I cannot. Mr. Hawthorne has relations and personal friends who look to him, I think, with great desires. I can demand nothing for mine.

Though the great Reform Bill of Lord John Russell was deferred by him the other night to another period on account of war, yet reforms on every point in social life are going on here, or *moving* to go on. Nothing seems to escape some eye that has suddenly opened. The Earl of Shaftesbury is one of God's Angels of Benefits. The hideous condition of the very poor and even of tradesmen is being demonstrated to the nation; a condition in which, a writer in the London "Athenæum" says, " Virtue is *impossible* " ! From this most crying and worst evil, up through all things, sounds the trumpet of reform.

Such abuse of the good President as there is, is sickening. I hope those who vilify him for doing what he considers his duty have a quarter of his conscience and uprightness. He is a brave man. . . . He wrote Mr. Hawthorne that he had no hope of being popular during the first part of his administration at least. He can be neither bribed, bought, nor tempted in his political course ; he will do what he thinks constitutional and right, and find content in it. . . . I wish our Senators had as good manners as the noble lords of Parliament. But we are perfect savages in manners as yet, and have no self-control, nor reverence. The dignity and serenity of maturer age will, I trust, come at last to us. . . .

I never dreamed of putting myself into a picture, because I am not handsome enough. But I will endeavor that you have Mr. Hawthorne and Rose-bud, some time or other. Mr. Hawthorne looks supremely handsome here ; handsomer than anybody I see. Every other face looks coarse, compared ; and his air and bearing are far superior to those of any Englishman I have seen. The English say that they should suppose he were *an Englishman*—till he speaks. This is a high compliment from *the English*. They look at him as much as they can, covertly ; as much as they can without being uncivil and *staring*, as if they wanted to assure themselves that he really were so wondrous handsome. He does not observe this ; but it is nuts to me, and *I* observe it. The lofty, sumptuous apartments become him very much. I always thought he was born for a palace, and he shows that he was.

We have had some delightful experiences, and have seen some interesting people, some literary celebrities, and beautiful English life within jealous stone walls, draped with ivy inside. We see why *comfort* is an essentially English word, and we understand Shakespeare and all the old poets properly now we are on the scene.

CHAPTER X

DOUGLAS, MONA, July 18.

MY DEAR FATHER, — I little dreamed that I should next address you from the Isle of Man! Yet here we all are, with one grievous exception, to be sure; for Mr. Hawthorne, after fetching us one day, and staying the two next, went away to the tiresome old Consulate, so conscientious and devoted is he; for his clerk assured him he might stay a little. Yet I know that there are reasons of state why he should not; and therefore, though I am nothing less than infinitely desolate without him, and hate to look at anything new unless he is looking too, I cannot complain. But is it not wonderful that I am here in this remote and interesting and storied spot? — the last retreat of the little people called fairies, the lurking-place of giants and enchanters. . . . At Stonehenge we found a few rude stones for a temple. I could not gather into a small enough focus the wide glances of Julian's great brown, searching eyes to make him see even what there was; and when finally he comprehended that the circle of stones once marked out a temple, and that the Druids really once stood there, he curled his lip, scornfully exclaiming, "Is that all?" and bounded off

273

to pluck flowers. I think that, having heard of Stonehenge and a Druid temple which was built of stones so large that it was considered almost miraculous that they were moved to their places, he expected to see a temple touching the sky, perhaps. . . . Mr. Hawthorne came back the next Friday, much to our joy, and on Saturday afternoon we walked to the Nunnery with him, which was founded by St. Bridget. A few ruins remain, overgrown with old ivy vines of such enormous size that I think they probably hold the walls together. . . . Julian and Una were enchanted with the clear stream, and Julian was wild for turtles; but there are no reptiles in the Isle of Man. . . . I kept thinking, "And *this* is the rugged, bare, rocky isle which I dreaded to come to, — this soft, rich, verdant paradise!" It really seems as if the giants had thrown aloft the bold, precipitous rocks and headlands round the edge of the island, to guard the sylvan solitudes for the fairies, whose stronghold was the Isle of Man. I should not have been surprised at any time to have seen those small people peeping out of the wild foxgloves, which are their favorite hiding-places. So poetical is the air of these regions that mermaids, fairies, and giants seem quite natural to it. In the morning of the day we went to the Nunnery Mr. Hawthorne took Julian and went to the Douglas market, which is held in the open air. . . . My husband said that living manners were so interesting and valuable that he would not miss the scene for even Peel

Castle. One day, when Una and I went to shop in Douglas, we saw in the market square a second-hand bookstall. I had been trying in vain to get "Peveril of the Peak" at the library and bookstores, and hoped this sales-counter might have it. So I looked over the books, and what do you think I saw? A well-read and soiled copy of the handsome edition of Mr. Hawthorne's "Blithedale Romance"! Yes, even in Mona. We have heard of some families in England who keep in use two copies of "The Scarlet Letter;" but I never dreamed of finding either of these books *here*.

Sunday was the perfectest day in our remembrance. In the morning Mr. Hawthorne walked to Kirk Braddon, and the afternoon we spent on Douglas Head. It is quite impossible to put into words that afternoon. Such softness and splendor and freshness combined in the air; such a clearest sunshine; such a deep blue sea and cloudless blue heaven; such fragrance and such repose. We looked from our great height upon all the beauty and grandeur, and in Mr. Hawthorne's face was a reflection of the incredible loveliness and majesty of the scene. Una was a lily, and Julian a magnolia. I think that for once, at least, Mr. Hawthorne was satisfied with weather and circumstances. Towards sunset the mountains of Cumberland were visible, for the first time during our visit, on the horizon, which proved that even in England the air was clear that day. A pale purple outline of waving hills lay on the silvery sea, which, as it grew later, became opaline in hue . . . .

. . . This morning, soon after ten, we summoned a boat, and were rowed to St. Mary's Rock, which has a good beach on one side, and spent two hours there. There was a delicious air and bright sunshine, and we found innumerable pretty pearl shells among the pebbles; and Julian bathed in the sea. Rosebud enjoyed it very much, and kept close to me all the time. I asked her why she kept so near mamma, and she replied, " Oh, dear mamma, I cannot help it." Once she put her little foot into a pool, and I had to take off her sock and shoe to dry them in the sun. Her snowy little foot and pink toes looked, on the rocks, like a new kind of shell, and I told her I was afraid a gentleman who was seeking shells on the other side of the island would come and take it for a conch shell, and put it in his pocket for his little children. She shouted at this; and then threw back her head, with a silent laugh, like Leatherstocking, showing all her little pearly teeth, — so pretty with her rosy cheeks and streaming hair. I actually seem in a dream, and not here in bodily presence. I cannot *imagine* myself here; much less realize it. Through the mist Douglas looked like a vast leviathan asleep on the sea, as we approached. It is a pity that steam should come near such a place, for its bustle is not in harmony with the vast repose.

I suppose the world could scarcely furnish another such stately and salubrious spot as exactly this; for the climate of the Isle of Man is extremely mild and genial. From my parlor windows, in the Fort Anne Hotel, I look out on the beautiful crescent harbor from a good height. . . . Mountains rise above high hills on the horizon in soft, large, mellow lines, which I am never weary of gazing at. The hills are of precious emerald stone; the sea is an opal; the distant mountains are a pile of topazes; and the sky is turquoise and gold. But why attempt to put into ink such a magnificent setting as this? No jewels could be compared to it. God alone could mingle these colors and pencil these grand lines. . . .

ROCK PARK, August 2.

DEAR ELIZABETH, — We returned last Saturday, after a delightful visit to Mona of a fortnight. We had constantly splendid weather, and there was one day which Mr. Hawthorne and I concluded we had never seen equaled in any hemisphere. . . . I took Una and Julian to Glen Darragh to see the ruins of a Druidical temple. . . . We ascended Mount Murray . . . and a magnificent landscape was revealed to us; a fertile valley of immense extent. . . . But before we arrived at Glen Darragh we came to Kirk Braddon, an uncommonly lovely place. I knew that in the churchyard were two very old Runic monuments, so we alighted. . . . The family residence of the late Duke of Atholl is situated at the extremity

277

of a flat meadow ; and as far as I could see, it did
not seem a very princely residence. But in this
country I am often struck with the simplicity and
freedom from show which those of *real* rank are
contented with. They seem really to agree with
Burns that "the *man's the gowd*." At Knowsley, the residence of the Earls of Derby, the inside of the mansion was very simple, and they are
the proudest nobles of England.

We finally arrived at Glen Darragh, and I
gazed about in vain to see the ruins of a temple.
. . . We came at last to some mounds of earth,
with rough stones on their tops, but I could discover no design or order to them, and was quite
cast down. But then I saw more, at a short distance, of better hope, and I ran to them, and
found they were stones placed in a circular form,
inclosing about fourteen yards diameter. These
stones, however, were unhewn and of moderate
size. And this was all. I broke off a crumb of
one of the stones, and looked around me. It was
quite desolate, for a large space. Not a tree or
a shrub grew near, but grand mountains rose up
on every side. Glen Darragh means the vale of
oaks, but not an oak could be seen. The singular destruction of trees in this be-battled, be-con-
quered island is unaccountable. Why invaders
should uproot such innocent adorners of the earth
is a mystery. It is said that the Druids found a
great many pine woods there, and that they uprooted them and planted their favorite oaks. But
pines, oaks, Druids, temples, and all are gone now,

except these few stones. I wondered whether any terrible human sacrifices had been offered on the spot where I was standing. The mountains were the same, and the sky was the same; but all else had changed since those fearful days. . . . Of course Rome was here, for where did that proud queen *not* set her imperial foot ? But the only sign of her left is at Castletown : it is an ancient altar. I looked out of the chamber window one night, and at twelve o'clock the golden flush of sunset still glowed in the west, and in the east was an enormous star. We often see Venus very large at home, but this was three times as large as we ever see it. I do not know what this star was. It must have been Venus, however. The star of beauty should surely rise over such a day as this had been. Once we rowed about the island, and it was truly superb — this circumnavigation. We were near enough to the shore to see every house and animal and tree, but far off from dangerous rocks. We passed St. Manghold's Head. The saint was an Irish prince, converted by St. Patrick, and became so eminent for sanctity that St. Bridget came from Ireland to receive the veil from him. It is the most eastern point of the island, and its summit is crested with rocks. Under one is a spring, called St. Manghold's Well, which is thought to have medicinal virtues ; and if any one who drinks the waters sits at the same time in the saint's chair, — a rude stone seat near, — they will certainly prove beneficial. We landed at Ramsey, and walked through the town. Towns fade into utter insignificance in that island. Nature is so grand there that houses and streets seem impertinences, and make no account, unless some stately castle towers up. The towns look like barnacles clinging to a majestic ship's sides. . . . This evening Mr. Hawthorne brings me news of the death of L. Howes! We were thinking yesterday what a mournful change had come over that family since we used to go every Saturday evening and see them, in most charming family group, all those bright, intelligent, happy faces gathered round the centretable or fireside, beaming with life, and mind, and heart. . . .

Julian enjoyed the rocks and beaches and seabathing at Mona greatly, and on his return here was homesick for it all for two days. Una grew so homesick for Rockferry that she could hardly be kept away till I was ready to come, though she also enjoyed the sea and the island very much. But I think she has inhabitiveness to a great degree. As to Rose, she was like a sunbeam from morning to night. . . . I have a slight journal of my visit to the Isle of Man, written at the earnest request of Mr. Hawthorne.

Rose is in no danger of forgetting you. We talk to her about you a great deal, and she is always referring to " When I was in 'Morica." Miss Martineau is about Liverpool, and while I was at the island Mr. Bright took Mr. Hawthorne to see her. She was extremely agreeable and brilliant. She has become quite infidel in her

opinions. . . . It must be either a fool or a mad-
man who says there is no GOD. . . . I had a delightful visit from the Cochrans, and went with
them to Chester. Martha was deeply affected by
the Cathedral, especially by the cloisters. Tears
filled her eyes. After luncheon, we went to see
a Roman bath and a Roman crypt, the last discovered within a few months. The bath is back
of, and beneath, a crockery shop. We saw first
a cold bath. It was merely an oblong stone basin,
built round a perpetual spring. A high iron rail-
ing now guards it, and we looked into what seemed
almost a well, where the Romans used to plunge.
. . . The black water reflected the candle and
glittered far below. It might be the eye of one
of the twentieth legion. We then went into a
shop and asked for the crypt. The men pointed
to a door, which we opened, and nearly tumbled
down some stone steps. By degrees our eyes
became owlish, and we gradually saw, as if loom-
ing out of past ages, the beautiful arches of the
roof, and the columns on each side. . . .

My mother gives a glimpse of the vicissitudes
of the Consulate, — that precinct which I pictured
as an ogre's lair, though the ogre was temporarily
absent, while my father, like a prince bewitched,
had been compelled by a rash vow to languish in
the man-eater's place for a term of years : —
"In the evening Mr. Hawthorne told me that
there were suddenly thrown upon his care two
hundred soldiers who had been shipwrecked in the

San Francisco, and that he must clothe and board them and send them home to the United States. They were picked up somewhere on the sea and brought to Liverpool. Mr. Hawthorne has no official authority to take care of any but *sailors* in distress. He invited the lieutenant to come and stay here, and he must take care of the soldiers, even if the expense comes out of his own purse." [Later.] "Mr. Hawthorne sent to Mr. Buchanan (the Ambassador) about the soldiers, and he would share no responsibility, though it was much more a matter pertaining to his powers than to a consul. . . . Mr. Hawthorne has supplied them with clothes and lodgings, and has finally chartered for their passage home one of the Cunard steamers! Such are his official reverses."

"Last Friday I received a note from the wife of the U. S. Consul at London, inviting me and the children to go with Mr. Hawthorne to town, to see the Queen open Parliament. It was such a cordial invitation that it was nearly impossible to refuse; but we could not go, Mr. Hawthorne was so busy with these soldiers, and with trials in the police courts; so that he could not leave his post." [Still later.] "As to shipwrecked *sailors*, there seems no end to them; and for all Mr. Hawthorne's costs for them he is, of course, repaid. His hands are full all the time. But in the history of the world, it is said, there never were so many shipwrecks as there have been this last winter. The coasts of Great Britain seem to have been nothing but stumbling-blocks in the way of every ship. . . . I have seen, in an American paper, a passage in which the writer undertakes to defend my husband from some dirty aspersions. It seems that some one had told the absolute falsehood that he had shirked all responsibility about the shipwrecked soldiers, and his defender stated the case just as it was, and that *Mr. Buchanan* declined having anything to do with the matter. The government *will* make the chartering of the steamer good to Mr. Hawthorne. . . . He has been very busily occupied at the Consulate this winter and spring, — so many disasters at sea, and vagabonds asking for money. He has already lost more than a hundred pounds by these impostors. But he is very careful indeed, and those persons who have proved dishonest were gentlemen in their own esteem, and it was difficult to suspect them. But he is well on his guard now ; and he says the moment he sees a coat-tail he knows whether the man it belongs to is going to beg ! His life in the Consulate is not charming. He has to pay a great penalty for the result of his toil. Not that he has any drudgery, but he is imprisoned and in harness. He will not let me take a pen in my hand when he is at home, because at any rate I see him so little."

Such paragraphs as the one I add, from a little letter of my sister's, often appear ; but in this instance it was the glad exclamation of release, just before we removed to Italy : —

" Papa will be with us on Monday, free from the terrors of the old Consulate. Perhaps you can imagine what infinitely joyful news that is to us; and to him, too, as much, if not more so; for he has had all the work, and we have only suffered from his absence."

The letters proceed : —

MY DEAR FATHER, — It was delightful to see your handwriting this week, written with the same firmness as ever. It gives me unspeakable satisfaction to know that the drafts Mr. Hawthorne sent contribute to your ease, and supply you with embellishments and luxuries, which in sickness are necessaries. I only wish I could put strength into your limbs, as well as provide you with a stuffed chair to repose them upon. Mr. Hawthorne has wished, you see, to prevent your having any anxiety about little wants. It will be all right for the present, and future too. . . . I suppose the War will affect everything in a disastrous manner, except the End, and *that* God will take into His own hands for good, no doubt, though not as either party proposes.

Here in England we are wholly occupied with the War. No one thinks or talks of anything else. Every face is grave with sorrow for the suffering and slaughter, and then triumphant with pride and joy at the incredible heroism of the troops. . . . In his sermon before the last, Mr. Channing brought out my dearest, inmost doctrines and faith; the sovereignty of good ; the unfallen ideal in man ; the impossibility of God's ever for one moment turning from man, or being averse to him ; the essential transitoriness of evil. . . . I deeply regret that Una and Julian cannot hear the sermons for the little people, for I think it would do much towards saving their souls.

My mother's loss in the death of her father was a great grief, which fell upon her at this time. She wrote to my aunt : —

DEAR ELIZABETH, — If anything could have softened such a blow, it would have been the divine way in which my husband told me. If a seraph *can* look more radiant with love — a flaming love, veiled with most tender, sorrowing sympathy — than he did, I am sure I cannot conceive of it, and am quite contented not to. I saw and felt in a moment how beyond computation and desert I was still rich, — richest. Father's sincerity, his childlike guilelessness, his good sense and rectitude, his unaffected piety, — all and each of his qualities made him interesting to my husband. I really do not believe any one else ever listened to his stories and his conversation with as much love and interest. Whatever is real and simple and true attracts my husband both as a poet and as a man. Genuine nature he always springs to. Father was entirely unspoiled by the world — as pure of it as a dewdrop. This indeed made him a rare person. He seems to stand meekly in the presence of God. Where more archangelic intellect — divine genius — would tremble and faint, simple goodness will feel quite at home, with its one talent become two talents, and its faith and hope blossomed into reality. By and by I shall perhaps have a vivid sense of his presence, as I did of mother's, six weeks after her departure.

We have been out, for the first time, walking in the garden. The morning was beautiful. The budding shrubbery was on every side, and daisies and wallflowers and auriculas blooming even while a thin veil of snow lay in some places.

Una, in writing home to America, portrays the family peace, and the little landscapes of the quieter corners of our "Old Home:" —

"We have got to England at last. It does not seem as if we were in England, but in Boston or Salem. There is not so much noise here as there was in Boston.

"Mamma has told you about Mr. Rathbone's place, but I do not think she has told you about one place by the wall. The wall is run over with all sorts of vines, and there are summer-houses close up by the wall, and a little brook rippling in front, and a great many mighty trees in front, so that not a ray of the sun could peep through.

"On Sunday, the great Easter Sunday, we went to the Chapel of the Blind, and stayed through the Communion service. Mamma received the sacrament. The sermon was very tiresome. It was about the skins that Adam and Eve wore. . . . I was very much interested in Chester, and all the old things I saw there, especially the Cathedral. As we walked round the cloisters you could almost fancy you saw the monks pacing slowly round, and looking now and then on the beautiful dewy green grass which is in the middle of the cloisters. On Monday my dear godpapa [Mr. O'Sullivan] went to London. Mamma got up at half past four and set on the table some chicken - pie, some oranges, and what she thought to be stout, and some flowers which I had gathered in the morn-ing, and gave all these to him.

"Rose is sitting on papa's knee, and through her golden hair I can see her little contented face. She has got down now, and is engaged in a lively dis-cussion with Julian about her name. Julian has been dancing round with the heat, for he thought dancing round would keep him cool. Rose is sit-ting in mamma's lap now, and she looks so jolly. Her very rosy round face and her waving flowing hair make her look so pretty. She is very sharp, and she has a great deal of fun in her. She has learnt 'Hark, the lark,' 'The Cuckoo,' and 'Where the bee sucks, there suck I.' She says them very prettily, and she has a sweet, simple way of saying what she knows."

Thoughts of her own country recall the joys of Lenox : —

"I have been nutting a great many times in Berkshire. Papa and mamma, Julian and I, all took large baskets and went into the woods, and there we would stay sometimes all day, picking walnuts and chestnuts. Perhaps where we were there were mostly walnuts ; but still there were a good many chestnuts. We had a very large oven in which we put as many of our nuts as we could, and the rest we put into large bags. We, and the rats and mice, had nice feasts on them every winter.

"Papa bought Julian a pop-gun to console him when we were going away to visit the Brights, for he had not been invited. He was very good about it indeed, and fired off his pop-gun in honor of mamma's going away.

"Papa gave Julian a new boat a little while ago, a yacht, and mamma has painted it beautifully in oils. I am going to make the sails for it.

"Please call me Primrose in your letters. Rose is called Periwinkle. Papa bought her an image of Uncle Tom and Eva, sitting on a bank, and Uncle Tom is reading the Bible. Eva has on a plaid apron, and has yellow cheeks, and is not very pretty. Uncle Tom is not either. Baby was very much pleased."

To return to my mother's records : —

RHYL, NORTH WALES.

Dr. Drysdale thought we needed another change of air, and so we came south this time. . . . The sun sinks just beside Great Orme's Head, after turning the sea into living gold, and the heights into heaps of amethyst. On the right is only sea, sea, sea. . . . I intended to go to the Queen's Hotel, and knew nothing about the manner of living in the lodging fashion. So we have to submit to German silver and the most ordinary table service. . . . Ever since our marriage we have always eaten off the finest French china, and had all things pretty and tasteful; because, you know, I would never have *second-best* services, considering my husband to be my most illustrious guest. But now! It is really laughable to think of the appointments of the table at which the Ambassador to Lisbon and the American Consul sat down last Saturday, when they honored me with their presence. And we did laugh, for it was of no consequence, — and the great bow window of our parlor looked out upon the sea. We did not come here to see French china and pure silver forks and spoons, but to walk on the beach, bathe in the ocean, and drive to magnificent old castles, — and get rid of whooping-cough. I had the enterprise to take all the children and Mary, and come without Mr. Hawthorne; for he was in a great hurry to get me off, fearing the good weather would not last. He followed on Saturday with Mr. O'Sullivan, who arrived from Lisbon just an hour before they both started for Rhyl. . . . Julian's worship of nature and natural objects meets with satisfaction here. . . .

The following was also written from Rhyl : —

"While the carriage stopped I heard the rapturous warble of the skylark, and finally discovered him, mounting higher still and higher, pressing upwards, and pouring out such rich, delicious music that I wanted to close my eyes and shut out the world, and listen to nothing but that. Not even Shelley's or Wordsworth's words can convey an adequate idea of this song. It seems as if its little throat were the outlet of all the joy that had been experienced on the earth since creation ; and that with all its power it were besieging heaven with gratitude and love for the infinite bliss of life. *Life, joy, love.* The blessed, darling little bird, quivering, warbling, urging its way farther and farther ; and finally swooning with excess of delight, and sinking back to earth ! You see I am vainly trying to help you to an idea of it, but I cannot do it. I do not understand why the skylark should not rise from our meadows as well, and the nightingale sing to our roses."

Society and the sternness of life were, however, but a hair's-breadth away : —

"Monday evening Mr. Hawthorne went to Richmond Hill to meet Mr. Buchanan. The service was entirely silver, plates and all, and in a high state of sheen. The Queen's autograph letter was spoken of (which you will see in the 'Northern Times' that goes with this) ; and as it happens to be very clumsily expressed, Mr. Hawthorne was much perplexed by Mr. Buchanan's asking him, before the whole company at dinner, 'what he thought of the Queen's letter.' Mr. Hawthorne replied that it showed very kind feeling. 'No,' persisted the wicked Ambassador ; 'but what do you think of the *style ?*' Mr. Hawthorne was equal to him, or rather, conquered him, however, for he said, 'The Queen has a perfect right to do what she pleases with her *own English.*' Mr. Hawthorne thought Miss Lane, Mr. Buchanan's niece, a very elegant person, and far superior to any Eng-

lish lady present. The next evening Mr. Hawthorne went to another dinner at Everton ; so that
on Wednesday, when we again sat down together,
I felt as if he had been gone a month. This second
dinner was not remarkable in any way, except that
when the ladies took leave they *all* went to him
and requested to shake hands with him !

" No act of the British people in behalf of the
soldiers has struck me as so noble and touching
as that of the reformed criminals at an institution
in London. They wished to contribute something
to the Patriotic Fund. The only way they could
do it was by *fasting.* So from Sunday night till
Tuesday morning they ate nothing, and the money
saved (three pounds and over) was sent to the
Fund ! Precious money is this."

In Rockferry, my first remembered home, the
personality of my father was the most cheerful
element, and the one which we all needed, as the
sunshine is needed by an English scene to make
its happiness apparent. If he was at all " morbid,"
my advice would be to adopt morbidness at once.
Perhaps he would have been a sad man if he had
been an ordinary one. Genius can make charming
presences of characters that really are gloomy and
savage, being so magical in its transmutation of
dry fact. People were glad to be scolded by Carlyle, and shot down by Dr. Johnson. But I am
persuaded by reason that those who called Hawthorne sad would have complained of the tears of
Coriolanus or Othello ; and, with Coriolanus, he
could say, " It is no little thing to make mine

eyes to sweat compassion." It was the presence
of the sorrow of the world which made him silent.
Who dares to sneer at that? When I think of my
mother, — naturally hopeful, gently merry, ever
smiling, — who, while my father lived, was so glad
a woman that her sparkling glance was never
dimmed, and when I have to acknowledge that
even she did not fill us children with the zest of
content which he brought into the room for us,
I must conclude that genius and cheer together
made him life-giving ; and so he was enchanting
to those who were intimate with him, and to many
who saw him for but a moment. Dora Golden,
my brother's old nurse, has said that when she
first came to the family she feared my father was
going to be severe, because he had a way of looking at strangers from under bent brows. But the
moment he lifted his head his eyes flashed forth
beautiful and kindly. She has told me that my
mother and she used to think at dusk, when he
entered the room before the lamps were lit, that
the place was illuminated by his face; his eyes
shone, his whole countenance gleamed, and my
mother simply called him "our sunlight."

My sister's girlish letters are evidence of the
enthusiasm of the family for my father's companionship, and of our stanch hatred for the Consulate because it took him away from us so much.
He read aloud, as he always had done, in the easiest, clearest, most genial way, as if he had been
born only to let his voice enunciate an endless
procession of words. He read " The Lady of the

Lake" aloud about this time, and Una wrote expressing our delight in his personality over and above that in his usefulness : " Papa has gone to dine in Liverpool, so we shall not hear ' Don Quixote ' this evening, or have papa either." Little references to him show how he was always weaving golden threads into the woof of daily monotony. Julian, seven years old, writes to his grandfather, "Papa has taught Una and me to make paper boats, and the bureau in my room is covered with paper steamers and boats." I can see him folding them now, as if it were yesterday, and how intricate the newspapers became which he made into hulls, decks, and sails. At one time Una bursts out, in recognition of the unbroken peace and good will in the home, " It will certainly be my own fault if I am not pretty good when I grow up, for I have had both example and precept."

The nurse to whom I have just referred has said that when Julian was about four, sometimes he would annoy her while she was sewing; and if his father was in the room, she would tell Julian to go to him and ask him to read about Robbie, who was Robinson Crusoe. He would sit quietly all the time his father read to him, no matter for how long. But her master finally told Dora not to send Julian to him in this way to hear " Robinson Crusoe," because he was " tired of reading it to him." The nurse was a bit of a genius herself, in her way, and not to be easily suppressed, and when her charge became fidgety, and she was in a hurry, she made one more experiment with Robbie. Her master turned round in his chair, and for the first time in four years she saw an angry look on his face, and he commanded her "never to do it again." At three years of age Julian played pranks upon his father without trepidation. There was a " boudoir " in the house which had a large, pleasant window, and was therefore thought to be agreeable enough to be used as a prison-house for Una and Julian when they were naughty. Julian conveyed his father into the boudoir, and shut the door on him adroitly. It had no handle on the inner side, purposely, and the astonished parent was caged. "You cannot come out," said Julian, "until you have promised to be a good boy." Through the persistent dignity with which Hawthorne behaved, and with which he was always treated by the household, Julian had felt the down of playful love.

Here are letters written to me while I was in Portugal with my mother, in 1856 : —

MY DEAR LITTLE ROSEBUD, — I have put a kiss for you in this nice, clean piece of paper. I shall fold it up carefully, and I hope it will not drop out before it gets to Lisbon. If you cannot find it, you must ask Mamma to look for it. Perhaps you will find it on her lips. Give my best regards to your Uncle John and Aunt Sue, and to all your kind friends, not forgetting your Nurse.

Your affectionate father,

N. H.

My dear little Rosebud, — It is a great while since I wrote to you; and I am afraid this letter will be a great while in reaching you. I hope you are a very good little girl; and I am sure you never get into a passion, and never scream, and never scratch and strike your dear Nurse or your dear sister Una. Oh no! my little Rosebud would never do such naughty things as those. It would grieve me very much if I were to hear of her doing such things. When you come back to England, I shall ask Mamma whether you have been a good little girl; and Mamma (I hope) will say : ' Yes; our little Rosebud has been the best and sweetest little girl I ever knew in my life. She has never screamed nor uttered any but the softest and sweetest sounds. She has never struck Nurse nor Una nor dear Mamma with her little fist, nor scratched them with her sharp little nails; and if ever there was a little angel on earth, it is our dear little Rosebud!" And when Papa hears this, he will be very glad, and will take Rosebud up in his arms and kiss her over and over again. But if he were to hear that she had been naughty, Papa would feel it his duty to eat little Rosebud up! Would not that be very terrible?

Julian is quite well, and sends you his love. I have put a kiss for you in this letter; and if you do not find it, you may be sure that some naughty person has got it. Tell Nurse I want to see her very much. Kiss Una for me.

Your loving   PAPA.

The next letter is of later date, having been written while the rest of the family were in Manchester : —

MY DEAR LITTLE PESSIMA, — I am very glad that Mamma is going to take you to see "Tom Thump;" and I think it is much better to call him Thump than Thumb, and I always mean to call him so from this time forward. It is a very nice name, is Tom Thump. I hope you will call him Tom Thump to his face when you see him, and thump him well if he finds fault with it. Do you still thump dear Mamma, and Fanny, and Una, and Julian, as you did when I saw you last? If you do, I shall call you little Rose Thump; and then people will think that you are Tom Thump's wife. And now I shall stop thumping on this subject.

Your friend little Frank Hallet is at Mrs. Blodget's. Do you remember how you used to play with him at Southport, and how he sometimes beat you? He seems to be a better little boy than he was then, but still he is not so good as he might be. This morning he had some very nice breakfast in his plate, but he would not eat it because his mamma refused to give him something that was not good for him; and so, all breakfast-time, this foolish little boy refused to eat a mouthful, though I could see that he was very hungry, and would have eaten it all up if he could have got it into his mouth without any-

body seeing. Was not he a silly child? Little
Pessima never behaved so, — oh no!

There are two or three very nice little girls at
Mrs. Blodget's, and also a nice large dog, who is
very kind and gentle, and never bites anybody;
and also a tabby cat, who very often comes to me
and mews for something to eat. So you see we
have a very pleasant family; but, for all that, I
would rather be at home.

And now I have written you such a long letter
that my head is quite tired out; and so I shall
leave off, and amuse myself with looking at some
pages of figures.

Be a good little girl, and do not tease Mamma,
nor trouble Fanny, nor quarrel with Una and
Julian; and when I come home I shall call you
little Pessima (because I am very sure you will
deserve that name), and shall kiss you more than
once.   N. H.

If he said a few kind words to me, my father
gave me a sense of having a strong ally among
the great ones of life; and if I were ill, I was
roused by his standing beside me to defy the illness. When I was seriously indisposed, at the
age of three, he brought me a black doll, which I
heard my mother say she thought would alarm
me, as it was very ugly, and I had never seen a
negro. I remember the much-knowing smile with
which my father's face was indefinitely lighted up
as he stood looking at me, while I, half unconscious to most of the things of this world, was

nevertheless clutching his gift gladly to my heart. The hideous darky was soon converted by my nurse Fanny (my mother called her Fancy, because of her rare skill with the needle and her rich decorations of all sorts of things) into a beautifully dressed footman, who was a very large item in my existence for years. I thought my father an intensely clever man to have hit upon Pompey, and to have understood so well that he would make an angel. All his presents to us Old People, as he called us, were either unusual or of exquisite workmanship. The fairy quality was indispensable before he chose them. We children have clung to them even to our real old age. The fairies were always just round the corner of the point of sight, with me, and in recognition of my keen delight of confidence in the small fry my father gave me little objects that were adapted to them : delicate bureaus with tiny mirrors that had reflected fairy faces a moment before, and little tops that opened by unscrewing them in an unthought-of way and held minute silver spoons. Once he brought home to Julian a china donkey's head in a tall gray hat such as negroes and politicians elect to wear, and its brains were composed entirely of borrowed brilliancy in the shape of matches. We love the donkey still, and it always occupies a place of honor. He brought me a little Bacchus in Parian marble, wearing a wreath of grapes, and holding a mug on his knee, and greeting his jolly stomach with one outspread hand, as if he were inwardly smiling as he is outwardly. This is a vase for flowers, and the white smile of the god has gleamed through countless of my sweetest bouquets.

My father's enjoyment of frolicking fun was as hilarious as that accorded by some of us to wildest comic opera. He had a delicate way of throwing himself into the scrimmage of laughter, and I do not for an instant attempt to explain how he managed it. I can say that he lowered his eyelids when he laughed hardest, and drew in his breath half a dozen times with dulcet sounds and a murmur of mirth between. Before and after this performance he would look at you straight from under his black brows, and his eyes seemed dazzling. I think the hilarity was revealed in them, although his cheeks rounded in ecstasy. I was a little roguish child, but he was the youngest and merriest person in the room when he was amused. Yet he was never far removed from his companion, — a sort of Virgil, — his knowledge of sin and tragedy at our very hearthstones. It was with such a memory in the centre of home joys that the Pilgrim Fathers turned towards the door, ever and anon, to guard it from creeping Indian forms.

On Sundays, at sundown, when the winter rain had very likely dulled everybody's sense of more moderate humor, the blue law of quietness was lifted from the atmosphere ; and between five and six o'clock we spread butterfly wings again, and had blind man's buff. We ran around the large centre-table, and made this gambol most tempest-

uously merry. If anything had been left upon
the table before we began, it was removed with
rapidity before we finished. There was a distinct
understanding that our blindfolded father must
not be permitted to touch any of us, or else we
should be reduced forthwith to our original dust.
The pulsing grasp of his great hands and heavy
fingers, soft and springing in their manipulation
of one's shoulders as the touch of a wild thing,
was amusingly harmless, considering the howls
with which his onslaught was evaded as long as
our flying legs were loyal to us. My father's
gentle laughter and happy-looking lips were a revelation during these bouts. I remember with
what awe I once tied the blinding handkerchief
round his head, feeling the fine crispness of his
silky hair, full of electricity, as some people's is
only on frosty days; yet without any of that
crinkly resistance of most hair that is full of energy. But there were times when I used to stand
at a distance and gaze at his peaceful aspect, and
wonder if he would ever open the floodgates of
fun in a game of romp on any rainy Sunday of
the future. If a traveler caught the Sphinx hum-
ming to herself, would he not be inclined to sit
down and watch her till she did it again ?

I have referred to his large hand. I shall never
see a more reassuring one than his. It was broad,
generous, supple. It had the little depressions
and the smoothness to be noticed in the hands of
truest charity; yet it had the ample outlines of
the vigorously imaginative temperament, so dif-

ferent from the hard plumpness of coarseness or brutality. At the point where the fingers joined the back of the hand were the roundings-in that are reminiscent of childhood's simplicity, and are to be found in many philanthropic persons. His way of using his fingers was slow, well thought out, and gentle, though never lagging, that most unpleasant fault indicative of self-absorbed natures. When he did anything with his hands he seemed very active, because thoroughly in earnest. He delighted me by the way in which he took hold of any material thing, for it proved his self-mastery. Strength of will joined to self-restraint is a combination always enjoyable to the onlooker ; but it is also evidence of discomfort and effort enough in the heroic character that has won the state which we contemplate with so much approval. I remember his standing once by the fire, leaning upon the mantelpiece, when a vase on the shelf toppled over in some way. It was a cheap, lodging-house article, and yet my father tried to save it from falling to the floor as earnestly as he did anything which he set out to do. His hand almost seized the vase, but it rebounded ; and three times he half caught it. The fourth time he rescued it as it was near the floor, having become flushed and sparkling with the effort of will and deftness. For years that moment came back to me, because his determination had been so valiantly intense, and I was led to carry out determinations of all sorts from witnessing his self-respect and his success in so small a matter. People of power *care* all the time. It is their life-blood to succeed; they must encourage their precision of eye and thought by repeated triumphs, which so soothe and rejoice the nerves.

He was very kind in amusing me by aid of my slate. That sort of pastime suited my hours of silence, which became less and less broken by the talkative vein. His forefinger rubbed away defects in the aspect of faces or animals with a lion-like suppleness of sweep that seemed to me to wipe out the world. We also had a delicious game of a labyrinth of lines, which it was necessary to traverse with the pencil without touching the hedges, as I called the winding marks. We wandered in and around without a murmur, and I reveled in delight because he was near.

Walking was always a great resource in the family, and it was a half-hearted matter for us unless we were at his side. His gait was one of long, easy steps which were leisurely and not rapid, and he cast an occasional look around, stopping if anything more lovely than usual was to be seen in sky or landscape. It is the people who love their race even better than themselves who can take into their thought an outdoor scene. In England the outdoor life had many enchantments of velvet sward upon broad hills and flowers innumerable and fragrant. A little letter of Una's not long after we arrived in Rockferry alludes to this element in our happiness : —

" We went to take a walk to-day, and I do not think I ever had such a beautiful walk before in all my life. Julian and I got some very pretty flowers, such as do not grow wild in America. I found some exquisite harebells by the roadside, and some very delicate little pink flowers. And I got some wild holly, which is very pretty indeed ; it has very glossy and prickery leaves. I have seen a great many hedges made of it since I have been here ; for nothing can get over it or get through it, for it is almost as prickery as the Hawthorne [the bush and the family name were always the same thing to us children], of which almost all the hedges in Liverpool, and everywhere I have been, are made ; and there it grows up into high trees, so that nothing in the world can look through it, or climb over it, or crawl through it ; and I am afraid our poor hedge in Concord will never look so well, because the earth round it is so sandy and dry, and here it is so very moist and rich. It ought to be moist, at any rate, for it rains enough." But later she writes on "the eighteenth day of perfect weather," and where can the weather seem so perfect as in England?

After breakfast on Christmas we always went to the places, in that parlor where Christmas found us (nomads that we were), where our mother had set out our gifts. Sometimes they were on the large centre-table, sometimes on little separate tables, but invariably covered with draperies; so that we studied the structure of each mound in fascinated delay, in order to guess what the humps and hubbles might indicate as to the nature of the objects of our treasure-trove. The happy-faced mother, who could be radiant and calm at once, — small, but with a sphere that was not small, and blessed us grandly, — received gifts that had been arranged by Una and the nurse after all the other El Dorados. were thoroughly veiled, and our hearts stood still to hear her musical cry of delight, when, having directed the rest of us to our presents, she at last uncovered her own. Our treasures always exceeded in number and charm our wildest hopes, although simplicity was the rule. Whatever my mother interested herself about, she accomplished with a finish and spirit that distinguished her performance as a title on a reputation distinguishes common clay. She threw over it the faithful ardor which is akin to miracle : the simplest twig in her hand budded ; her dewdrops were filled with all the colors of the rainbow, because with her the sun always shone. She writes a description of our happy first Christmas in England, in which are these passages : "We had no St. Nicholas or Christmas-tree ; and so, after all had gone to bed, I arranged the presents upon the centre-table in the drawing-room. . . . From a vase in the middle a banner floated with an inscription upon it : 'A Merry Christmas to all !' Una had given Rose a little watch for her footman Pompey ; Mrs. O'Sullivan had sent her a porcelain rosary, which was put in a little box ; and Mr. Bright had sent her an illuminated edition of 'This is the House that Jack Built.' Julian found a splendid flag from Nurse. This flag was a wonder. . . .

The stripes were made of a rich red and white striped satin, which must have been manufactured for the express purpose of composing the American flag. The stars were embroidered in silver on a dark blue satin sky. On the reverse, a rich white satin lining bore Julian's cipher, surrounded with silver embroidery. . . . The children amused themselves with their presents all day. But first I took my new Milton and read aloud to them the Hymn of the Nativity, which I do every Christmas." "How easy it is," my mother writes of a Christmas-tree for poor children, "with a small thing to cause a great joy, if there is only the will to do it!" But most deeply did we delight in the presents given to our beloved parents, whom we considered to be absolutely perfect beings; and there was nothing which we ever perceived to make the supposition unreasonable. In one of Una's girlish letters she declares: "I will tell you what has given me almost — nay, quite as great pleasure as any I have had in England; that is, that Mamma has bought a gold watch-chain. She bought it yesterday at Douglas." We had such thorough lessons in generosity that they sometimes took effect in a genuine self-effacement, like this. A letter from my mother joyfully records of my brother: —

"Julian was asking Papa for a very expensive toy, and his father told him he was very poor this year, because the Consulate had not much business, and that it was impossible to buy him everything that struck his fancy. Julian said no more;

and when he went to bed he expressed great condolence, and said he would not ask his father for
anything if he were so poor, but that he would
give him all his own money (amounting to fivepence halfpenny). When he lay down, his face
shone with a splendor of joy that he was able
thus to make his father's affairs assume a brighter
aspect. This enormous sum of money which Julian had he intended, at Christmas-time, to devote
to buying a toy for baby or for Una. He intended
to give his all, and he could no more. In the
morning, he took an opportunity when I was not
looking to go behind his father, and silently handed
him the fivepence halfpenny over his shoulder.
My attention was first attracted by hearing Mr.
Hawthorne say, ' No, I thank you, my boy ; when
I am starving, I will apply to you ! ' I turned
round, and Julian's face was deep red, and his lips
were quivering as he took back the money. I
was sorry his father did not keep it, however. I
have never allowed the children to *hoard* money.
I think the flower of sentiment is bruised and
crushed by a strong-box ; and they never yet have
had any idea of money except to use it for another's benefit or pleasure. Julian saw an adver-
tisement in the street of the loss of a watch, and
some guineas reward. ' Oh,' said he, ' how gladly
would I find that watch, and present it to the
gentleman, and say, No reward, thank you, sir ! ' "

My sister, who was made quite delicate, at first,
by the English climate, and acquired from this
temporary check and the position of eldest child

a pathetic nobility which struck the keynote of her character, writes from Rockferry : " This morning of the New Year was very pleasant. It was almost as good as any day in winter in America. I went out with Mamma and Sweet Fern [Julian]. The snow is about half a foot deep. Julian is out, now, playing. I packed him up very warmly indeed. I wish I could go out in the new snow very much. Julian is making a hollow house of snow by the rhododendron-tree." What not to do we learned occasionally from the birds. "The little robins and a thrush and some little sparrows have been here this morning ; and the thrush was so large that she ate up the crumbs very fast, and the other poor little birds did not dare to come near her till she had done eating." My father used to treat the Old and the New Year with the deepest respect. I never knew the moments to be so immense as when, with pitying gentleness, we silently attended the Old Year across the ghostly threshold of midnight, and my father at last rose reverently from his chair to open the window, through which, at that breath, the first peals would float with new promise and remembering toll.

We children were expected to come into the presence of the grown people and enjoy the interesting guests whom we all loved. My father was skillful in choosing friends : they were rare, good men, and he and they really met ; their loves and interests and his were stirred by the intercourse, as if unused muscles had been stretched. I

could perceive that my father and his best cronies
glowed with refreshment. Mr. Bennoch was a
great favorite with us. He was short and fat,
witty and jovial. He was so different in style and
finish from the tall, pale, spiritual Henry Bright
(whom my mother speaks of as "shining like a
star" during an inspiring sermon) that I almost
went to sleep in the unending effort to understand
why God made so sharp a variety in types. Mr.
Bennoch wrote more poetry than Mr. Bright did,
even, and he took delight in breathing the same
air with writers. But he himself had no capacity
more perfected than that of chuckling like a whole
brood of chickens at his own jokes as well as those
of others. The point of his joke might be ob-
scure to us, but the chuckle never failed to satisfy.
He was a source of entire rest to the dark-browed,
deep-eyed thinker who smiled before him. The
only anecdote of Mr. Bennoch which I remember
is of a Scotchman who, at an inn, was wandering
disconsolately about the parlor while his dinner
was being prepared. A distinguished traveler —
Dickens, I think — was dashing off a letter at the
centre-table, describing the weather and some of
the odd fellows he had observed in his travels.
"And," he wrote, "there is in the room at the
present moment a long, lank, red-headed, empty-
brained nincompoop, who looks as if he had not
eaten a square meal for a month, and is stamping
about for his dinner. Now he approaches me as I
sit writing, and I hear his step pause behind my
chair. The fool is actually looking over my shoul-

der, and reading these words " — A torrent of Scotch burst forth right here : "It 's a *lee,* sir, — it 's a *lee !* I never read a *worrd* that yer *wrort !* " Screams from us ; while Mr. Bennoch's sudden aspect of dramatic rage was as suddenly dropped, and he blazed once more with broad smiles, chuckling. I will insert here a letter written by this dear friend in 1861 : —

80 WOOD STREET, LONDON.

MY DEAR HAWTHORNE, — A few lines just received from Mr. Fields remind me of my too long silence. Rest assured that you and yours are never long out of our thoughts, and we only wish you were here in our peaceful country, far removed from the terrible anxieties caused by wicked and willful men on one side, and on the other permitted by the incompetents set over you. How little you thought, when you suggested to me the propriety of old soldiers only going into battle, that you should have been absolutely pre-dicting the unhappy course of events ! Do you remember adding that "a premium should be offered for men of fourscore, as, with one foot in the grave, they would be less likely to run away " ? I observe that the "Herald" advises that "the guillotine should be used in cropping the heads of a lot of the officers, beginning at the city of Washington, and so make room for the young genius with which the whole republic palpitates." . . . Truly, my dear Hawthorne, it is a melan-choly condition of things. Let us turn to a far more agreeable subject ! It is pleasant to learn that, amid all the other troubles, your domestic anxieties have passed away so far as the health of your family is concerned. The sturdy youth will be almost a man, and Una quite a woman, while Rosebud will be opening day by day in knowledge and deep interest. I hear that your pen is busy, and that from your tower you are looking upon old England and estimating her influences and the character of her people. Recent experiences must modify your judgment in many ways. A romance laid in England, painted as you only can paint, must be a great success. I struggle on, and only wish I were worthy the respect my friends so foolishly exhibit.

With affectionate regards to all, ever yours truly, F. Bennoch.

On November 17, 1854, my mother writes : —
"Last evening a great package came from Mr. Milnes [Lord Houghton], and it proved to be all his own works, and a splendid edition of Keats with a memoir by Mr. Milnes. This elegant gift was only a return of favors, as Mr. Hawthorne had just sent him some American books. He expended three notes upon my husband's going to meet him at Crewe Hall, two of entreaty and one of regret; but he declares he will have him at Yorkshire. Mrs. Milnes is Lord Crewe's sister. The last note says : 'The books arrived safely, and alas! alone. When I get to Yorkshire, to my own home, I shall try again for you, as I may

find you in a more ductile mood. For, seriously, it would be a great injustice — not to yourself, but to us — if you went home without seeing something of our domestic country life : it is really the most special thing about our social system, and something which no other country has or ever will have.' "

Another note from Lord Houghton is extant, saying : —

DEAR MR. HAWTHORNE, — Why did not you come to see us when you were in London ? You promised to do so, but we sought you in vain. I wanted to see you, mainly for your own sake, and also to ask you about an American book which has fallen into my hands. It is called " Leaves of Grass," and the author calls himself Walt Whitman. Do you know anything about him ? I will not call it *poetry*, because I am unwilling to apply that word to a work totally destitute of art ; but, whatever we call it, it is a most notable and true book. It is not written *virginibus puerisque ;* but as I am neither the one nor the other, I may express my admiration of its vigorous virility and bold natural truth. There are things in it that read like the old Greek plays. It is of the same family as those delightful books of Thoreau's which you introduced me to, and which are so little known and valued here. Patmore has just published a continuation of " The Angel in the House," which I recommend to your attention. I am quite annoyed at having been so long within the same four seas with you, and having seen you so little. Mrs. Milnes begs her best remembrances. I am yours very truly,

RICHD. MONCKTON MILNES.
16 UPPER BROOK STREET, June 30.

It is a perpetual marvel with some people why some others do not wish to be looked at and questioned. Dinner invitations were constantly coming in, and were very apt to be couched in tones of anxious surprise at the difficulty of securing my father. An illustration may be found in this little note from Mr. Procter (father of Adelaide Procter) : —

32 WEYMOUTH STREET, Tuesday morning.

DEAR MR. HAWTHORNE, — It seems almost like an idle ceremony to ask you and Mrs. Hawthorne to dine here on Friday; but I cannot help it. I have only *just* returned from a circuit in the country, and heard this morning that you were likely to leave London in a few days.

Yours always sincerely,
B. W. PROCTER.

It was desirable to meet such people as Mr. Procter, and I have heard enthusiastic descriptions, with which later my mother amused our quiet days in Concord, of the intellectual pleasures that such friendships brought, and of the sounding titles and their magnificent accessories, with human beings involved, against whom my parents were now sometimes thrust by the rapid tide of celebrity. But my father was never to be found in the track of admiring social gatherings except by the deepest scheming. In her first English letters my mother had written: " It is said that there is nothing in Liverpool but *dinners*. Alas for it!" The buzz of greeting was constant. It must have been delightful in certain respects. She sent home one odd letter as a specimen of hundreds of similar ones which came to my father from admirers. Yet very soon individuals make a crowd, and the person who attracts their attention is more nearly suffocated than the rest quite realize. His attempts at self-preservation are not more than half understood, and, if successful, are remembered with a dash of bitterness by the onlookers.

To her husband in Liverpool, Mrs. Hawthorne writes : —

LONDON, September 19.

MY DEAREST, — At half past three Mrs. Russell Sturgis came in her sumptuous barouche. We drove all through the fashionable squares and streets and parks, and all through Kensington, even to the real Holland House. But Leigh Hunt's book went all out of my head when I tried to think what he said about it. Mrs. Sturgis knows him very well, and often visits him in his humble cottage. Oh, dear me! Such superb squares and terraces as I saw! Mrs. Sturgis told me where Sir E. B. Lytton, and many noted and noble persons, lived. We drove through Mayfair, but I did not see Miss Cushman's house, 1 Bolton Row. We certainly had a fine time. At five we got back, and I found the Ambassador's card, and Miss Lane's, inviting us there this evening.

September 20. I was just hurrying off with Mr. Bright when I wrote the two lines of postscript in my letter this morning, in answer to your note, — so like you ; so tender and kind. Since I must go away, I ought not to have said a word ; but you must ascribe what I said and say to infinite love only ; for it is only because of this that I do not look forward with delight to a winter in Lisbon with the O'Sullivans. I could not be happy if you made any sacrifice for me ; and as our interests are indissoluble, it would be my sacrifice, too. So I will be good, and not distress you with more regrets. I once thought that no power on earth should ever induce me to live without you, and especially thought that an ocean should never roll between us. But I am overpowered by necessity ; and since my life is of importance to you, I will not dare to neglect any means of preserving it.

This morning baby was dressed in a beautiful embroidered white frock and blue sash, blue kid shoes, laced with blue ribbon, and blue silk sack fastened with a blue girdle, and a hat trimmed with blue and gray. Her long curls streamed out beneath. She was thus arrayed to visit Portland Place and the Sturgis children. Una looked very lovely in her summer cloud-muslin.

Mr. Bright came at twelve o'clock, bringing five or six superb photographs of Cologne; I never saw any so splendid. Then we started for the Crystal Palace. It has been one of the divinest days — one of our days, like that at Stratford-on-Avon. When we got into the cab, however, Mr. Bright proposed to go to the Houses of Parliament first, and then at last concluded to give up the Crystal Palace, and see the sights of London instead. So we drove to the old St. James's Palace Yard. But a police-officer said we could only go in on Saturday, and then by a ticket from the Lord Chamberlain. I knew *that*, but supposed Mr. Bright had some other means of gaining admittance. He had not, nevertheless. He took us (Julian was with me) over Westminster Bridge. . . . We went into the Photographic Exhibition of persons and places at the Crimea, which was just like taking up groups of the army and putting them before one's eyes. It must be of wonderful interest to the relatives and friends of those who are there. The room was full of fine-looking, aristocratic people. From this we drove to Kensington Gardens; and I must say, my dear lord, that I never imagined any place so grand and majestic, so royal and superb, as those grounds. The trees — oh, the trees — every one of them kings, emperors, and Czars; so tall, so rich, and the lawn beneath them so sunny-velvet green, all made illustrious by the clearest warm sunshine, and a soft, sweet air. The magnificent groves of trees all round; and far off in the terminus, the towers and pinnacles of the Parliament Houses, and Westminster Abbey towers, rise into the clear sky over the blue waters of the Serpentine. A pretty yacht, with one white wing, slowly moved along. Large, princely lambs grazed on the sunny lawns. I think that thou wouldst have asked no more in the way of a park. We sat down on a felled tree and talked awhile. I would almost give a kingdom to sit on the tree again, with thee. Was not Mr. Bright good and lovely to devote his only whole day in London to me? He certainly is the most amiable and hospitable of mortals.   THY DOVE.

My mother writes of Miss Bacon, who put Lord Bacon in that place in her heart where Shakespeare should have been : —

MY DEAREST, — I have been reading Miss Bacon's manuscript this afternoon, and it is marvelous. She reveals by her interpretation of Lord Bacon more fully to me what I already divined dimly of the power of Christ over nature; and it is the first word that I have found spoken or written which is commensurate with my actual idea. I felt as if I wanted to take this manuscript and all the others, and run off to some profound retreat, and study it all over, and reproduce it again with my own faculties. Oh, that I could read them with you! I almost begin to love the pain with which I delve after the thoughts presented in such a close and difficult handwriting.

To Miss Peabody : —
"Miss Bacon cannot speak out fairly [upon the subject of Bacon and Shakespeare], though there is neither the Tower, the scaffold, nor the pile of fagots to deter her. But she is a wonder and a benefactor, — and let us not criticise her style ; or rather, it is no matter whether we did or not, so much remains for her. I did not see her. I was just going to take Una and call upon her, when she went to Stratford.

"I hope Mr. Plumly has not forgotten his project of beneficence [towards her]. It must be a foretaste of heaven to have money to give away."

317

CHAPTER XI

TOURIST letters describe Wordsworth's house and country at Rydal : —

MY DEAR ELIZABETH, — I had a hope that when I left Rock Park I should be clothed with wings, and be able to write letters and journal and to draw. But I have been particularly wingless during the whole six weeks of our absence, and have done literally nothing but use my eyes. At Windermere we left Una, Rose, and Nurse at a charming, homelike house, and Mr. Hawthorne, Julian, and I went farther north. We went first to Rydal and Grasmere, and at Grasmere Hotel, which is nearly opposite the grave of Wordsworth, I had set my heart upon writing you a long letter about those sacred places, especially sacred to you, the true lover of Wordsworth. On a most superb afternoon we took an open carriage at Lowood Hotel, where we had been staying for several days, and drove to Grasmere Hotel, where we left our luggage and then drove back to Rydal Water. We alighted just at the commencement of the lake, intending to loiter and enjoy it at leisure. The lake surprised me by its extreme smallness, — in America we should never think of calling it a lake ;

but it receives dignity from the lofty hills and mountains that embosom it, and I thought it was irreverent in Mr. Hawthorne to say he " could carry it all away in a porringer." It has several very small islands in it, and one rather larger, which is a heronry. The lake and all the parks and grounds around belong to Sir Richard le Fleming, who is Lord of the Manor and of a very ancient family in those regions. We presently came to a fine old crag by the shore, up which were some friendly steps ; and we were entirely sure that Wordsworth had often gone up there and looked off upon his beloved Rydal from the summit. We went up and sat down where we knew he must have sat, and there I could have dreamed for many hours. The gleam, the shadow, and the peace supreme were there, and I thought with an infinite joy how human beings have the power to consecrate the earth by genius, heroic deeds, and even homely virtues. The gorgeous richness of the vegetation, the fresh verdure, the living green of the lawns and woodlands, flooded and gilded by the sunshine, made me wonder whether the Delectable Mountain could be much more beautiful, and made me realize deeply the poetic rapture, the noble, sustained enthusiasm of Wordsworth in his descriptions of natural scenery. It is only for perhaps a week in June that we in America can obtain an idea of the magnificent richness and freshness of English scenery. How can I find language airy and delicate enough to picture to you the *fields* of harebells, tossing their lovely heads on their threadlike stems, and bringing heaven to earth in the hue of their petals! Then the pale golden cuckoo-buds, the yellow gorse, the stately foxglove, standing in rows, like prismatic candelabra, all along the roadside, — and ah me, alas! — the endless trees and vines of wild eglantine, with blossoms of every shade of pink, from carmine to the faintest blush, wreathing themselves about and throwing out into your face and hands long streamers of buds and blossoms, so rarely and exquisitely lovely! One wonders whether it can be true or whether one is dreaming on the Enchanted Plain. I loved Wordsworth as I never could have done if I had not been in the very place that knew him, and seen how and why he worshiped as he did, what really seems there the perpetual Morning of Creation.

At the right of the doorstep a superb fuchsia-tree stood, and I asked the man to pluck me one of the jewel blossoms. But he declined to approach so near, as he feared to disturb Mrs. Wordsworth. And he did not introduce us into her presence, because he said Lady le Fleming had told him never to disturb her with visitors, but only show them the outside of the house. He said Lady le Fleming built the house and it was hers, as well as everything else round about. But we might have gone in, we now find, and Mrs. Wordsworth likes very much to see people. So this intelligent man led us through the pretty gardens and grounds, up and up and up innumerable steps in successive short flights, through many

wickets, till I began to think we could never reach
our goal. Finally we came to a spot of constant
shade where was a singularly shaped rock — a kind
of slab — thrusting itself out from the wall, in
which a brass plate was inserted with an inscription by Wordsworth, which we read. It expressed
that he had pleaded for this rock as often as he
had for other natural objects.

The gardener opened a wicket, after passing
the deep, shady nook, and said, "This is Mr.
Wordsworth's garden." I looked about and saw
troops of flowers, and sought for the white foxglove, which was a favorite of his, and found it ;
and the air was loaded with a fine perfume, which
I discovered to be from large beds of mignonette.
In those paths he walked and watched and tended
his plants and shrubs. Presently, after so much
mounting of steps, and threading of embowered
paths and lanes of flowers, we were ushered into
the grounds immediately around the actual house.
And the man first took us upon that memorable
terraced lawn, in great part made by Wordsworth's own hands. It is circular, and the turf,
like thick-piled velvet, yielding to the feet and of
delicious green — smooth and soft. Perhaps it is
thirty feet in diameter, and double, with a very
high step. Beneath it is a gravel walk, and then
a hedge of thick shrubs. Julian flung himself at
full length on the velvet sward, and Mr. Hawthorne and I sat down on the even tops of two
stumps of trees, evidently intended for seats, as
one meets them everywhere, arranged for that

purpose. But how am I to tell you what I saw from them?

Wordsworth must have described it some-where. It was his beloved view. Richer could not have been the Vale of Cashmere. The moun-tains take most picturesque forms, and after throwing against the sky bold and grand outlines, they so softly curve down into the lovely dells that they seemed doing homage to beauty, lordly and gentle. And far away at the end of the val-ley, Windermere, Queen of the Lakes, reposed, gleaming silvery blue. This fair, open eye com-pleted the picture. In that was the soul revealed. I wished I had had my sketch-book to draw just the outlines, but was not too sorry, because I intended to go again, and then I would have it. Now I was content to gaze alone.

The attractions of London are fully admitted by Mrs. Hawthorne, in various letters, from which I gather these sentences : —

"At last I have found myself in London soci-ety. I suppose Ellen and Mary [her nieces] would like to know what I wore on one occasion. I had on a sky-blue glacé silk, with three flounces, which were embroidered with white floss, making a very silvery shine. The dress had low neck and short sleeves ; but I wore a jacket of starred *blonde* with flowing sleeves ; and had round me also a shawl of Madeira lace, which, though very airy, fleecy, and cloud-looking, is warm and soft. My headdress was pearl, in the shape of bunches of grapes and leaves, mingled with blue ribbon, with a wreath of pearl-traced leaves round my hair, which was rolled in coronet fashion. Was not that a pretty dress?

" Mr. Hawthorne was invited to Monckton Milnes' to a *déjeuner*, and met there Macaulay, Mr. and Mrs. Browning, Lord Stanley, the Marquis of Lansdowne, Lord Goderich, etc. He enjoyed it very much; and the venerable old Marquis seemed bent on doing him honor and showing him respect. He insisted upon Mr. Hawthorne's taking precedence of himself on every occasion. It is an immense disappointment to me that we cannot spend some months within daily reach of London, because I want Mr. Hawthorne to take a very full draught of it. But I shall persuade him to go up to the grim, glorious old city by himself, if possible."

My mother had been so seriously attacked by bronchitis as to endanger her lungs, which led to a visit of six months to Lisbon and Madeira, my father remaining at the Consulate. While in exile, she writes to him : —

"I am all the time tumbling into fathomless reveries about going home.

"Dearest, I have an idea! Next winter, if you wish to remain in England, and my coughing continues, I will tell you how I might do, and be most happy and comfortable. I might remain in my chamber all winter, and keep it at an even temperature, and exercise by means of the portable gymnasium. I am sure the joy of your pre-

sence would be better than any tropic or equa-
tor without you. And I hate to be the means of
your resigning from the Consulate."

We also went to Southport for my mother's
health. Here she writes : —

MY DEAR ELIZABETH, — The Doctor will not
let me walk more than thirty minutes at a time.
Here there are no carriages with horses, but with
donkeys, sometimes two or three abreast. They
will go out to the edge of the deep sea. The donkeys walk, unless they take it into their heads
to run a little. One day I mounted Una and
Julian on donkeys, while Rose and I were in the
carriage. One little girl belabored the two sad-
dled donkeys, and one guided my two. They
were weather-beaten, rosy girls, one with a very
sweet young face. The elder conversed with me
awhile, and said the young gentleman's donkey
was twenty years old and belonged to her brother, who would surely die if they bartered it,
"because it is his, you know." She smiled reluctantly when I smiled at her, as if she had too
much care to allow herself to smile often, but evidently she was a sound-hearted, healthy, contented child, ready to shine back when shone
upon.

Mr. Hawthorne now knows what has been my
danger, and he is watchful of every breath I draw ;
and I would not exchange his guardianship for
that of any winged angel of the hosts. God has.
given him to me for my angel, only He makes

him visible to my eye, as He does not every one's angel. It seems as if even *I* never knew what felicity was till now. As the years develop my soul and faculties, I am better conscious of the pure amber in which I find myself imbedded.

The Doctor shows me that it is my DUTY to be self-indulgent, and I can be so with a quiet conscience, and shall soon be all right in body, as I am all right in mind and heart. Mr. Hawthorne *never* has *anything*. I do not believe there is another spirit so little disturbed by its body as his.

... Mr. Hawthorne, you may be sure, will take care of me. I should think he would suppose you thought he had no interest in the matter ; but he thinks of nothing else, and would give up the Consulate to-day if he saw it was best for me.

After so hard a beginning, I long for him to repose from anxiety for the future of our life. I only wish that for others as well as for ourselves the fables about this Consulate had been truths. Because what my husband would like would be to find always his right hand (unknown to his left) full of just what his fellow mortals might need, with no more end of means than there is of will to bestow. In him is the very poetry of beneficence, the pure, unalloyed fountain of bounty. It has been well tested here, where every kind of woe and want have besieged him.

That provoking Consular bill has been in force nearly two years, depriving us of our rights to the amount now of about $35,000, because ever since it became the law the times have been more prosperous. The year before that the business was miserable. I think it was unjust that the actual incumbents of the office should not have been allowed to fulfill their terms with the conditions upon which they commenced them. It was a bill hoisted in on the shoulders of the ministerial bill, which very strangely does not come in play till 1857.

December 11.

Mr. Hawthorne is dining in the suburbs of Liverpool this evening, with a Mr. William Browne, M. P., to meet Baron Alderson. It is only the second dinner he has been *obliged* to sacrifice himself to since we have been in Southport. This Mr. Browne is a venerable gentleman, who takes the trouble to go to the Consulate, and bend his white head in entreaty, and he can no more be refused, all things considered, than two and two can refuse to be four. So, at the present moment, there sits my lord at the gorgeous board, shining like a galaxy with plate and crystal. There was lately a banquet in honor of Mr. Browne, which went off magnificently. All Liverpool and part of the county shared in it; and the town was hung with banners from end to end, and business was suspended. It was a superb day of bright sunshine and perfectly dry streets, and the procession of the selected guests, and then of subscribers, was immensely long. I believe fifteen hundred collated at St. George's Hall; and on an elevated dais the twenty invited guests sat. Mr. Hawthorne was one of these. He had received notice that Monckton Milnes was to give him a toast, and a speech would be expected. You may see by some papers that Mr. Milnes gave "The United States;" but this is a mistake. It was "Nathaniel Hawthorne." He was very cordial and complimentary; but he did not say, as the reporter of the "Post" wrote, "that the 'Scarlet Letter' *stuck* to the hearts of all who came in contact with it," as if it were a kind of adhesive plaster; but that it "*struck* to the hearts of all who read it." When Mr. Hawthorne rose there was such a thunder of applause and cheers that, after a while, he actually sat down till quiet was restored. Mr. Channing told me, day before yesterday, that his speech was admirable, and delighted all who knew him, and made the Americans proud of him. He sat beneath, but very near him. Was it not a burning shame that I was not there? Many ladies were present in the galleries, and one of them sent a footman to Mr. Hawthorne, requesting a flower or a leaf as a memento. The modest and generous Mr. Browne [who had just made a public bequest] was overwhelmed with the reverberations of gratitude on every side. Mr. Hawthorne said he liked Lord Stanley, though he was rather disappointed in his appearance. The latter had to respond to "The House of Stanley." Lord Derby was to come, but was unable. Before the banquet, the corner-stone was laid. What a wise way this is — for rich men to make bequests during life. I hope many will do likewise.

Yes, I have read about a thousand times over of Mr. Peabody's gift to Baltimore. We have a great many American papers, and the English papers repeat everything of importance. Mr. Browne has done the same thing in Liverpool.

December 18. Mr. Hawthorne had a stupid time enough at Mr. Browne's dinner at Richmond Hill. Mr. Browne himself is always stupid, and Mrs. Browne never says a word. The judges were dumb and lofty with their own grandeur, and communicated no ideas. Do you know how very grand the judges are when *in acto?* Do you know that they are then kings, and when the Queen is present they still have precedence? So Imperial is Law in this realm. In going down to dinner, therefore, at Mr. Browne's (whose dinner they kept waiting exactly an hour) they led the way, followed humbly by the High Sheriff of the county, who is always the first dignitary except where the judges lead. Then went the Mayor, attended by one of his magnificent footmen in the Town livery, which is so very splendid and imposing that "each one looks like twenty generals in full military costume," as Mr. Hawthorne says; with scarlet plush vests, innumerable cordons and tassels of gold, small-clothes, and white hose, and blue coats embroidered with gold flowers. No crowned emperor ever felt so blindingly superb, and how they ever condescend to put down their feet on the floor is a wonder. Mr. Hawthorne followed next to the Mayor. There being no conversation, there was ample time to look at the truly gorgeous appointments of the table, upon which no china appeared, but only massive plate. The épergne was Phœbus Apollo in his chariot of the sun, with four horses galloping perpetually along the table without moving. The dessert-plates were bordered with wreaths of flowers and fruits in high relief, all of silver. Perhaps Mr. Browne's wits have turned to silver, as Midas's surroundings into gold. Mr. Hawthorne has gone to another dinner this evening at the Mayor's. It is a state dinner to my lords the judges. Baron Alderson nearly expires with preëminence on these occasions, and perhaps he will cease to breathe to-night. These are heavy hours to Mr. Hawthorne. London society has put him even more out of patience than usual with Liverpool dinners, and I know he is wishing he were at home at this moment. Last evening he was reading to me the rare and beautiful "Espousals" of Coventry Patmore. Have you seen "The Angel in the House" yet? It takes a *truly* married husband and wife to appreciate its exquisite meaning and perfection; but with your miraculous power of sympathy and apprehension, I think you will enjoy it, next to us.

This evening, as I wrote, Prince Rose-red entered, holding aloft a clay head which he had been modeling. It was a great improvement upon the first attempts, and resembled Chevalier Daddi, Una's music-teacher in Lisbon. He put it upon the grate to bake, and then lay down on the rug, with his head on a footstool, to watch the process. But before it was finished I sent him to bed. It is after ten now, and the Chevalier has become thoroughly baked, with a crack across his left cheek. In all sorts of athletic exercises, in which a young Titan is required, Julian is eminent. Monsieur Huguenin, the gymnast, said that in all his years of teaching athletics, he had never met but once with his equal. Yet he moves in dancing in courtly measures and motions, and when he runs, he throws himself on the wind like a bird, and flits like a greyhound. Julian's great head is a delicately organized one. I am obliged to have all his hats made expressly for him, and my hatter, Mr. Nodder, says he never saw such a circumference in his life. I always look upon his head as one of the planets.

Our house has been robbed by two notorious thieves. They had much better have risked their lives in stealing the Hungarian Baron Alderson, whose full dress is incrusted with forty thousand pounds' worth of diamonds and emeralds. We have met with a greater loss than these robbers caused us. Mrs. Blodget has all our luggage at her house in Liverpool ; and one of her servant-men opened two of my trunks, which were in the cellar, and stole almost every piece of plate we possess — all the forks and spoons, and so on. He has confessed, while ill in a hospital. But Mr. Hawthorne will not prosecute him.

Have you read Froude's history, just published,

from the period of the fall of Wolsey to the death
of Elizabeth ? His style is wholly unlike that of
the stately, but rather tiresome unchangeable *can-
ter* of Macaulay's. Macaulay takes care of his
style, but Froude is only interested in his theme.
I do not suppose any one historian has yet climbed
up to the pinnacle of perfect impartiality, — unless my darling Herodotus, who has the simplicity of a child, and no theories at all. But Macaulay's style tires me. He is so *ferociously* lucid
that he confuses me, as with too much light. It
is the regular refrain of his brilliant sentences
that finally has the effect of a grand jangle of
musical instruments.

The Manchester Exhibition framed a particularly rare spectacle : —

MANCHESTER.

MY DEAR ELIZABETH, — We are now at Old
Trafford, close by the Palace of Art Treasures,
which we have come here expressly to see. There
is no confusion, no noise, no rudeness of any kind,
though there are thousands of the second-class
people there every day. If you shut your eyes,
you only hear the low thunder of *movement*. . . .
Yesterday we were all there, and met — now,
whom do you think? Even *Tennyson*. He is
the most picturesque of men, very handsome and
careless-looking, with a wide-awake hat, a black
beard, round shoulders, and slouching gait ; most
romantic, poetic, and interesting. He was in the
saloons of the ancient masters. Was not that

rare luck for us? Is it not a wonder that we should meet? His voice is also deep and musical, his hair wild and stormy. He is clearly the "love of love and hate of hate," and "in a golden clime was born." He is the Morte d'Arthur, In Memoriam, and Maud. He is Mariana in the moated grange. He is the Lady Clara Vere de Vere and "rare, pale Margaret." There is a fine bust of him in the exhibition, and a beautiful one of Wordsworth. . . . Ary Scheffer's Magdalen, when Christ says, "Mary!" is the greatest picture of his I have ever seen. Ary Scheffer himself was at the exhibition the other day. . . .

Again Mr. Hawthorne, Una, and I were at the Palace all day. We went up into the gallery of engraving to listen to the music; and suddenly Una exclaimed, "Mamma! there is Tennyson!" He was sitting by the organ, listening to the orchestra. He had a child with him, a little boy, in whose emotions and impressions he evidently had great interest; and I presumed it was his son. I was soon convinced that I saw also his wife and another little son, — and all this proved true. It was charming to watch the group. Mrs. Tennyson had a sweet face, and the very sweetest smile I ever saw; and when she spoke to her husband or listened to him, her face showered a tender, happy rain of light. She was graceful, too, and gentle, but at the same time had a slightly peasant air. . . . The children were very pretty and picturesque, and Tennyson seemed to love them immensely. He devoted himself to them, and was absorbed in their interest. In him is a careless ease and a noble air which show him of the gentle blood he is. He is the most romantic-looking person. His complexion is *brun*, and he looks in ill health and has a hollow line in his cheeks. . . . Allingham, another English poet, told Mr. Hawthorne that his wife was an admirable one for him, — wise, tender, and of perfect temper ; and she looks all this ; and there is a kind of adoration in her expression when she addresses him. If he is moody and ill, I am sure she must be a blessed solace to him. When he moved to go, we also moved, and followed him and his family faithfully. By this means we saw him stop at his own photograph, to show it to his wife and children ; and then I heard them exclaim in sweet voices, "That is papa !" Passing a table where catalogues were sold, . . . his youngest son stopped with the maid to buy one, while Tennyson and his wife went on and downstairs. So then I seized the youngest darling with gold hair, and kissed him to my heart's content ; and he smiled and seemed well pleased. And I was well pleased to have had in my arms Tennyson's child. After my raid I went on. . . .

Of this glimpse of the great poet fortunately accorded to our family my father writes in the " Note-Books : " "Gazing at him with all my eyes, I liked him very well, and rejoiced more in him than in all the other wonders of the exhibition." Again my mother refers to the interesting experience : —

MY DEAR ELIZABETH, — My last letter I had not time to even double up myself, as Mr. Hawthorne was booted and spurred for Liverpool before I was aware, and everything was huddled up in a hasty manner. It was something about Tennyson's family that I was saying. I wanted you to know how happy and loving they all seemed together. As Tennyson is in very ill health, very shy and moody, I had sometimes thought his wife might look worn and sad. I was delighted, therefore, to see her serene and sweet face. I cannot say, however, that there was no solicitude in it, but it was a solicitude entirely penetrated with satisfied tenderness. . . .

I did not reply to your last long letter to me about slavery. . . . There is not a single person whom I know or ever talked with who advocates slavery. Your letters to me would be far more appropriate to a slaveholder. . . . I do not see how they apply to me at all. . . .

There has been the customary misinterpretation of calm justice in the case of my father's moderation during the wild ardor of abolition. This sort of ardor is very likely necessary in great upheavals, but it is not necessary that every individual should join the partisans (while they slash somewhat promiscuously) at the expense of his own merciful discretion. My mother writes in eloquent exposition of her husband's and her own loyalty to the highest views in regard to the relations of all members of the human family, but she never convinced the hot fidelity of the correspondents of her own household. I will add a letter and note, from Hawthorne to Miss Peabody, partly upon this subject : —

LIVERPOOL, August 13th, '57.

DEAR E., — I return this manuscript pamphlet on the Abolition question, for I do not choose to bother Sophia with it ; and yet should think it a pity to burn so much of your thought and feeling. You had better publish it. I speak trustingly, though not knowingly, of its merits ; for to tell you the truth, I have read only the first line or two, not expecting much benefit even were I to get the whole by heart. No doubt it seems the truth of truth to you; but I do assure you that, like every other Abolitionist, you look at matters with an awful squint, which distorts everything within your line of vision ; and it is queer, though natural, that you think everybody squints, except yourselves. Perhaps they do ; but certainly *you* do.

As regards Goodrich's accounts of the relations between him and me, it is funny enough to see him taking the airs of a patron ; but I do not mind it in the least, nor feel the slightest inclination to defend myself, or be defended. I should as soon think of controverting his statement about my personal appearance (of which he draws no very lovely picture) as about anything else that he says. So pray do not take up the cudgels on my behalf ; especially as I perceive that your recollections are rather inaccurate. For instance, it was Park Benjamin, not Goodrich, who cut up the "Story-teller." As for Goodrich, I have rather a kindly feeling towards him, and he himself is a not unkindly man, in spite of his propensity to feed and fatten himself on better brains than his own. Only let him do that, and he will really sometimes put himself to some trouble to do a good-natured act. His quarrel with me was, that I broke away from him before he had quite finished his meal, and while a portion of my brain was left ; and I have not the slightest doubt that he really felt himself wronged by my so doing. Really, I half think so too. He was born to do what he did, as maggots to feed on rich cheese.

Sophia has enjoyed herself much for some months past, and enjoyment seems to agree with her constitution, for her health and vigour have been very satisfactory. Neither did I ever have a better time in my life, than during our recent tours in England and Scotland. Between us, we might write an immense book of travels. I have six or seven volumes of journals, written during my residence in England ; but unfortunately, it is written with so free and truth-telling a pen that I never shall dare to publish it. Perhaps parts of it shall be read to you, some winter evening, after we get home ; but I entirely yield the palm to Sophia on the score of fullness and accuracy of description. [Considerably more of the letter is cut off, and the following fragment of another letter is pasted over a portion of the first.]

LIVERPOOL, October 8th, '57.

DEAR E., — I read your manuscript Abolition pamphlet, supposing it to be a new production, and only discovered afterwards that it was the one I had sent back. Upon my word, it is not very good ; not worthy of being sent three times across the ocean ; ·not so good as I supposed you would always write, on a subject in which your mind and heart were interested. However, since you make a point of it, I will give it to Sophia, and will tell her all about its rejection and return.

Pictures of Leamington and its vicinity were sent home, as follows : —

No. 10 LANSDOWNE CIRCUS, LEAMINGTON, WARWICKSHIRE, September 9, 1857.

MY DEAR ELIZABETH, — Do not suppose that we are among horses, mountebanks, and clowns by my date. On the contrary, we are in a charming little paradise of gardens, with a park in the centre, towards which all these gardens converge. It is such a paradise as the English only know how to make out of any given flat bit of land. Fancy a circle of houses at the end of a street. They are white stucco houses, with balconies leading out of the drawing-rooms, in which to sit and enjoy the gardens, made up of sunny green lawns, bright rainbow flowers, and dark green shrubbery and trees. The park is full of lovely trees and evergreens, with lawns and gravel-walks. We are in profound quiet. Nothing but a bird's note ever

breaks our stillness. The air is full of mignonette,
roses, and wallflowers. It is autumn; but the grass
and foliage are like those of early spring or summer.

In Manchester, which we have lately visited, I
found that the foul air of the manufactories made
me cough more, and the moment Mr. Hawthorne
perceived it, he decided to come away. Nothing
but the Palace of Art would ever have made us
think of being one hour in such a nasty old ugly
place. I could never be weary of looking at some
of the masterpieces, to the end of my days. I
should think the Good Shepherd would convert
the Jew, Baron L. R., to Christianity; for it is his.
No words can possibly do justice to that, or to the
Madonna in Glory. . . .

September 12. To-day we went to Kenilworth.
There was not blue sky enough to encourage Mr.
Hawthorne at first; but at eleven o'clock we set
forth in very good sunshine, and delicious air. By
a short turn out of our Circus we came into a street
called Regent's Grove, on account of a lovely
promenade between noble trees for a very long
distance, almost to the railroad station; and Una
and I walked that way, leaving Mr. Hawthorne
and Julian to follow, as we wished to saunter.
They overtook us, having gone down the Parade,
which is the principal street, containing hotels and
shops; and it crosses at right angles Warwick
Street, which reaches for several miles, until it
arrives at Warwick Castle itself.

The bright greens of England seem to be lined

338

with gold ; and in the autumn, the leaves merely turn their golden linings.

The approach to the domain of Kenilworth is through roads with trees, winding along, and also across a narrow river, which we should call a brook, glimpses of the castle towers appearing at every turn.

The grass was very wet, and I had no india-rubbers, and Mr. Hawthorne went off with Una to buy me some, being resolved to make them, I believe, if he could not find any in the only shop not explored, for we had already tried for them. He returned with the only pair in Kenilworth that would fit me — and the last pair the shopman had left in his box. . . . The ivy, after climbing up the sides of the Castle in a diffusive embrace, reaches the crumbling battlements ; and to conceal the gnawing teeth of time there, it rises into perfect trees, full and round, where it does not find it lovelier to trail over and hang in festoons and wreaths and tassels. Ivy and time contend for the mastery, and have a drawn battle of it. Enormous hawthorn-trees, large as our largest horse-chestnuts, also abound around the Castle, and are now made rich and brilliant with scarlet haws. Mr. Hawthorne and I were filled with amazement at their size. Instead of the rich silk hangings which graced the walls when Elizabeth entered the banqueting-room, now waved the long wreaths of ivy, and instead of gold borders, was sunshine, and for music and revel — SILENCE — profound, not even a breeze breaking it. For we had again one of those brooding, still days which we have so often been fortunate enough to have among ruined castles and abbeys. Bare stone seats are still left around Elizabeth's boudoir, upon which, when softly cushioned with gold, she sat, and saw a fair prospect. The park and chase extended twenty miles !

Nothing but music can ever equal or surpass architecture in variety of utterance. Music is poetry to the ear, architecture to the eye, and poetry is music and architecture to the soul, for it can reproduce both. Music, however, seems to be freer from all shackles than any other art ; and I remember that in one of my essays for Margaret Fuller, I made it out to my own satisfaction to be the apex of expression. The old Glasgow verger of whom I wrote you had not got so far as to see that it needed the "Kist of Whistles," as he called the organ, to make his beloved Cathedral soar and glow with life and praise to its utmost capacity. But I cannot say that it does not sing, even without a sound, in its immortal curves, as Ruskin calls those curves that return in no conceivable time or space. Cathedrals sing, and they also *pray*, with pointed arches for folded hands. Julian liked these ruins better than any he had seen, he said ; and he climbed up on the dismantled turret of Leicester's buildings, and settled himself among the ivy like some rare bird with wonderful eyes. His hair had grown very long, and clustered round his head in hyacinthine fashion, and I think my lord would have been glad to call him his princely boy. [Such things he never allowed himself to say.] All the princeliness that lies in clustering curls Julian has lost to-day, for a hair-dresser has cropped him like a Puritan.

As for myself, fine weather, flower-filled lanes, sturdy walks, and the zest of environs that aroused the rest of the family through association as well as loveliness, seemed to awaken in my mind a vivid era that was exciting if laborious. I had night-vigils which were delightfully entertained by a faculty for hearing quite splendid music, — music that my imagination composed with a full orchestra of admirable brilliancy ; and I was also able to see in perfect distinctness a splendid bazaar, filled with any quantity of toys, which I could summon at will. But this pastime required a great deal of will-power, a peculiar subtlety of condition, and could only be kept up for a few moments at a time ; and in the course of several months the charming capacity was modified to that of being able to evoke most clearly scenes where imaginary characters, more real than actual companions, leaped into being, and talked and moved to any extent. I suppose numbers of people have this faculty, and it is a sovereign protection against *ennui ;* or would be, if remedies could always be relied upon. I mention these matters to prove that I moderately possessed artistic perception. I can see, nevertheless, quite well, that I must have been a very stupid child most of the time, and that the befogged state of my mind was certainly a pity and perhaps a shame. Yet there was a sort of advantage in it: fogs choose with much good sense what they will emphasize; and the intellect bereft of fussy clearness may have a startling grasp that reminds one of occult methods. My observations could not pretend to so much, but they caught truths not very often stared into capture by a little girl; and my father interested me more, and was more frequently the subject of my meditations, than any one else.

In Leamington there seemed to be some opportunity for quiet pursuits. In the first place, there were great preparations for Christmas; which means, that my sister Una made a few little hand-worked presents in complete secrecy, and there was a breathless spending of a few sixpences. If a good deal of money was used by my parents, it was never distributed with freedom, but for those luxuries which would gather the least rust; and not a little was exchanged for heavenly treasure itself, in charity that answered appeals too pathetic to disregard. And we children learned — though we did not learn to save money, because our parents could not — to go without the luxuries money oftenest brings; a lesson that comes to happy fruition in maturer life, if there is need of it. I say happy, because we look back with joy to the hours spent in toughening the sinews of endurance. I remember that long and Penelope-like were my own Christmas preparations; but what they evolved is a matter as lost to thought as a breeze on the desert, in spite of the clearness with which I remember the gifts from my sister and our genteel Nurse, Fanny, who was with us again, and shone more sweetly than ever in Leamington. The handsomest objects we had were given us by Fanfan, or Fancy, as my mother called her. My mother writes, "Our Twelfth Cake was a superb little illuminated Book of Ruth, which never can be eaten up, and will be a joy forever to all our posterity after us, and to our contemporaries."

I will insert here an account of how perfect the smoothness of English mechanism may be : —

13 CHARLES STREET, BATH.

MY DEAR ELIZABETH, —We asked the porter at the depot to tell us of a good hotel, and he sent us to York House. After being deposited in it, with our stones round our necks (as I call our luggage), we found it was not only the first hotel in Bath, but one famous throughout the land. A terrible fear came over me that a year's income would scarcely defray our expenses even for one day and night; but as we did not arrive till five, we could not leave till the next day. So we had nothing to do but to take it grandly. We were put in possession of a lordly sitting-room, hung with crimson. There was nothing gaudy, but a solid richness. Papa and Mamma were the Duke and Duchess of Maine [in remembrance of a lordly claim at Raymond], Julian was Lord Waldo, and Una, Lady Raymond. The finest cut crystal, and knives and forks with solid silver handles, and spoons too heavy to lift easily, delicate rose and gold china, and an entire service of silver dishes, came upon the table. Our attendants were the Sublime and the Pensive, in the form of two men. The Sublime had a bosom full of linen lilies in peculiarly wide bloom; while the Pensive was adorned rather with snowdrops. Their footfalls were descending snowflakes, their manners devout, solemn, and stately. It was really quite delicious, just for a short time; and it was impossible not to be convinced that we at least came over with William the Conqueror; or we might be descended in a straight line from Prince Bladud, who flourished in Bath eight hundred years before the Christian era. At all events, we were the noblest in the land, and received the salaams of the Sublime and the Pensive as obviously due to our exalted rank. As I looked at my husband, so kingly in aspect by nature, of such high courtesy in manner; and at Una, princesslike, with her sweet dignity, I did not at all wonder at the stolen glances of our waiters; that *looking without looking* for which a thoroughbred English waiter is so remarkable. Lord Waldo also "bore it well;" and as to the Lady Rose, she might have bloomed in a royal conservatory. Sumptuous wax candles, in richly chased silver candlesticks, lighted us up in the evening. Whenever I left the sitting-room for my chamber, the Sublime was suddenly at the door to open and shut it for me, bowing down with all his lilies.

Ah, me! But how can I describe the York

House table! Such Apician food, so delicately touched with fire! And who can ever sing adequately the graceful curves in which the Pensive swept off the covers, at the sound of some inaudible music — inaudible except to his ear — as soon as we were all seated! I felt so grand that I was ready to shout with laughter — having gone full circle from the sublime to the ridiculous several times. I felt the ducal coronet on my brow, flashing fine flames from diamonds and emeralds. His Grace's diadem put my eyes out (as it often does, even when not in York House, and we not all in full dress). The weather was dull and cold, and a glorious fire blazed in the large grate, fed and tended by a third noiseless apparition, *the Soft*, in the shape of a boy, who gently deposited black boulders of coal without raising any dust, and with a brush delicately invited away the ashes from the bars and the hearth, and *poked* as one would kiss a sleeping babe. The eyes of the Soft did not wander; they were kept snug beneath their lids with well-trained reverence; and this genius of the fire always appeared as soon as the glow began to fade, as if by inspiration. In my large chamber, draped with white muslin over rose color and drab damask, a superb fire glowed. I must make an end of this nonsense.

The next day I drove about Bath to get apartments, — the first hour in vain; and everybody said the city was full, and we should not succeed. The children cried out to stay in York House, enjoying the luxury. But again I took a Bath

chair, and with Fanny the nurse at my side to
talk for me, and Rosebud to look out for signs of
"To Let," we tried again, and found this modest
house ; where, such is the simplicity of my nature, I am ten times as comfortable and at home
as at even York House, with its shaded grandeur.
Yet I am very fond of splendor, I have to confess ; and, moreover, our surprise was great when,
upon demanding the account, the Sublime brought
on a silver salver charges actually more moderate than those of many inferior hotels all about
England.

I will proceed here with our visit to Redcar,
though that occurred in 1859, when we had returned from Rome.

Redcar is in the midst of a stately region, grand
with an outline of hard-bosomed, endless beach
and vast sky, of sea and sand-hills, where my father
stands forth very distinctly in my memory. When
he went out at fixed hours of the day, between the
hours for writing, he walked over the long, long
beach, and very often with my brother and myself ;
stopping now and then in his firm, regal tread to
look at what nature could do in far-stretching
color and beckoning horizon line. Along the sand-
hills, frolicking in the breeze or faithfully clinging
in the strong wind to their native thimbleful of
earth, hung the cerulean harebells, to which I ardently clambered, listening for their chimes. In
the preface to "Monte Beni," the compliment paid
to Redcar is well hidden. My father speaks of

reproducing the book (sketched out among the dreamy interests of Florence) " on the broad and dreary sands of Redcar, with the gray German Ocean tumbling in upon me, and the northern blast always howling. in my ears." Nothing could have pleased him better as an atmosphere for his work ; all that the atmosphere included he did not mean to admit, just then. And London was not so very far away.

On September 9, 1859, my mother says in her diary, " My husband gave me his manuscript to read." There are no other entries on that day or the next, except, " Reading manuscript." On the 11th she says, " Reading manuscript for the second time." The diary refers to reading the manuscript on the third day, but on the two following days, in which she was to finish as much of the romance as was ready, there are wholly blank spaces. These mean more than words to me, who know so well how she never set aside daily rules, and how unbrokenly her little diaries flow on. She writes home : —

" Mr. Hawthorne has about finished his book. More than four hundred pages of manuscripts are now in the hands of the publishers. I have read as much as that, but do not yet know the dénouement. He is very well, and in very good spirits, despite all his hard toil of so many months. As usual, he thinks the book good for nothing, and based upon a very foolish idea which nobody will like or accept. But I am used to such opinions, and understand why he feels oppressed with disgust of what has so long occupied him. The true judgment of the work was his *first* idea of it, when it seemed to him worth the doing. He has regularly despised each one of his books immediately upon finishing it. *My* enthusiasm is too much his own music, as it were. It needs the reverberation of the impartial mind to reassure him that he has not been guilty of a *bêtise*.

"Mr. Hawthorne had no idea of portraying me in Hilda. Whatever resemblance one sees is accidental."

On November 8 (we were then in Leamington once more) she records in very large script, " My husband to-day *finished his book*, ' The Romance of Monte Beni.' "

My mother was especially fortunate in finding the smallest rose-tinted and most gleaming among the shells which we came across upon the sands, and of these a few superlative but almost invisible specimens were long the cherished possession of her English work-box. She often went with me to the sands, spending much time there; her diary saying: "Superb, calm day. I went on sands with Rosebud to gather shells. Stayed three hours." Or: "Most superb day possible. I went on the sands with Rose, and sat all the morning in a sand-chair, reading, while Rose played. It was a divine day; the air like rose petals, the sky cerulean, the sea sapphire. I felt so serene and quiet; — a great calm." Then comes the inevitable contrast: "Tremendous sea. Rose and I went on the sands to gather shells." These shells, which we could none of us find in so perfect a state as my mother could, were object-lessons to me in the refinements of art, as the harebells were in the refinements of nature; for were not the dancing flowers alive, and the stirless shells the passive work of thought?

Sometimes she read Disraeli's "Sibyl," while I built a sand fortress round her; or she read "Venetia," "Oliver Twist," "The Life of Mary II.," "Romany Rye," and "The Lives of the Last Four Popes." She remembered Pio Nono with unflagging interest, and mentions his serious illness, and then his recovery. She read "a queer biography of Wordsworth by Hood," and she regarded Carlyle's diction in the "French Revolution" as "rubbishy."

Besides the pilgrimages in search of shells, another pursuit was inaugurated by my mother, in her breathlessly calm way, which was the finding of multitudinous seaweeds of every eccentricity of style. The Yankee elm, the English oak, the kitchen-garden herb, or Italian stone-pine, the fern, and tresses, as they seemed, of women's fair or dusky hair, were all so cleverly imitated by the seaweeds that one might have supposed them to be the schoolbooks of the sea; or the latest news there, regarding the nature of the dry world. Many spare moments were given to mounting these pretty living pictures of growths. My lack of success in producing a single very neat specimen was, I grieve to admit, hardly bettered by any of us; my father joining in the scientific excess only so far as to turn his luminous eyes upon our enthusiasm, with his genial "h'm-m" of permission.

Excursions were made to Whitby, Wilton Castle, and other places; and I made an excursion on my own account, which kept me lame for some time. "Rose fell and hurt her knees and elbow, following a monkey." But my most considerate mother would never have let me perceive the humorous and possibly unintelligent aspect of my adventurous spirit; and the next day she tenderly inscribes the historical fact, "Poor baby lame."

Here are a few words of testimony, from my sister, to the charm of this shore: —

REDCAR, October 4, 1859.

Our last day in Redcar, dearest aunt Lizzie; and a most lovely one it is. The sea seems to reproach us for leaving it. But I am glad we are going, for I feel so homesick that I want constant change to divert my thoughts. How troublesome feelings and affections are! When one ought to forget, they are strongest.

Your loving niece,

U. H.

I thought that the petty lodging in which we were established was an odd nook for my father to be in. I liked to get out with him upon the martial plain of sand and tremendous waves, where folly was not, by law of wind and light of Titan power, and where the most insignificant ornament

350

was far from insignificant : the whorl of an exquisite shell, beautiful and still, as if just dead ; or
the seaweeds, that are so like pictures of other
growths. I felt that this scene was a worthy one
for the kind but never familiar man who walked
and reflected there. We enjoyed a constant outdoor life. But in those uninspired hours when
there was no father in sight, and my mother was
resting in seclusion, I played at grocer's shop on
the sands with a little girl called Hannah, whom
I then despised for her name, her homely neat
clothes, her sweetness and silence, and in retrospect learned to love. As we pounded brick,
secured sugary-looking sands of different tints,
and heaped up minute pebbles, a darkly clad,
tastefully picturesque form would approach, — a
form to which I bowed down in spirit as, fortunately for me, my father. He would look askance
at my utterly useless, time-frittering amusement,
which I already knew was withering my brain and
soul. In his tacit reproach my small intellect
delighted, and loftier thoughts than those of the
counter would refresh me for the rest of the day ;
and I thankfully returned to the heights and
lengths of wide nature, full of color and roaring
waves.

CHAPTER XII

ITALIAN DAYS: I

My first frequent companionship with my father began in Italy, when I was seven years old. We entered Rome after a long, wet, cold carriage journey that would have disillusionized a Doré. As we jolted along, my mother held me in her arms, while I slept as much as I could ; and when I could not, I blessed the patient, weary bosom upon which I lay exhausted. It was a solemn-faced load of Americans which shook and shivered into the city of memories that night. In "Monte Beni," as he preferred to call "The Marble Faun," my father speaks of Rome with mingled contempt for its discomforts and delighted heartiness for its outshining fascinations. "The desolation of her ruin" does not prevent her from being "more intimately our home than even the spot where we were born." A ruin or a picture could not satisfy his heart, which accepted no yoke less strong than spiritual power. Rome supplies the most telling evidence of human failure, because she is the theatre of the greatest human effort, both in the ranks of Satan and of God ; and she visibly mourns her sins of mistake at the feet of spiritual victory, Saints Peter and Paul. (As a Catholic, I could hardly win the respect of the

352

gentle reader if I were so un-American as to fear
to stand by my belief.) And while the observer
in Rome may well feel sad in the midst of remind-
ers of the enormous sins of the past, there is an
uplifting, for the soul eager to perceive the truth,
in all her assurances of that mercy which is the
cause of religion. If the Holy See was established
in Rome because it was the city where the worst
wickedness upon earth, because the most intelligent, was to be found, we may conclude that the
old emperors, stormy and grotesque, are responsible for its melancholy "atmosphere of sin," to
which Hilda alludes as a condition of the whole
planet; and not the popes who have prayed in
Rome, nor the people who believe there. In
printed remarks about Italy both my parents say
that she most reminds them of what is highest.

But, whether chilly or warm, the Eternal City
did not at once make a conquest of my father's
allegiance, though before he bade it farewell,
it had painted itself upon his mind as sometimes
the sunniest and most splendid habitation for a
populace, that he knew. In the spring my sister wrote : —

"We are having perfectly splendid weather
now, — unclouded Italian skies, blazing sun, everything warm and glorious. But the sky is too
blue, the sun is too blazing, everything is too
vivid. Often I long for the more cloudy skies
and peace of that dear, beautiful England. Rome
makes us all languid. We have to pay a fearful price for the supreme enjoyment there is in

standing on the very spots made interesting by poetry or by prose, imagination, or (which is still more absorbing) truth. Sometimes I wish there had never been anything done or written in the world ! My father and I seem to feel in this way more than the rest. We agree about Rome as we did about England."

In the course of the winter my mother had written of our chilly reception thus : —

No. 37 VIA PORTA PINCIANA, 2D PIANO,
PALAZZO LARAZANI, ROME.

MY DEAR ELIZABETH, — I could not have believed I could be in Rome a day without announcing it to you in words and expressions which would have the effect at least of the bell of St. Peter's or the cannon of St. Angelo. . . . But my soul has been iced over, as well as the hitherto flowing fountains of the Piazza di San Pietro. I have not been able to expand like corn and melons under a summer sun. Nipped have been all my blossoming hopes and enthusiasms, and my hands have been too numb to hold a pen. Added to this, Mr. Hawthorne has had the severest cold he ever had, because bright, keen cold he cannot bear so well as damp ; and Rosebud has not been well since she entered the city. It is colder than for twenty years before. We find it enormously expensive to live in Rome ; our apartment is twelve hundred a year.

But I am in Rome, Rome, *Rome !* I have stood in the Forum and beneath the Arch of

Titus, at the end of the Sacra Via. I have wandered about the Coliseum, the stupendous grandeur of which equals my dream and hope. I have seen the sun kindling the open courts of the Temple of Peace, where Sarah Clarke said, years ago, that my children would some time play. (It is now called Constantine's Basilica.) I have climbed the Capitoline and stood before the Capitol, by the side of the equestrian statue of Marcus Aurelius, — the finest in the world [my father calls it "the most majestic representation of kingly character that ever the world has seen "], — once in front of the Arch of Septimius Severus. I have been into the Pantheon, whose sublime portico quietly rises out of the region of criticism into its own sphere, — a fit entrance to the temple of all the gods. How wise was the wise and tact-gifted Augustus to reject the homage of Agrippa, who built it for his apotheosis, and to dedicate it to the immortal gods! It is *now* dedicated to the Immortal God.

And I have been to St. Peter's! There alone in Rome is perpetual summer. You have heard of the wonderful atmosphere of this world of a basilica. It would seem to be warmed by the ardent soul of Peter, or by the breath of prayer from innumerable saints. One drops the hermetical seal of a curtain behind, upon entering, and behold, with the world is also shut out the bitter cold, and one is folded, as it were, in a soft mantle of down, as if angels wrapped their wings about us. I expanded at once under the invisible sun. There have been moments when I have felt the spell of Rome, but every one says here that it dawns gradually upon the mind. It would not have been so with me, I am convinced, if I had been *warm*. Who ever heard of an icicle glowing with emotion ? What is Rome to a frozen clod ? . . .

We were not able to seize upon the choicest luxuries of living, as our accommodations, even such as they were, proved to be expensive enough to hamper us. We had all expected to be blissful in Italy, and so the inartistic and inhuman accessories of life were harder to bear there than elsewhere. I remember a perpetual rice pudding (sent in the tin ten-story edifices which caterers supply laden with food), of which the almost daily sight maddened us, and threw us into a Burton's melancholy of silence, for nothing could prevent it from appearing. We all know what such simple despairs can do, and, by concerted movement, they can make Rome tame. If we had sustained ourselves on milk, like Romulus and Remus, and dressed in Russian furs, we might have had fewer vicissitudes in the midst of the classic wonders on all sides. But spring was faithful, and at its return we began to enjoy the scenes of most note within and beyond the walls : the gleaming ruins, and fresh, uncontaminated daisies that trustfully throve beside some of them ; the little fountains, with their one-legged or flat-nosed statues strutting ineffectually above them, — fountains either dry as dead revelers or tinkling a pathetic sob into a stone trough ; the open views where the colors of sunlit marble and the motions of dancing light surrounded the peasants who sprang up from the ground like belated actors in a drama we only keep with us out of childish delight.

My father had never looked so serious as he did now, and he was more slim than in England. He impressed me as permeated by an atmosphere of perception. A magnetic current of sympathy with the city rendered him contemplative and absorbent as a cloud. He was everywhere, but only looked in silence, so far as I was aware. "The Marble Faun" shows what he thought in sentences that reveal, like mineral specimens, strata of ideas stretching far beyond the confines of the novel. While he observed Rome, as he frequently mentions, he felt the sadness of the problems of the race which there were brought to a focus. Yet it is a singular fact that, notwithstanding this regret for her human pathos, perhaps the best book he ever wrote was created among the suggestive qualities of this haven of truth, — the book which inculcates the most sterling hope of any of his works. I saw in my walks with him how much he enjoyed the salable treasures and humble diversions of the thoroughfare, as his readers have always perceived. Ingenuous simplicity, freedom from self-consciousness and whitewash, frank selfishness on a plane so humble that it can do little harm, — all this is amusing and restful after long hours with transcendental folk. In regard to the tenets of these, my mother writes to her sister : —

"I am just on the point of declaring that I hate transcendentalism, because it is full of immoderate dicta which would disorganize society, and should never be uttered, in my opinion, except behind the veil, among priests. As to displaying before the great, innocent eyes of a girl like Una all the horror of a slave-auction — a convent is better than such untimely revelations. Now, you must not think I am a Catholic. I know the Lord withholds the pure from seeing what they should not — blessed be the Lord! — but I will not be the one to put what should not be seen before the eyes of the pure."

My father looked in good spirits as we moved along. When he trafficked with an Italian fruit-vender, and put a few big hot chestnuts into his pocket, with a smile for me, I (who found his smile the greatest joy in the world) was persuaded that really fine things were being done. The slender copper piece which was all-sufficient for the transaction not only thrilled the huckster with delight, but became precious to me as my father's supple, broad fingers held it, dark, thin, small, in a respectful manner. He caressed it for a moment with his large thumb, — he who was liberal as nature in June, — and when the fruit-vender was wrought up to the proper point of ecstasy he was allowed to receive the money, which he did with a smile of Italian gracefulness and sparkle, while my father looked conscious of the mirthfulness of the situation with as lofty a manner as you please. As for the peasant women we met, under their little light-stands of head - drapery, they were easily comprehensible, and expressed without a shadow of reserve their vanity and tiger blood by an openly proud smile and a swing of the brilliantly striped skirt. The handsomest men and women possible, elaborately dressed, shone beside tiers of the sweetest bunches of pale violets, or a solitary boy, so beautiful that his human splendor scintillated, small as he was, sat in the pose and apparel that the world knows through pictures, and which pigment can never well render any more than it can catch the power of a sunset or an American autumn. The marble-shops were very pleasant places. A whirring sound lulled the senses into dreamy receptiveness, as the stone wheel heavily turned with soft swiftness, giving the impression that here hard matter was controlled to a nicety by airy forces ; and a fragrance floated from the wet marble lather, while the polishing of our newly picked up mementos from the ruins went on, which was as subtle as that of flowers. A man or two, hoary with marble-dust and ennobled by the "bloom" of it, stood tall and sad about the wheel, and we handed to these refined creatures our treasures of giallo-antico and porphyry and other marbles picked up "for remembrance" (and no doubt once pressed by a Cæsar's foot or met by a Cæsar's glance), in order to observe the fresh color leap to the surface, — yellow, red, black, or green.

Far more were we thrilled at finding scraps of iridescent glass lachrymals, containing all the glories of Persian magnificence, while pathetically hinting of the tears of a Roman woman (precious only to herself, whatever her flatterers might aver) two thousand years ago.

The heart of Rome was acknowledged to be St. Peter's, and its pulse the Pope. The most striking effect the Holy Father produced upon me, standing at gaze before him with my parents, was when he appeared, in Holy Week, high up in the balcony before the mountainous dome, looking off over the great multitude of people gathered to receive his blessing. Those eyes of his carried expression a long way, and he looked most kingly, though unlike other kings. He was clothed in white not whiter than his wonderful pallor. My father implies in a remark that Pio Nono impressed him by a becoming sincerity of countenance, and this was so entirely my infantile opinion that I became eloquent about the Pope, and was rewarded by a gift from my mother of a little medallion of him and a gold scudo with an excellent likeness thereon, both always tenderly reverenced by me.

Going to the Pincian Hill on Sunday afternoons, when my father quite regularly made me his companion, was the event of my week which entertained me best of all. To play a simple game of stones on one of the gray benches in the late afternoon sunshine, with him for courteous opponent, was to feel my eyes, lips, hands, all

my being, glow with the fullest human happiness.
When he threw down a pebble upon one of the
squares which he had marked with chalk, I was
enchanted. When one game was finished, I trembled lest he would not go on with another. He
was never fatigued or annoyed — outwardly. He
had as much control over the man we saw in him
as a sentinel on duty. Therefore he proceeded
with the tossing of pebbles, genially though quietly, not exhibiting the least reluctance, and
uttering a few amused sounds, like mellow wood-
notes. Between the buxom groups of luxuriant
foliage the great stream of fashion rolled by in
carriages, the music of the well-trained band pealing forth upon the breeze; and in the tinted distance, beyond the wall of the high-perched garden which surrounded us, the sunset shook out its
pennons. Through the glinting bustle of the
crowd and the richness of nature my father peacefully breathed, in half-withdrawn brooding, either
pursuing our pebble warfare with kindest stateliness, or strolling beside lovely plots of shadowed
grass, fragrant from lofty trees of box. An element by no means slight in the rejoicing of my
mind, when I was with him of a Sunday afternoon, was his cigar, which he puffed at very deliberately, as if smoking were a rite. The aroma
was wonderful. The classicism which followed my
parents about in everything of course connected
itself with my father's chief luxury, in the form
of a bronze match-box, given him in Rome by
my sister, upon which an autumn scene of har-

vest figures was modeled with Greek elegance, and to this we turned our eyes admiringly during the lighting of the cigar. There was a hunter returning to a home draped with the grape, bringing still more of that fruit, and a rabbit and bird, hung upon a pole, while his wife and child were ever so comfortably disposed upon the threshold, and the hunting-dog affectionately lapped the young matron's hand. An autumn was also depicted on the reverse, presumably a year earlier than the one just described, where two lovers stood among sheaves of wheat, their sickles in hand, and the youth held up a bunch of grapes which the maiden, down-looking, gently raised her arm to receive. At last it would grow too late to play another game, and my father's darkly clothed form would be drawn up, and his strongly beautiful face lifted ominously. Before leaving the hill we went to look over the parapet to the west, where stood, according to " Monte Beni," " the grandest edifice ever built by man, painted against God's loveliest sky." Quoit-players were no doubt rolling their disks upon the road below us ; and on the very first glance it almost always happened that a springing, vaporous-looking quoit would appear without one's seeing the man whose hand had sent it on its way. It was a refined pastime, immortalized by the Discobolus, which, however, cannot give the charm of the whirling quoit.

The entries in my mother's diary so abound in names and persons met day by day, names both unknown to the world and familiar to it, that it is

hard to understand how there was time for sight-
seeing or illness, or the reading which was kept
up. The wife of a distinguished sculptor in Rome
afterwards said in a letter that this year of 1859
was remarkable for its crowd of tourists, and
added that 1860 proved very quiet. It does not
sound quiet to hear that she had just enjoyed a
horseback ride with Mr. Browning ; but Americans
and English certainly did have rich enjoyment in
Italy in those days, and grew exacting. The jot-
tings of the diary stir the imagination quite pleasantly, beginning January 16, 1859 : "Mr. Browning called to visit us. Delightful visit. I read
Charlotte Brontë for the second time. — Mrs.
Story sent a note to my husband to invite him to
tea [my mother being housed with my sick sister]
with Mr. Browning. — Mr. Horatio Bridge spent
the evening. — Read 'Frederick the Great.'— Mr.
Motley called, and brought 'Paradise Lost' for
Una. — I went to the sunny Corso with my husband, who is far from well. Mrs. Story asks us
to dine with Mr. de Vere, Lady William Russell,
Mr. Alison, Mr. Browning, and other interesting
people. — Lovely turquoise day. I prepared Julian's Carnival dress. Went to the Hoars' balcony,
and the Conservatori passed in gorgeous array.
The George Joneses took Una to drive in the
Corso, and the Prince of Wales threw her a bouquet from his balcony. I read the 'Howadji in
Syria' as I sat at the Hoars' window. — I had
a delightful visit from E. Hoar. She saw the
Pope yesterday, and he blessed her. Mrs. Story

looked very pretty in a carriage at the Carnival, with a hat trimmed with a wreath of violets. — Mr. and Mrs. Story called for us to go to the Doria Villa. We had a glorious excursion, finding rainbow anemones and seeing wonderful views. Mr. Christopher Cranch joined us. — I went to the Vatican for the first time this year, with E. Hoar. We met there Mr. Hawthorne escorting Mrs. Pierce and Miss Vandervoort. We went through all the miles of sculpture. — Una and I called on Mrs. Pierce, Mrs. Browning, Mrs. Pickman, Mrs. Hoar, and met Mrs. Motley. In the afternoon I went with E. Hoar to Mr. Story's studio. Mrs. Pickman called on me. — Mr. Hawthorne and I and Julian went to call on Miss Cushman, and to Mr. Page's studio. Mr. Motley had made a long call early in the day, and teased Mr. Hawthorne to dine with him, to meet Lord Spencer's son. — Mrs. Story brought Una the first lilies-of-the-valley that have bloomed in Rome this year. I went with Rose to Trinità dei Monti to hear the nuns sing vespers. Coming out, I met Miss Harriet Hosmer. — Superb day. I went with my husband to call at Miss Hosmer's studio, and met the Hon. Mr. Cowper, who stopped to talk. Mr. Browning darted upon us across the Piazza, glowing with cordiality. Miss Hosmer could not admit us, because she was modeling Lady Mordaunt's nose. — Governor Seymour called. — I took Rose to a window in the Carnival. It was a mad, merry time. A gentleman tossed me a beautiful bouquet and a bonbon. —

Julian and I went to the Albani Villa with Mrs.
Ward and Mr. Charles Sumner. A charming
time. — In the twilight I went with Mr. Hawthorne to the Coliseum and the Forum. It grew
to lovely moonlight. — After dinner I went to the
Pincian gardens with Mr. Hawthorne and Julian.
It was moonlight. — Mr. Sumner made a long
call."

Among the friends much with us was the astro-
nomer, Miss Maria Mitchell, whom we had long
known intimately. She smiled blissfully in Rome,
as if really visiting a constellation; flashing her
eyes with silent laughter, and curling her soft, full,
splendid lips with fascinating expressions of satisfaction. I loved her for this, but principally because, while with us in Paris, it was she who had
with delicious comradeship introduced me to that
perfection of all infantile taste — French ginger-
bread, warm (on an outdoor counter) with the sunshine of the skies! She had the long list of
churches and ruins and pictures catalogued upon
her efficient tongue, and she and my mother ran
together like sisters to see the sights of beauty
and reminiscence; neither of them ever tired, and
never disappointed. Her voice was richly mellow,
like my father's, and her wit was the merry spray
of deep waves of thought. The sculptor, Miss
Harriet Hosmer, it was easy to note, charmed the
romancer. She was cheerfulness itself, touched
off with a jaunty cap. Her smile I remember as
one of those very precious gleams that make us
forget everything but the present moment. She

could be wittily gay ; but there was plenty of brain power behind the clever *mot*, as immensities are at the source of the sun-ray. There was a blessing in the presence of Miss Elizabeth Hoar, once engaged to that beloved brother of Mr. Emerson whom death had taken. She seemed to me (I plead guilty to fancifulness) like a tall, speaking monument, composed of diamonds and pearls. She talked a great deal, gently, with a penetrating sweetness of voice, and looking somewhat down, as those do who have just received the news of a bitter sorrow. She knew everything that was fine in history and poetry and art ; and to be near her, and to catch at moments the clear unfaltering challenge of her sad but brave eyes, was to live a little nobler one's self.

I will give here two letters from this friend, showing her strength of sympathy and tenderness : —

FLORENCE, May.

DEAR SOPHIA, — We are here after a journey entirely prosperous in every respect, driving through a country as lovely as it could be. Such wreaths of hawthorn, such hanging tassels of laburnum, such masses of delicate purple flowers draping the rocks and carpeting every broken ground, — golden broom on every hillside, scarlet poppies illuminating every field of grain, and the richest crimson clover, like endless fields of strawberries, — I never saw before. We have had just clouds enough to make beautiful shadows on the mountains. How I wish you and Una could be

floated on a cloud over the charming region. I
thought of the dear child at every new flower, but
not without a pang; for my only disappointment
in leaving Rome (no, the *other* was that I had not
seen Mr. Browning) was that I could not send
Una some flowers the morning of our departure.
I had *set my heart* upon it, but could not find
any pretty enough. Every fresh spray of hawthorn on our journey renewed the prick of my
disappointment. We should have liked to take
Julian along with us as our traveling artist, to
lay up the flowers for us in imperishable colors
[he already painted flowers remarkably]; we were
reminded of him very often. I saw dear little
Rose's patron, St. Rosa, in the Staffa Gallery
at Perugia, — very beautiful. I have much to
thank you for, dear Sophia, in all sorts of aid and
sympathy. Very charming is the recollection of
every meeting with you, from the first lovely Sunday at the Villa Doria; and then the day when
we visited the willful Queen of Egypt as she sat
waiting to be made again immortal in marble
[in Story's studio]. Those days in Rome were
made brighter to me by the sunshine of kindness
and a hearty sympathy, beginning with the day
which will be an exhilarating thought to me as
long as I live, when you showed me St. Peter's
Piazza under the blue sky; and then we passed
the wall of the Capitol, and looked down upon
ancient Rome. It was a *wonderful* day, Sophia,
and I shall never forget that *you* received me in
that city. I hope you will have many joyous days

before you leave Europe, so that you may all forget the many anxieties of the last three months. I wish to send my love to Mrs. Story. I enjoy *the thought* of her, and Mr. Story, very much. I have always loved them for their thorough kindness to Margaret [Fuller d'Ossoli], and now I have seen them I love them for themselves. Love and constant remembrance to Una and dear little Rose. You don't know how hard it is not to know about you, day by day. [Later.] I had your other letter in Genoa, and was rejoiced to get it. I had driven with Lizzie and Mr. May the very day before from Villeneuve to Montreux to call upon you, the people at Hotel Byron assuring us you were to spend a month at Montreux. However, the news from Una was precious, for it was the first intelligence we had had since we left the dear child in bed in Rome, with that trickish fever playing about her. I did not receive the note from Mr. Hawthorne. I am almost glad you are not going to take her back into the low ground at Concord this autumn. . . .

Many friends were in Rome, both as residents and as tourists, and in all my after-life our two winters there were the richest of memories, in regard both to personalities and exquisite objects, and to scenes of artistic charm. Yet, as I have said elsewhere, if the tall, slender figure of my father were not at hand, even my mother's constantly cheering presence and a talkative group of people could not warm the imagination quite enough. He says, in speaking of the Carnival, "For my part, though I pretended to take no interest in the matter, I could have bandied *confetti* and nosegays as readily and riotously as any urchin there." These few words explain his magnetism. The decorous pretense of his observant calm could not make us forget the bursts of mirth and vigorous abandon which now and then revealed the flame of unstinted life in his heart. And I, watching constantly as I did, saw a riotous throw of the *confetti*, a mirthful smile of Carnival spirits, when my father was radiant for a few moments with a youth's, a faun's merriment.

Having quoted a letter of my sister's which expresses his opinion and her own of the irksomeness of sight-seeing, however heroic the spot, I will add this little paragraph from the next winter's correspondence, when, though only fifteen, she wrote very well of Europe and America, concluding : "It shows you have not lived in Europe, dear aunt, and do not know what it is to breathe day after day the atmosphere of art, that you can think of our being satisfied. We have seen satisfactorily, but the longer we stay, the higher and deeper is our enjoyment, and the more are our minds fitted to understand and admire, and the nearer do our souls approach in thought and imagination to that fount of glory and beauty, from which the old artists drew so freely."

In art, Catholicity was utterly bowed down to by my relatives and their friends, because without it this great art would not have been. For, as scientists and dreamers have proved that gold cannot be made until we know as much as the earth, so uninspired artists have proved that religious art can only grow under conditions known solely to the heart that is Catholic. Every religious school of art which has departed from imitation of the Old Masters has forfeited holiness in depicting the Holy Family.

My mother's letters describing my sister's illness with Roman fever recall the many persons of interest whom we saw. She writes : " Carriages were constantly driving to the door with inquiries. People were always coming. Even dear Mrs. Browning, who almost never goes upstairs, came the moment she heard. She was like an angel. I saw her but a moment, but the clasp of her hand was electric, and her voice penetrated my heart. Mrs. Ward, also usually unable to go upstairs, came every day for five days. One day there seemed a cloud of good spirits in the drawing-room, Mrs. Ward, Mrs. Browning, Mrs. Story, and so on, all standing and waiting. Magnificent flowers were always coming, baskets and bouquets, which were presented with tearful eyes. The American minister constantly called. Mr. Aubrey de Vere came. Every one who had seen Una in society or anywhere came to ask. Mrs. Story came three times in one day to talk about a consultation. The doctor wished all the food prepared exactly after his prescription, and would accept no one's dishes. ' Whose broth is this ? ' ' This is Mrs. Browning's.' ' Then tell Mrs. Browning to write her poesies, and

not to meddle with my broths for my patient!'
'Whose jelly is this?' 'Mrs. Story's.' 'I wish
Mrs. Story would help her husband to model his
statues, and not try to feed Miss Una!' General
Pierce came three times a day. I think I owe to
him, almost, my husband's life. He was divinely
tender, sweet, sympathizing, and helpful." She
adds : " No one shared my nursing, because Una
wanted my touch and voice; and she was not
obliged to tell me what she wanted. For days, she
only opened her eyes long enough to see if I were
there. For thirty days and nights I did not go to
bed; or sleep, except in the morning in a chair,
while Miss Shepard watched for an hour or so.
Una had intervals of brightness and perfect consciousness. In one of these, she tied up a bouquet
of flowers with hands that almost shook the flowers
to pieces with their trembling, to send them to a
friend who was ill. She raised herself upon her
elbow, and wrote with a pencil a graceful note,
quoting her father's ' Wonder-Book ' in reference
to the bouquet."

I went with my father and mother to several
painters' and sculptors' studios (besides innumerable visits to churches and galleries), all filling my
mind with unfailing riches of memory. I hope I
shall be pardoned for giving the general effect of
this companionship and sight-seeing upon many
years of reflection in a strain that is autobiograph-
ical. The studio which I best remember was Mr.
Thompson's, he who had painted the portrait of
my father used in the editions of "Twice-Told

Tales." The room was very large, but not very high, and it had a great deal of shadow in it. I did not think he painted as well as Raphael; but I delighted in the smell of his pigments, which were intensely fragrant. I thought his still moist canvas upon the easel, of a little Peter and a well-groomed angel, infinitely amusing. It was history scrubbed, and rather reduced in size. I was half appalled, half fascinated, by my temerity in having such frivolous private opinions of a picture that my mother and father felt the excellence of with reverence and praise. A minute portrait of me was painted by Mr. Thompson; one for which I did not find it at all amusing to sit, as I had to occupy a stiff chair (I think it was even a high stool) without any of the family to keep me in heart, although I had almost never been left with friends in that way, and although I was by that time a perfect recluse in disposition. So I was under the impression that I was being punished by the invisible powers, which I was conscious of eminently deserving. The small painting shows this idea of Purgatorial arrest by a clever touch here and there, without depicting a frown or positive gloom. The patronizing demeanor of an artist at work upon a portrait, which we all know so well, — the inevitable effect of his faith in himself, the very breath of artistic endeavor, without which he would lounge through life asking, " Of what use is it to attempt ? " — made me furious, in my naughty, secret mind. I was not accustomed to being patronized ; my mother herself had never given me a command. Besides, I was out of temper to think that my quietly observant father had stood in admiration before that picture of the liberating of St. Peter, of which I wearied, liking it so cordially that he had uttered his conclusive, deeply sympathetic "Yes," when my mother gave voice to her praise ; whereas I had not had the grace to glow, but voted all the pictures bores in a lump. Mr. Thompson, below the average size, and harmlessly handsome, always wore the prevailing gleam of a smile that showed chiefly at the eyes, offset by a nimbus of gray and black hair.

I wondered, even at seven years of age, how sculptors in the flesh could come and carve original conceptions among the unspeakably successful attempts of those who were already thinnest dust, yet whose names have so much personality in them that a sovereign presence fills the place where they are spoken, — sculptors whose statues step as it were unexpectedly (themselves surprised) into sight, with none of the avoirdupois of later stone-work ; that heaviness which, in some of the finest of these modern figures, causes them to pause involuntarily, as if snowed upon. The high degree of smoothness of the old statues, as well as their mellowed whiteness, may give life ; added to that wonderful deep cutting in all crevices and detail of nature, such as gives, in literature, the life to Balzac's endlessly studied facts of situation. The sugary porousness of much of the inferior marble of to-day arrests the eye, and troubles it. Story's Cleopatra is smooth, close-fibred as glass, and the snowstorm has not been allowed to drift upon the folds of her robe, the interstices of her modeling. She, with a few others of still later date, comes near to the old art, which has as much possibility for our imaginative survey as the plot of "The Marble Faun," so marvelously, so intricately, so unslavishly finished. In looking at the Dying Gladiator, we wonder whether he has already passed on from mastering the thought of his approaching death to the remembrance of his wife and children; or whether upon the agony of the physical pang and the insult to courage, which his wound has brought him to endure, is yet to break the pathos of a hero's regret for the relinquished sweetness of love and home.

The Marble Faun suggests the problem as to whether he has for an instant stopped laughing, or will not immediately laugh; and what has a little while ago, or will suddenly cause, the animal fury of gladness to turn this jocund athlete into a dancing, bewilderingly enticing companion, chiming with guffaws and songs. Cleopatra's watchful melancholy partook also of classic momentariness, and I hoped she would spring to her feet. I liked very much to go to Mr. Story's studio, and I thought that for so slight a figure he was remarkably fearless.

The arches of triumph, which my mother studied reverently, seemed to me too premeditated and unnecessary; although an architect could no doubt have explained why, even to the present day, the little door for the little cat should supplement the big door of all space, which one would at first take to be a hero's best environment. Not thus unnecessary appeared the Coliseum ; haunted by wild beasts, especially lions, leaping (I imagined) in hobgoblin array from the cavernous entrances which were pointed out to me as connected in the days of triumphant tyranny with their donjons. Many tender thoughts filled my reflections as I saw pilgrims visiting, and kneeling before, the black cross in the centre, and the altars around the walls. I delighted to muse within the circular ruin, upon whose upper rim, jagged but sunlit, delicate vegetation found a repentant welcome. The circular form of the ruin is full of eloquence, as one approaches from the Forum. What would be grace in a smaller structure is tragedy in so immense a sweep, which melts into vagueness, or comes mountainously upon you, or swirls before you in a retreating curve that figures the never-changing change of eternity.

The tomb of Cecilia Metella, and other successive tombs of the Appian Way beyond the walls, gave me my first impression of death that really was death. There could be, I reflected, looking at the sepulchres of these old Romans, no pretty story about the poor folk having gone to heaven comfortably from their apparent bodies. Here were the ashes of them, after a thousand years, in contemptible little urns ; and they were expected to enjoy, in that much impaired state, sundry rusty bric-à-brac, dolls, and tear-vials of spookish iridescence, until, in the vast lapse of time, even a ghost must have got tired. Unaided by the right comment, I was dragged down considerably by those pagan tombs ; and as an antidote, the unexplained catacombs were not sufficiently elevating. I did not read the signs of the subterranean churches aright, any more than the uncultivated Yankee reads aright an Egyptian portraiture. Monkish skulls and other unburied bones, seen by the light of *moccoletti*, were to me nothing but forms of folly. The abounding life of Catholicity was hardly understood by our party, which for some reason seemed inclined to impute the most death to the faith which has the most form. We did not gather how this abounding life can afford, though making more of our little fleshly sojourn than any other patron, to compare a skull with the life of the spirit, and relegate it to ornamentation and symbol.

Through the streets of Rome trotted in brown garb and great unloveliness a frequent monk, brave and true ; and each of these, I was led by the feminine members of the family, to regard as a probable demon, eager for my intellectual blood. A fairer sight were the Penitents, in neat buff clothes of monastic outline, their faces covered with their hoods, whose points rose overhead like church steeples, two holes permitting the eyes to peep with beetle glistenings upon you. They went hurryingly along, called from their worldly affairs ; and my mother imparted to me her belief

that they were somewhat free of superstition because undoubtedly clean. Sometimes processions
of them, chanting, came slowly through the city,
bearing the dead to burial. I did not know, then,
that the chanting was the voicing of good, honest,
Bible-derived prayers ; I thought it was child's
play, useless and fascinating. In the churches
the chanting monks and boys impressed me dif-
ferently. Who does not feel, without a word to
reveal the fact, the wondrous virtue of Catholic
religious observance in the churches? The holiness of these regions sent through me waves
of peace. I stepped softly past the old men and
women who knelt upon the pavements, and gazed
longingly upon their simpler spiritual plane ; I
drew back reluctantly from the only garden where
the Cross is planted in visible, reverential substance. For the year ensuing this life in Rome,
I entertained the family with dramatic imitations
of religious chants, grumbling out at sundown the
low, ominous echoings of the priests, answered by
the treble, rapid and trustful, of the little choris-
ters, gladly picturing to myself as I did so the
winding processions in St. Peter's.

In the square beneath our windows, during
Lent, booths were set, and countless flat pancake-
looking pieces of dough were caught up by a white-
capped and aproned cook, with a long-handled
spoon, and fried in olive oil placed in a caldron
at the booth's door, to be served to passers in the
twinkling of an eye. I watched this process until
I grew to regard Lent as a tiresome custom. Hav-

ing tested the cakes, I found them to be indistinct in taste, for all their pretty buff tint, and the dexterous twist of the cook's wrist as he dumped them and picked them up. If they had been appetizing I should have been sharply interested in the idea of becoming a Catholic, but their entire absence of relish convinced me that the Italians lacked mental grasp and salvation at a single swoop : and this in spite of the fact that one of my mother's most valued friends, Mrs. Ward, had lately joined the Church. It was her husband who said of her, " Whatever church has Anna, has St. Anna ! " Perhaps the most exquisite speech ever uttered by a husband.

Before this serious season of pancakes, which was all Lent was to me at the time of which I speak, the Carnival had rushed upon my sight, carrying all our friends through its whirlpool. Every gay cloth, shawl, and mat that could be brought into service I had rejoiced to see displayed upon the balconies. A narrow, winding street the Corso seemed, being so full, and the houses so high ; and a merry blue strip of heaven far away overhead, glancing along the housetops, assured us space still existed. Sudden descents of flowers upon one's shoulders and lap in the carriage, from a window or a passer, or a kindly feeling stranger in another carriage, made one start in mirthful response. Sudden meetings with dear friends, or friends who seemed almost dear in the cheerful hurly-burly, became part of the funny scrimmage. At each side-street sat on a stony standing horse a beautifully proportioned and equipped guard, in gleaming helmet and calm demeanor.

To stand or sit at the windows beside the show was an experience full of pleasure ; and if the window was on a level·with the heads of the huddling passers, one could be in all the merriment yet not jostled ; one could easily pick out a pretty woman or a handsome man to whom to throw a bouquet ; and one could see energetic revelers, already well supplied with flowers, reaching high windows with bouquets by means of those wooden contrivances which can be extended or contracted at will, and look like impracticable ladders. The fair recipient at the lattice never failed to respond with an ecstatic smile if this Jacob's ladder had been sufficiently long to reach her welcoming hand. Meantime, many bunches of flowers, some large and elegant, some small and merely gay of color, were being thrown aloft or flung downward, making fountains and cataracts of flowers. Sometimes these bouquets fell into the street dejectedly, upon whose pavement little ragamuffins were always ready to pounce for them, and sell them again as fast as possible to passers who had exhausted their supply, had become mad with the Carnival, and caught sight, in that very moment, of some cherished comrade to whom they wished to throw a greeting. There was an intoxicating enjoyment in being singled out as the recipient of fragrant flowers, sent with a laugh of the eyes ; or of a handful of sugared almonds, tossed with a gay shout of compliment. If the passer who thus honored us was a complete stranger, meeting us for this one moment in racial kindness, we felt the untrammeled bonhomie which, God knows, we were expected to feel as a matter of course not for a moment only, but for life.

Upon all these things I delighted to think and afterwards to ponder, because I realized that they were of vital interest to the intelligence which was to me greatest and dearest.

CHAPTER XIII

ITALIAN DAYS: II

BETWEEN our two winters in Rome we spent the summer in Florence, to which we journeyed by carriage over a road that was hung like a rare gallery with landscapes of the most picturesque description, and bordered close at hand by many a blue or crimson or yellow Italian anemone with its black centre. This experience was all sunshine, all pastime. On the way, stopping at Lake Thrasymene, my mother wrote : —

May 29, 1858.

MY DEAR ELIZABETH, — I have just been watching the moon rise over the lake, exactly opposite the window of our parlor. We thought to go out and see the moonlight this evening, when I saw on the horizon what seemed a mighty conflagration, which I immediately supposed must be the moon, though I had never seen it look so red. The clouds were of a fiery splendor, and then the flaming rim of the moon appeared above the mountains, like the shield of some warrior of the great battle between Flaminius and Hannibal on this spot, rising with its ghostly invisible hero to see how it was now on the former field of blood. The "peace supreme" that reigns here this evening distances all thought of war and terror. We left Perugia this afternoon at three o'clock, with the finest weather. Our drive was enchanting all the way, along rich valleys and up mountains. And when climbing mountains we have two milk-white steers which majestically draw us along. Their eyes are deep wells of dark, peaceful light, that seem to express broad levels of rich waving grain, pure lapsing streams, olives and vines, and every other sign of plenty and quiet husbandry, with no end of dawns, twilights, and cool thickets. The golden age of rural life slumbers in their great orbs. Byron calls them "the purest gods of gentle waters."

June 7. Here we are, then, in enchanting Florence! I shall try to send you a journal by the Bryants, who are here now. The Brownings are close by, and we are going to see them soon. The language has yet to be made in which to describe beautiful, beautiful Florence, with its air of nectar and sherbet and soft odors, its palaces, Arno, and smooth streets, arched bridges, and all its other charms and splendors. . . .

We were hot in the city of Florence. My only consolation was to eat unnumbered cherries and apricots, for I did not as yet like the figs. My brother and I sometimes had a lurid delight in cracking the cherry and apricot stones and devouring the bitter contents, with the dreadful expectation of soon dying from the effects. Altogether I considered our sojourn in the town house, Casa del Bello, a morose experience; but it was, fortunately, short. My mother had a different feeling : she wrote home to America, " It is a delightful residence." Without doubt it contained much engaging finery. Three parlors, giving upon a garden, were absorbed into the "study" for my father alone ; and my mother was greatly pleased to find that fifteen easy-chairs were within reach of any whim for momentary rest between the campaigns of sight-seeing. To add to my own arbitrary shadow and regret of that time, the garden at the rear of the house was to me damp ; full of green things and gracefully drooping trees, doubtless, but never embracing a ray of sunshine. Yet it was hot ; all was relaxing ; summer prevailed in one of its ill-humored moods. To make matters worse, my brother had caught in this Dantesque garden a brown bird, whether because sick or lame I know not. But an imprisoned bird it certainly was ; and its prison consisted of a small, cell-like room, bare of anything but the heart-broken glances of its occupant. My father objected to the capture and caging of birds, and looked with cold disapproval upon the hospitable endeavor of my brother to lengthen the existence of a little creature that was really safer in the hands of Dame Nature. Presently the bird from the sad garden died, and then indeed Florence became intolerable to me ! I wandered through the long, darkish hall that penetrated our edifice from front to back, and I sometimes emerged into the garden's bosky sullenness in my unsmiling misery. Again my mother's testimony proves my mind to have been strangely influenced by what to her was "a garden full of roses, jessamine, orange and lemon trees, and a large willow-tree drooping over a fountain in its midst," with a row of marble busts along a terrace : altogether a place that should have filled me with kittenish glee. The " Note-Books," to be sure, suggest that it harbored malaria. I looked with painful disappointment upon the unceasing dishes of fresh purple figs, which everybody else seemed to enjoy. I saw pale golden wine poured from poetic bottles braided with strands of straw, like pretty girls' heads of flaxen hair ; and I was surprised that my father had the joyousness to smile, though sipping what he was later to call " Monte Beni Sunshine."

That nothing of misery might be excluded from my dismal round of woe, the only people whom I could go to see were the Powers family, living opposite to us. Mr. Powers petrified me by the *sang-froid* with which he turned out, and pointed out, his statues. Great artists are apt to be like reflections from a greater light, — they know more about that light than about themselves ; but Mr. Powers seemed to me to defy art to lord it over his splendid mechanical genius, the self he managed so well. To prove beyond a doubt that material could not resist him, he would step from the studio into an adjoining apartment, and strike off button-like bits of metal from an iron apparatus which he had invented. It was either buttons or Venuses with him, indifferently, as I supposed.

Gray to me, though "bright" to my mother, were the galleries and narrow halls of marble busts, where started back into this life old Medicean barbarians, of imperial power and wormlike ugliness; presided over, as I looked upon them in memory during my girlhood, by that knightly form of Michel Angelo's seated Lorenzo de' Medici, whose attitude and shadowed eyes seem to express a lofty disapproval of such a world.

A morning dawned when the interest in living again became vigorous. A delicate-looking, essentially dignified young gentleman, the Count da Montaüto, seeming considerably starved, but fascinatingly blue-blooded, appeared in our tiresome house. I heard that we were to remove to a villa at Bellosguardo, a hill distant fifteen minutes' drive from the city, where the summer was reasonable; and as the count owned this haunt of refreshment, I became enthusiastically tender in my respect for him. For years afterwards my sensibilities were exercised over the question as to where the count was put while we enjoyed the space and loveliness of Montaüto; I did not know that he had a palace in town. His sad, sweetly resentful glance had conveyed to me the idea, "Must I still live, if I live beneath my rank, and as a leaser of villas?"

One day, happy day, we toiled by carriage, between light-colored walls, sometimes too high for

any view, — that once caused my mother a three
hours' walk, because of a misturn, — over little
hot, dusty roads, out and up to the villa. My father
and brother had already walked thither; and my
brother's spirits, as he stood beside the high iron
gateway, in front of the gray tower which was the
theme, or chief outline, of the old country-seat,
were pleasant to witness, and illustrated my own
pent-up feelings. He shouted and danced before
the iron bars of the gate like a humanized note of
music, uncertain where it belonged, and glad of it.

Our very first knowledge of Montaùto was rich
and varied, with the relief from pretentiousness
which all ancient things enjoy, and with the ap-
pealing sweetness of time-worn shabbiness. The
walls of the hall and staircase were of gray stone,
as were the steps which led echoingly up to the
second story of the house. My sister exclaims in
delight concerning the whole scene: "This villa,
— you have no idea how delightful it is! I think
there must be pretty nearly a hundred rooms in
it, of all shapes, sizes, and heights. The walls are
never less than five feet thick, and sometimes
more, so that it is perfectly cool. I should feel
very happy to live here always. I am sitting in
the loggia, which is delightful in the morning
freshness. Oh, how I love every inch of that
beautiful landscape!" The tower and the adjacent
loggia were the features that preëminently sated
our thirst for suggestive charm, and they became
our proud boast and the chief precincts of our
daily life and social intercourse. The ragged gray

giant looked over the road-walls at its foot, and beyond and below them over the Arno valley, rimmed atop with azure distance, and touched with the delicate dark of trees. Internally, the tower (crowned, like a rough old king of the days of the Round Table, with a machicolated summit) was dusty, broken, and somewhat dangerous of ascent. Owls that knew every wrinkle of despair and hoot-toot of pessimism clung to narrow crevices in the deserted rooms, where the skeleton-like prison frameworks at the unglazed windows were in keeping with the dreadful spirits of these unregenerate anchorites. The forlorn apartments were piled one above the other until the historic cylinder of stone opened to the sky. In contrast to the barrenness of the gray inclosures, through the squares of the windows throbbed the blue and gold, green and lilac, of Italian heavens and countryside.

At the dangers of the stairway my father laughed, with flashing glances. He always laughed (it was a sound peculiarly passionate and low, full, yet unobtrusive) at dangers in which he could share himself, although so grave when, in the moral turmoil, he was obliged to stand and watch uneven battle ; not the less sorry for human nature because weakness comes from our ignoring the weapons we might have used. But on those trembling stairs he approved of the risk we ran, while cautioning me not to drop through one of the holes, and then stumbled within an inch of breaking his own neck, and laughed again.

"While gropingly descending these crazy steps one dusky evening, I gratified Julian exceedingly by hitting my nose against the wall," he admits in the "Note-Books." Who would not enjoy seeing a monarch come to so humble a contact with the bulwarks of his tower? Especially if he were royal enough not to take offense at one's mirth, as this one never did. Reaching the topmost heights of the stone pile, shaggy with yellow moss, we eagerly pressed to the battlements and drank in the view, finding all Florence spread out before us, far down from the breeze and light and prospect of our perch, — understanding the joy of falcons that are long hooded, and then finally *look*.

On one side of the tower was the lawn, hemmed round by a somewhat high semicircular stone wall. In front of it was Florence, pinnacled and roof-crowded, across the gentle valley. Not far away rose Galileo's rival tower, and the habitations of one or two friends. On another side of the keep the valley dipped more decidedly; and in the foreground clustered a collection of trees upon a grassy slope, divided from the villa lawn by a low wall, over which my father and mother sometimes bought grapes, figs, pomegranates, and peaches grown upon the place, which were smilingly offered by the count's *contadini*. These from their numbers were unrecognizable, while their prices for the exquisite fruit were so small that it was a pleasure to be cheated. Behind the tower stretched lengthily the house, its large

388

arched doorway looking upon all comers with a frown of shadow. Still further behind basked a bevy of fruit gardens and olive-tree dotted hillsides with their vines of the grape. We used to sit on the lawn in the evenings, and sometimes received guests there ; looking at the sky, moon, comet, and stars ("flowers of light," my mother called them) as if they were new. Any mortal might have been forgiven for so regarding them, in the sapphire glory of an Italian night. My mother's untiring voice of melodious enthusiasm echoed about the group in ejaculations of praise.

In connection with the comet my elders spoke of war and misery, of which it was accused of being the messenger. My child's heart already knew the iron truth, and was not astonished at the intrusion of such a thought, that beauty and peace must always entertain the herald of the other country — the dark one. There was a sadness about Italy, although it lay under "the smile of God," as my father calls its sunshine. He and my mother often mention this shadow, as before remarked, in their records. At times the cause seems to them to come from the "incubus" of the Catholic religion, although they both believed it capable of being wholly perfect. Glorious scenes were constantly soothing this sense of human sorrow, scenes such as cannot be found in regions outside the Church. In the Basilica of San Spirito my mother came upon several visible lovelinesses of elaborate devotion, which with her limpid purity of justice she enthusiastically notes down. She entered the church one day for coolness and rest, and, recognizing its "noble" beauties, she described, in her journal already printed, "a function going on before one of the side-chapels — the burial service of a child. The coffin was covered with a white satin pall, embroidered with purple and gold. The officiating priests were in robes of white satin and gold, and the altar was alight with candles, besides those borne by young boys in white tunics. This scene in the aisle was a splendid picture in the soft gloom of the church ; and when the organ burst forth in a kind of tender rapture, rolling pearly waves of harmony along the large spaces, and filling the dome with the foam and spray of interlacing measures, it seemed as if angels were welcoming the young child to heaven." The pettiness of a brief burial service in a private parlor or in a meagre meeting-house would not have touched her heart so profoundly, because it would not have recalled heaven so impressively in all its grandeur and tenderness. She evidently perceived here the sweet and even cheering veracity of a devotion that is glad to remember all the possibilities of reverent observance, each motion and aspect of which have a reference to God and to religious history. Again San Spirito gave her an insight into the dignity of painstaking worship. "While we were walking about, the priests and monks of the Order of St. Augustine, who have a convent attached, came in a procession from the sacristy, and knelt down in their sweeping black robes upon the marble pavement, in two lines, one behind the other, and chanted aloud their Ave Maria. It was a wonderful picture." She still clung to the Puritanical idea that in religion itself, "What looks so wondrous, wondrous fair, His providence has taught us to fear. . . . Angels only are fit to live as monks pretend to live." But she contradicts this theory. No one was more adapted than she to perceive the godliness of the monastic sacrifice, when she realized the object of it. Among her dearest friends and verified ideals were Mr. George Bradford, who always reminded me of a priest of the true type; and Miss Hoar, whose vestal soul, celebrating constant rites over the memory of her dead betrothed, made her the image of a nun. This welcome delicacy and loftiness of self-consecration my mother also observed in the ranks of the sometimes harshly criticised friars. At Fiesole, "A young monk unveiled the picture for us. He was very courteous, and had an air of unusual goodness and sincerity. He is one of those who 'bear witness.' As a matter of course I offered him a fee for his trouble, but he made a sad and decided gesture of refusal, that was very surprising and remarkable; for it was impossible to gainsay him, and I felt embarrassed that I had thought of the gold that perishes in the presence of the heavenly picture and the holy youth. I wish I knew his history." I also wish she had known it, for it would have unveiled for her the most beautiful facts about other holy youths of our own day, as well as similar facts of earlier days, — truths whose purity would have rapt her thought even more deeply than Fra Angelico's purity in art, uncurtained by brave and humble hands for her sight. It is to be observed that her views and tacit beliefs and my father's are identical. They did not really believe that Italy was under an "incubus;" they felt the physical weight of Catholicity, or the Cross, and half guessed its spiritual spring.

Some of the rooms at Montaüto I studiously avoided. The forlorn cavern of a parlor, or ball-room, I remember to have seen only once. There was a painful vacuum where good spirits ought to have been. Along the walls were fixed seats, like those in the apse of some morally fallen cathedral, and they were covered with blue threadbare magnificence that told the secrets of vanity. Heavy tables crowded down the centre of the room. I came, saw, and fled. The oratory was the most thrilling place of all. It opened out of my sister's room, which was a large, sombre apartment. It was said to attract a frequently seen ghost by the force of its profound twilight and historic sorrows; and my sister, who was courageous enough to startle a ghost, highly approved of this corner of her domain. But she suddenly lost her buoyant taste for disembodied spirits, and a rumor floated mistily about that Una had seen the wretched woman who could not forget her woes in death. In "Monte Beni" this oratory is minutely pictured, where "beneath the crucifix . . . lay a human skull . . . carved in gray alabaster, most skillfully done . . . with accurate imitation of the teeth, the sutures, the empty eye-caverns." Everywhere the intense picturesqueness gave material, at Montaùto, for my father's romance. Stella, whom he invited into the story without changing her name, was a sympathetic object in my now somewhat alarmed and lonely days. I call her an "object," because I could not understand a word she said, and she soon gave up opening her lips when we were together. She looked kind, in spite of her rocky hardness of Italian feature, and she fed me on dried melon-seeds when I was at the lowest tide of depression. Sometimes she was to be found at the well, close to the entrance-arch. There the faithful servant let down a bucket by its heavy chain with a doomsday clank. The sunlight revealed the smallness and brilliancy and number of her black braids and the infinite multitude of her wrinkles, as well as the yellowness of her dangling gold earrings and the texture of her parchment-like arms, which were the color of glossy brown leaves. Sometimes she would awaken me from soporific melancholy by allowing herself to be found upon her knees in her bedroom, a bare and colorless abode, her great black crucifix hanging in majestic solitude upon the wall above her handsome old head. I thought her temporarily insane to pray so much, and at all to an audience; but I recognized the gentleness of the attacks, and I somehow loved her for them. Even to the ignorance of error truth can be beautiful. An extremely attractive little Italian maid, of sixteen or less, used also to be found on her knees before the crucifix.

Stella was obliged to drive this dark-eyed butterfly to her devotions. If I discovered her, I had no reverence, and tried unmercifully to interrupt her soft whispers. Stella's loving revenge for my wickedness was to give me a tiny wax sleeping *Bambino*, surrounded by flowers under a convex glass, whose minute face had a heaven of smiling forgiveness in it. Often I surreptitiously studied the smile on the sleeping face. I felt that He loved us even during His sleep ; and I cherished the gaze of shining gladness with which Stella herself had placed this treasure in my hand, which could so simply quicken sluggish thought.

To give a clearer glimpse of the villa, which with our life there became one of the most precious of our memories, and a glimpse also of one or two people and events, I will insert this letter from my mother : —

August 14, 1858.

MY DEAR ELIZABETH, — Una and Rose were getting pale for the first time in their lives, and Mr. Hawthorne was languid and weary of the city life, and an English lady, a friend of the Brownings, told us of this villa, which the Count da Montaüto wished to let this summer, though never before, and so we tried for it and got it. It is a most enchanting situation, and the villa is immensely large and very nice. We have an old mediæval tower at the oldest end, in which Savonarola was confined, and from its summit we have a view which one might dream of, but seldom see. We are so high, however, that from the first floor we have a sweeping view, and look down on the most sumptuous valley of the Arno from our western windows, — a level plain, cultivated every inch with grapes and olives and other fruits ; and all round rise up soft hills, and the Apennines afar off where the sun sets. We see the noble white steers slowly moving in the valley, among the trees, ploughing as in the days of Cincinnatus. An infinite peace and quiet reign. We hear birds, and in the evening the cue owl utters his melodious, melancholy one note. The world does not disturb us. The air is as pure and fresh as air can possibly be, blowing from the sweet, carefully tended plain, and sweeping down from the mountains. Near us is the villa and tower of Aurora Leigh, just at the end of our estate, and farther off is Galileo's tower, where he studied the heavens. Northeast from us lies the beautiful Florence, burning in the bottom of the cup of hills, with all its domes and campaniles, palaces and churches. Fiesole, the cradle of Florence, is visible among the heights at the east, and San Miniato, with its grove of cypresses, is farther off to the south. There is no end of beauty and interest, and the view becomes ideal and poetic the moment the sun begins its decline ; for then the rose and purple mists drape the hills, and mountains — the common earth — turn to amethysts, topazes, and sapphires, and words can never convey an idea of the opaline heavens, which seem to have illimitable abysses of a penetrable substance, made up of the light of pearls.

395

Literally and carefully I speak of the *light* of pearls, with the opaline changes. I am quite happy that I have seized the image. The effect is of a roundness with the confused yet clear outline of a pearl, an outline which also is not one, and the light looks living and absorbing. One evening, after the sun went down, rays of blue and rose came from it in a half-wheel shape, so ineffably delicate that if we looked too pryingly they were not there, but if we glanced unawares there they were. It was more like the thought of them than the realities. This summer we have our first sight of Italian sunsets, for we were assured we should have fever if we were out at the hour in Rome. We began by watching them from the bridges over the Arno, which are perhaps the finest points of view, because the river is added. It flows east and west, and so we have all the glory by standing on either of the bridges. The arches, the reflections in the waters, the city's palaces and churches, the distant hills, all come in for a part of the pomp and splendor, — all that man can do, all that God has done, for this lovely land.

Una's chamber is in the tower [but approached from the house], a large, lofty, vaulted chamber, with an oratory attached, full of Madonnas, pyxes, "and all sorts," as Mr. Browning says. There is a regular chapel besides. Mr. Hawthorne has a delightful suite of study, saloon, dressing-room, and chamber, away from all the rest of the family.

August 25. Last evening Miss Ada Shepard
and I went to a neighboring villa to see some
table-turning, which I have never seen, nor anything appertaining to spirits. Mr. Frank Boott
was there and a Fleming, Una's drawing-master.
We tried patiently for two hours with the table,
but though it trembled and wavered, nothing
came of it; so Miss Shepard then took a pencil
and paper for the spirits to write, if they would.
[The attempt on Miss Shepard's part was now,
and always afterwards, successful. My mother
speaks of several somewhat vulgar spirits who
caused great merriment.] Then Ada felt quite
a different and new power seize her hand, rapidly
writing : " Who ? " " Mother." " Whose mother ? " " Mrs. Hawthorne's. My dear child, I
am with you. I wish to speak to you. My dearest child, I am *near* you. I am oftener with you
than with any one." Ada's hand was carried
forcibly back to make a strong underline beneath
" near," and it was all written with the most eager
haste, so that it agitated the medium very much,
and me too ; for I had kept aloof in mind, because
Mr. Hawthorne has such a repugnance to the
whole thing. Mrs. Browning is a spiritualist.
Mr. Browning opposes and protests with all his
might, but he says he is ready to be convinced.
Mrs. Browning is wonderfully interesting. She
is the most delicate sheath for a soul I ever saw.
One evening at Casa Guidi there was a conversation about spirits, and a marvelous story was told
of two hands that crowned Mrs. Browning with a

wreath through the mediumship of Mr. Hume. Mr. Browning declared that he believed the two hands were made by Mr. Hume and fastened to Mr. Hume's toes, and that he made them move by moving his feet. Mrs. Browning kept trying to stem his flow of eager, funny talk with her slender voice, but, like an arrowy river, he rushed and foamed and leaped over her slight tones, and she could not succeed in explaining how she *knew* they were spirit hands. She will certainly be in Rome next winter, unless she goes to Egypt. You would be infinitely charmed with Mrs. Browning, and with Mr. Browning as well. The latter is very mobile, and flings himself about just as he flings his thoughts on paper, and his wife is still and contemplative. Love, evidently, has saved her life. I think with you that " 'Aurora Leigh' overflows with well-considered thought ; " and I think all literature does not contain such a sweet baby, so dewy, so soft, so tender, so fresh. Mr. Hawthorne read me the book in Southport, but I have read it now again, sitting in our loggia, with Aurora's tower full in view. . . .

This loggia opened widely to the air on two sides, so that the opalescent views were framed in oblong borders of stone that rested our rejoicing eyes. Under the stone shade, in the centre of the Raphaelesque distances, many mornings were passed ideally. Visitors often joined us here. Among them was Miss Elizabeth Boott, afterwards Mrs. Duveneck, who came with her little

sketch-book. She made a water-color portrait of
my father, which, as the young artist was then
but a girl, looked like a cherub of pug-nosed, pink
good nature, with its head loose. I can see that
little sketch now, and I feel still a wave of the
dizziness of my indignation at its strange depic-
tion of a strong man reduced to dollhood. Miss
Boott being a true artist in the bud, there was, of
course, the eerie likeness of some unlike portraits.
It became famous with us all as the most startling semblance we had ever witnessed. I sincerely wish that the ardor with which the young
girl made her sketch could have been used later
on a portrait, which certainly would have been
superbly honest and vigorous, like all the work
that has come from her wonderfully noble nature
and her skillful perception. Another young lady
appeared against the Raphaelesque landscape.
She was very pretty in every way, and my mother
was delighted to have her present, and showered
endearing epithets upon her. Her large brown
eyes were alluring beyond words, and her features
pathetically piquant and expressive. Her face
was rather round, pale, and emphatically saddened
by the great sculptor Regret. She sat in picturesque attitudes, her cheek leaning against her
hand, and her elbow somewhere on the back or
arm of her chair; yet her positions were never
excessive, but eminently gentle. She had been
disappointed in love, and one was sure it was not
in the love of the young man. She was too
pretty to die, but she could look sad, and we all

liked to have her with us, and preferred her charming misery to any other mood.

The roads going to and fro between the cream-colored stone walls of the surrounding country were unsparingly hot. I can feel now the flash of sunbeams that made me expect to curl up and die like a bit of vegetation in a flame. I tried to feel cooler when I saw the peasant women approaching, bent under their loads of wheat or of brush. If they had no shading load, it made me gasp to observe that their Tuscan hats, as large as cart-wheels and ostensibly meant to shadow their faces, were either dangling in their hands or flapping backward uselessly. It seemed to be no end of a walk to Florence, and the drive thither was also detestable, — all from the heat and dust, and probably only at that time of year. The views of many-colored landscape, hazy with steaming fields, were lovely if you could once muster the energy to gaze across the high road-walls when the thoroughfare sank down a declivity. After a while there were cottages, outside of which ancient crones sat knitting like the wind, or spinning as smoothly as machines, by the aid of a distaff. Little girls, who were full-fledged peasant women in everything but size, pecked away at their knitting of blue socks, proud of their lately won skill and patient of the undesired toil. They were so small and comely and conformable, and yet conveyed such an idea of volcanic force ready to rebel, that they entranced me. Further inside the heart of the city upstarted the intoxications of sin and the terrible beggars with their maimed children. I never lost the impressions of human wrong there gathered into a telling argument. The crowded hurry and the dirty creatures that attend commercial greed and selfish enjoyment in cities everywhere weltered along the sidewalks and unhesitatingly plunged into the mud of the streets. It seemed to me even then that something should be done for the children maimed by inhuman fathers, and for their weeping mothers too. My father did not forget in his art the note he found in beautiful Florence, though it was too sad to introduce by a definite exposition, and falls upon the ear, in "Monte Beni," like a wordless minor chord.

I sometimes went with my mother when she called at Casa Guidi, where the Brownings lived. I had a fixed idea that Galileo belonged to their family circle; and I had a vision of him in my mind which was quite as clear as Mrs. Browning ever was (although I sat upon her lap), representing him as holding the sun captive· in his back yard, while he blinked down upon it from a high prison of his own. The house, as I recall it, seemed to have a network of second-story piazzas, and the rooms were very much shadowed and delightfully cool. Mr. Browning was shining in the shadow, by the temperate brightness of mind alone, and ever talking merrily. Cultivated English folk are endowed with sounding gayety of voice, but he surpassed them all, as the medley of his rushing thought and the glorious cheer of

his perception would suggest. Mrs. Browning
was there : so you knew by her heavy dark curls
and white cheeks, but doubted, nevertheless, when
you came to meet her great eyes, so dreamy
that you wondered which was alive, you or she.
Her hand, usually held up to her cheek, was absolutely ghostlike. Her form was so small, and
deeply imbedded in a reclining - chair or couch-
corner, that it amounted to nothing. The dead
Galileo could not possibly have had a wiser or
more doubtfully attested being as a neighbor. If
the poor scientist had been there to assert that
Mrs. Browning breathed, he would probably have
been imprisoned forthwith by another incredulous
generation. My mother speaks, on her second
visit to Rome, of the refreshment of Mr. Browning's calls, and says that the sudden meetings
with him gave her weary nerves rest during the
strain of my sister's illness. She could not have
rejoiced in his spirited loveliness more than the
little girl by her side, who sometimes languished
for direct personal intercourse in all the panorama
of pictures and statues, and friends absorbed in
sight-seeing. I had learned to be grateful for art
and ruins, if only they were superlative of their
kind. I put away a store of such in my fancy.
But Mr. Browning was a perfection which *looked
at me*, and moved vigorously ! For many years
he associated himself in my mind with the blessed
visions that had enriched my soul in Italy, and
continued to give it sustenance in the loneliness
of my days when we again threw ourselves upon

the inartistic mercies of a New England village. He grouped himself with a lovely Diana at the Vatican, with some of Raphael's Madonnas and the statue of Perseus, with Beatrice Cenci and the wildflowers of our journeys by *vettura*, besides a few other faultless treasures deeply appreciated by me. We all noticed Mr. Browning's capacity for springing through substances and covering space without the assistance of time.

My mother says in her little diary of Rome, "I met Mr. Browning; or rather, he rushed at me from a distance, and seemed to come through a carriage in his way." It was as if he longed to teach people how to follow his thoughts in poetry, as they flash electrically from one spot to another, thinking nothing of leaping to a mountain-top from an inspection of "callow nestlings," or any other tender fact of smallest interest. Not one of all the cherubs of the great masters had a sunnier face, more dancing curls, or a sweeter smile than he. The most present personality was his; the most distant, even when near, was the personality he married. I have wondered whether the Faun would have sprung with such untainted jollity into the sorrows of to-day if 'Mr. Browning had not leaped so blithely before my father's eyes. "Browning's nonsense," he writes, "is of a very genuine and excellent quality, the true babble and effervescence of a bright and powerful mind; and he lets it play among his friends with the faith and simplicity of a child."

I think I must be right in tracing one of the

chief enchantments of the story of Dr. Grimshawe
to these months upon the hill of Bellosguardo.
For at Montaüto one of the terrors was the cohort
of great spiders. There is no word in the diction-
ary so large or so menacing as a large spider of
the Dr. Grimshawe kind. Such appear, like excla-
mations, all over the world. I saw one as huge
and thrilling as these Italian monsters on the
Larch Path at the Wayside, a few years later;
but at Montaüto they really swaggered and remained. We perceive such things from a great
distance, as all disaster may be perceived if we
are not more usefully employed. A presentiment
whispers, " There he is ! " and looking unswerv-
ingly in the right direction, there he is, to be
sure. I could easily have written a poor story,
though not a good novel, upon the effectiveness
of these spiders, glaring in the chinks of bed-cur-
tains, or moving like shadows upon the chamber
wall or around the windows, and I can guess my
father's amusement over them. They were as
large as plums, with numerous legs that spread
and brought their personality out to the verge of
impossibility. I suppose they stopped there, but
I am not sure. No wonder the romancer humor-
ously added a touch that made a spider of the
doctor himself, with his vast web of pipe-smoke!

The great romance of "Monte Beni" is thus
referred to by Mr. Motley and his wife; I give
a few sentences written by the latter, a friend of
many years' standing, and I insert Mr. Motley's
letter entire : —

DEAREST SOPHIA, — My pen continues to be
the same instrument of torture to me that you
remember it always was in my youth, when I used
to read your letters with such wonder and delight.
This spell is still upon me, for I appreciate the
magic of your mind now as much as I did then,
and have treasured up every little bit of a note
that you wrote me in Rome. I like your fresh
feminine enthusiasm, and always feel better and
happier under its influence. . . . I am glad that
you were so much pleased with Lothrop's letter
of praise and thanksgiving; a poor return at best
for the happiness we had derived from reading
Mr. Hawthorne's exquisite romance. . . . I shall
not now attempt to add any poor words of mine
to his expressive ones, except to assure you of my
deep sympathy for the infinite content and joy
you must feel in this new expression of your husband's genius. We were so much pleased to find
that he was willing to come to us in London,
which we hardly dared to hope for. . . . At least
I can promise to *attend* to him as little as possible. . . . We have taken for the season a small
house in Hertford Street, 31, which belongs to
Lady Byron, who has fitted it up for her grand-
daughter, Lady Annabella King. . . . The eldest
brother, Lord Ockham, is a mechanic, and is now
working in a machine-shop in Blackwall Island,
where he lives. This eccentric course is rather,
I fear, the development of a propensity for low
company and pursuits than from anything Peter

the Greatish there is about him. His father, who is the quintessence of aristocracy, has cast him off. . . . Lothrop was very much gratified by all the fine things you said about him, and so was I ; for praise from you means something and is worth having, because it comes from the heart. There is another volume written, . . . but another must be written before either is published.

Ever your affectionate   M. E. M.

The "letter of praise and thanksgiving" referred to above is as follows : —

WALTON-ON-THAMES.

MY DEAR HAWTHORNE, — I can't resist the impulse to write a line to you, in order to thank you for the exquisite pleasure I have derived from your new romance. Everything that you have ever written, I believe, I have read many times · and I am particularly vain of having admired "Lights from a Steeple," when I first read it in the "Boston Token," several hundred years ago, when we were both younger than we are now ; and of having detected and cherished, at a later day, an " Old Apple Dealer," whom I believe that you have unhandsomely thrust out of your presence, now you are grown so great. But the romance of " Monte Beni " has the additional charm for me that it is the first book of yours that I have read since I had the privilege of making your personal acquaintance. My memory goes back at once to those (alas, not too frequent, but that was never my fault) walks we used to take along the Tiber or in the Campagna, during that dark period when your Una was the cause of such anxiety to your household and to all your friends ; and it is delightful to get hold of the book now, and know that it is impossible for you any longer, after waving your wand, as you occasionally did then, indicating where the treasure was hidden, to sink it again beyond the plummet's sound. I admire the book exceedingly. I don't suppose that it is a matter of much consequence to you whether I do or not, but I feel as much disposition to say so as if it were quite an original and peculiar idea of my own, and as if the whole world were not just now saying the same thing. I suppose that your ears are somewhat stunned with your praises, appearing as you. do after so long an interval ; but I hope that, amid the din, you will not disdain the whisper from such sincere admirers as I am myself, and my wife and daughter are. I don't know which of the trio is the warmest one, and we have been fighting over the book, as it is one which, for the first reading at least, I did not like to hear aloud. I am only writing in a vague, maundering, uncritical way, to express sincere sympathy and gratitude, not to exhibit any dissenting powers, if I have any. If I were composing an article for a review, of course I should feel obliged to show cause for my admiration, but I am now only obeying an impulse. Permit me to say, however, that your style seems, if possible, more perfect than ever. Where, oh where is the godmother who gave you to talk pearls and diamonds? How easy it seems till anybody else tries! Believe me, I don't say to you half what I say behind your back; and I have said a dozen times that nobody can write English but you. With regard to the story, which has been slightly criticised, I can only say that to me it is quite satisfactory. I like those shadowy, weird, fantastic, Hawthornesque shapes flitting through the golden gloom which is the atmosphere of the book. I like the misty way in which the story is indicated rather than revealed. The outlines are quite definite enough, from the beginning to the end, to those who have imagination enough to follow you in your airy flights; and to those who complain, I suppose nothing less than an illustrated edition, with a large gallows on the last page, with Donatello in the most pensive of attitudes, his ears revealed at last through a white nightcap, would be satisfactory.

I beg your pardon for such profanation, but it really moves my spleen that people should wish to bring down the volatile figures of your romance to the level of an every-day novel. It is exactly the romantic atmosphere of the book in which I revel. You who could cast a glamour over the black scenery and personalities of ancient and of modern Massachusetts could hardly fail to throw the tenderest and most magical hues over Italy, and you have done so. I don't know that I am

especially in love with Miriam or Hilda, or that I
care very much what is the fate of Donatello ; but
what I do like is the air of unreality with which
you have clothed familiar scenes without making
them less familiar. The way in which the two
victims dance through the Carnival on the last
day is very striking. It is like a Greek tragedy
in its effect, without being in the least Greek.
As I said before, I can't single out any special
scene, description, or personage by which to
justify or illustrate my feeling about the book.
That I could do better after a second reading,
when it would be easy to be coldly critical. I
write now just after having swallowed the three
volumes almost at a draught ; and if my tone is
one of undue exhilaration, I can only say it was
you gave me the wine. It is the book — as a
whole — that I admire, and I hope you will forgive my saying so in four pages instead of four
words.

Is there any chance of our seeing you this summer ? We expect to be in London next month.
It will be very shabby of you not to let us have a
glimpse of you ; but I know you to be capable of
any meanness in that line. At any rate, you can
have little doubt how much pleasure it will give
us. Pray don't answer this if it is in the least a
bore to you to do so. I know that you are getting notes of admiration by the bushel, and I have
no right to expect to hear from you. At the
same time it would be a great pleasure to me to

hear from you, for old (alas, no, — new) acquaintance' sake.

I remain very sincerely yours,

J. L. MOTLEY.

Of the discussions about "Monte Beni" I remember hearing a good deal, as my mother laughingly rehearsed passages in letters and reviews which scolded about Hawthorne's tantalizing vagueness and conscienceless Catholicity. My parents tried to be lenient towards the public, whose excitement was so complimentary, if its usually heavy inability to analyze its best intellectual wine was fatiguing. My father never for a moment expected to be widely understood, although he no doubt hoped to be so in certain cases. He must have easily deduced something in the way of chances for appreciative analysis from prevalent literature. He struck me as a good deal like an innocent prisoner at the bar, and if I had not been a member of his family I might have been sorry for him. As it was, I felt convinced that he could afford to be silent, patient, indifferent, now that his work was perfected. My mother put into words all that was necessary of indignation at people's desire for a romance or a "penny dreadful" that would have been temporary and ineffective. Meantime, such rewards as Mr. Motley offered weighed down the already laden scales on the side of artistic wealth.

Perhaps it will not be impertinent for me to remark, in reference to this admirable and delightful letter, that its writer here exemplifies the best feelings about Hawthorne's art without quite knowing it. We see him bubbling glad ejaculations in the true style of an Omar Khayyám who has drained the magic cup handed to him. It is delicious to hear that he was not sure he cared about the personages of a story that had clutched his imagination and heart, until he reeled a little with responsive enchantment; though it is hard to say about what he cared if not about the romancer's powerful allies, who carried his meaning for him. Mr. Motley tries to attribute to the scenes he knew so well in reality, under their new guise of dreamy vividness, the spell which came, I believe, from the reality of moral grandeur, in both its sin and its holiness, but which we so entirely ignore every precious hour by sinking to the realities of bricks and common clay. Miriam and Donatello may seem at first glance like visions; but I have always been taught that their spell lay in our innate sense that they were ourselves, as we really are. The wine of great truth is at first the most heady of all, making its revelations shimmer.

411

CHAPTER XIV

THE WAYSIDE

In order to give an idea of how it happened that our family could return from Europe to Concord with a few great expectations, I will rehearse somewhat of the charm which had been found in the illustrious village when my father and mother first knew it. There a group of people conversed together who have left an echo that is still heard. There also is still heard "the shot fired round the world," which of course returned to Concord on completing its circuit. But even the endless concourse of visitors, making the claims of any region wearisomely familiar, cannot diminish the simple solemnity of the town's historical as well as literary importance; and indeed it has so many medals for various merit that it is no wonder its residents have a way of speaking about it which some of us would call Bostonian. Emerson, Thoreau, Channing, and Alcott dispersed a fragrance that attracted at once, and all they said was resonant with charity and courage.

The first flash of individuality from Emerson could hardly fail to suggest that he resembled the American eagle; and he presided over Concord in a way not unlike our glorious symbol, the Friend of Light. It must have been exhilarating to look forward to many years in Emerson's hamlet. My earliest remembered glimpse of him was when he appeared — tall, side-slanting, peering with almost undue questioning into my face, but with a smile so constant as to seem like an added feature, dressed in a solemn, slender, dark overcoat, and a dark, shadowing hat — upon the Concord highroad; the same yellow thoroughfare which reaches out to Lexington its papyrus-strip of history. At the onset of Emerson — for psychic men do attack one with their superiority — awe took possession of me; and, as we passed (a great force and a small girl) I wondered if I should survive. I not only did so, but felt better than before. It then became one of my happiest experiences to pass Emerson upon the street. A distinct exaltation followed my glance into his splendid face. Yet I caviled at his self-consciousness, his perpetual smile. I complained that he ought to wait for something to smile at. I could not be sure that he was privately enjoying some joke from Greek fun-makers, remembered under a Concord elm. After a time, I realized that he always had something to smile *for*, if not to smile *at;* and that a cheerful countenance is heroic. By and by I learned that he always could find something to smile at, also; for he tells us, "The best of all jokes is the sympathetic contemplation of things by the understanding, from the philosopher's point of view." But, in my unenlightened state, when I saw him begin to answer some question, however

trivial, with this smile, slowly, very slowly growing, until it lit up his whole countenance with
a refulgent beam before he answered (the whole
performance dominated by a deliberation as great
and brilliant as the dawn), I argued that this good
cheer was out of proportion ; that Emerson should
keep back a smile so striking and circumstantial
for rare occasions, such as enormous surprise ; or,
he should make it the precursor to a tremendous
roar of laughter. I have yet to learn that any
one heard him laugh aloud, — which pastime he
has called, with certainly a familiar precision that
indicates personal experience, a " pleasant spasm,"
a " muscular irritation."

In maturer years I believed that his smile
brought refreshment, encouragement, and waves
of virtue to those who saw it. To be sure, it was
a sort of questioning ; sometimes even quizzical ;
sometimes only a safeguard ; but it was eminently
kind, and no one else could do it. His manner was patronizing, in spite of its suavity ; but it
grew finer every spring, until it had become as
exquisitely courteous as Sir Philip Sidney's must
have been. The arch of his dark eyebrows sometimes seemed almost angry, being quickly lifted,
and then bent in a scowl of earnestness ; but as
age advanced this sternness of brow grew to
be, unchangeably, a calm sweep of infinite kindness.

It was never so well understood at The Wayside
that its owner had retiring habits as when Alcott
was reported to be approaching along the Larch

Path, which stretched in feathery bowers between
our house and his. Yet I was not aware that the
seer failed at any hour to gain admittance, — one
cause, perhaps, of the awe in which his visits were
held. I remember that my observation was attracted to him curiously from the fact that my
mother's eyes changed to a darker gray at his
advents, as they did only when she was silently
sacrificing herself. I clearly understood that Mr.
Alcott was admirable; but he sometimes brought
manuscript poetry with him, the dear child of his
own Muse, and a guest more unwelcome than the
enfant terrible of the drawing-room. There was
one particularly long poem which he had read aloud
to my mother and father; a seemingly harmless
thing, from which they never recovered. Out of the
mentions made of this effusion I gathered that it
was like a moonlit expanse, quiet, somnolent, cool,
and flat as a month of prairies. Rapture, convic-
tion, tenderness, often glowed upon Alcott's features and trembled in his voice. I believe he was
never once startled from the dream of illusive joy
which pictured to him all high aims as possible of
realization through talk. Often he was so happy
that he could have danced like a child; and he
laughed merrily like one; and the quick, upward
lift of his head, which his great height induced
him to hold, as a rule, slightly bent forward, — this
rapid, playful *lift*, and the glance, bright and eager
though not deep, which sparkled upon you, were
sweet and good to see. Yet I have noticed his
condition as pale and dolorous enough, before the

event of his noble daughter's splendid success. But such was not his character; circumstances had enslaved him, and he appeared thin and forlorn by incongruous accident, like a lamb in chains. He might have been taken for a centenarian when I beheld him one day slowly and pathetically constructing a pretty rustic fence before his gabled brown house, as if at the unreasonable command of some latter-day Pharaoh. Ten years afterward he was, on the contrary, a Titan : gay, silvery-locked, elegant, ready to begin his life over again.

Alcott represented to me a fairy element in the up-country region in which I so often saw him. I heard that he walked the woods for the purpose of finding odd coils of tree-roots and branches, which would on the instant suggest to him an ingenious use in his art of rustic building. It was rumored that nobody's outlying curios in this line were safe under his eye, and that if you possessed an eccentric tree for a time, it was fated to close its existence in the keeping of Alcott. I imagined his slightly stooping, yet tall and well-grown figure, clothed in black, and with a picturesque straw hat, twining itself in and out of forest aisles, or craftily returning home with gargoyle-like stems over his shoulders. The magic of his pursuit was emphasized by the notorious fact that his handiwork fell together in the middle, faded like shadows from bronze to hoary pallor ; its longevity was a protracted death. In short, his arbors broke under the weight of a purpose, as poems become

doggerel in the service of a theorist. Truly, Alcott
was completely at the beck of illusion; and he
was always safer alone with it than near the hard
uses of adverse reality. I well remember my as-
tonishment when I was told that he had set forth
to go into the jaws of the Rebellion after Louisa,
his daughter, who had succumbed to typhus fever
while nursing the soldiers. His object was to
bring her home; but it was difficult to believe that
he would be successful in entering the field of
misery and uproar. I never expected to see him
again. Almost the only point at which he nor-
mally met this world was in his worship of apple-
trees. Here, in his orchard, he was an all-admi-
rable human being and lovely to observe. As
he looked upon the undulating arms or piled the
excellent apples, red and russet, which seemed to
shine at his glance, his figure became supple, his
countenance beamed with a ruby and gold akin to
the fruit. In his orchard by the highroad, with
its trees rising to a great height from a basin-
shaped side lawn (which may originally have been
marshy ground), he seemed to me a perfect soul.
We all enjoyed greatly seeing him there, as we
wended to and from our little town. No doubt
the garden of children at the beginning of his
career inspired him likewise; and in it he must
have shown the same tender solicitude and benevolence, and beamed upon his young scholars with
a love which exquisitely tempered his fantastical
suppositions.

He often spoke humbly, but he never let peo-

ple think he was humble. His foibles appeared
to me ridiculous, and provoked me exceedingly, —
the brave cat of the proverb must be my excuse,
— but I awakened to the eternal verity that some
such husks are rather natural to persons of purely
distinctive minds, perhaps shielding them. And
I think one comes to value a bent blessed with
earnest unconsciousness; a not too clever Argus
vision; a childlike gullibility and spontaneity.
This untarnished gullibility and gentle confidence,
for all his self-laudations, Alcott had, and when
he did not emerge either from his apple orchard or
his inspirations he was essentially wholesome, full
of an ardent simplicity, and a happy faith in the
capacities given him by his Creator. So that his
outline is one of much dignity, in spite of the
somewhat capricious coloring of his character; the
latter being not unlike the efforts of a nursery
artist upon a print of "The Father of His Country," for whom, as he stands proudly upon the
page, a green coat and purple pantaloons were
not intended, and are only minor incidents of
destiny.

Mr. Ellery Channing was, I am sure, the towns-
man who was most gladly welcome. My parents
felt great admiration and friendliness for him,
and it would be a sacrifice on my own part not
to mention this companion of theirs, although I
must beg his pardon for doing so. There is no
doubt that Concord would have hung with several
added pounds of weight upon our imaginations
if it had not been for him. Over his tender-heart-

edness, as I saw him in the old days, played delicious eccentricities, phosphorescent, fitful, touch-
me-not antics of feeling. I was glad to meet the
long glance of his gray, dazzling eyes, lowered
gracefully at last. The gaze seemed to pass
through me to the wall, and beyond even that
barrier to the sky at the horizon line. It did not
disturb me; it had been too kindly to criticise,
or so I thought. No doubt Mr. Channing had
made his little regretful, uncomplimentary notes
in passing, but it was characteristic of his exquisite comradeship towards all that we did not fear
his eyes. I say comradeship, although the power
which I believed touched him with its wand
so mischievously had induced him to drop (as
a boy loses successively all his marbles) all his
devoted friends, without a word of explanation,
because without a shadow of reason; the only
thing to be said about it being that the loss was
entirely voluntary on the part of this charming
boy. He would cease to bow, as he passed. Then
he found the marbles again, pocketed them as if
nothing had happened, smiled, called, and hob-
nobbed. A man's high-water mark is his calibre;
and at high-water mark Mr. Channing's sea was
to us buoyant, rich-tinted, sunlit; a great force,
darkening and dazzling with beautiful emotions.
He was in those days devoted to the outer air, and
to the wonders of the nature we do not often
understand, even when we trap it and classify it.
He always invited his favorites to walk with him,
and I once had the honor of climbing a very high

hill by his side, in time to look at a Concord sunset, which I myself realized was the finest in the world.

Another peculiar spirit now and then haunted us, usually sad as a pine-tree — Thoreau. His enormous eyes, tame with religious intellect and wild with the loose rein, making a steady flash in this strange unison of forces, frightened me dreadfully at first. The unanswerable argument which he unwittingly made to soften my heart towards him was to fall desperately ill. During his long illness my mother lent him our sweet old music-box, to which she had danced as it warbled at the Old Manse, in the first year of her marriage, and which now softly dreamed forth its tunes in a time-mellowed tone. When he died, it seemed as if an anemone, more lovely than any other, had been carried from the borders of a wood into its silent depths, and dropped, in solitude and shadow, among the recluse ferns and mosses which are so seldom disturbed by passing feet. Son of freedom and opportunity that he was, he touched the heart by going to nature's peacefulness like the saints, and girding upon his American sovereignty the hair-shirt of service to self-denial. He was happy in his intense discipline of the flesh, as all men are when they have once tasted power — if it is the power which awakens perception of the highest concerns. His countenance had an April pensiveness about it; you would never have guessed that he could write of owls so jocosely. His manner was such as to suggest that he could mope and weep *with* them. I never crossed an airy hill or broad field in Concord, without thinking of him who had been the companion of space as well as of delicacy; the lover of the wood-thrush, as well as of the Indian. Walden woods rustled the name of Thoreau whenever we walked in them.

When we drove from the station to The Wayside, in arriving from Europe, on a hot summer day, I distinctly remember the ugliness of the un-English landscape and the forlornness of the little cottage which was to be our home. Melancholy and stupid days immediately followed (at least they were so in my estimation). I marveled at the amount of sand in the flower-borders and at the horrifying delinquencies of our single servant.

For some years I was eager to use all the eloquence I could muster in my epistles to girl friends, in England or anywhere, as to the paucity of life in Concord. Perhaps the following extracts from two letters, one written at Bath, England, and the other at Concord, and never sent, but kept by my mother from the flames with many more of my expressions in correspondence, may convey the feelings of the whole family : —

31 CHARLES STREET, BATH, ENGLAND.

DEAR HANNAH [Redcar Hannah], — When I go home I think that I shall never have such a nice time as when I go home; for I shall have such a big garden, and I shall have little and big girls to come and see me. Never on earth shall I have such a nice time as when I am at home.

After the transition : —

CONCORD, MASS.

I am in Concord now, and long to see you again, but I suppose that it is useless to think of it. I am going out, after I have done my lessons, to have a good time. — A very good time indeed, to be sure, for there was nothing but frozen ground, and I had to be doing something to keep myself warm, and I had to come back after a little while. I do not know how to keep myself warm. Happy are you who keep warm all the time in England. The frost has made thick leaves on our windows everywhere, and you can hardly see through them.

I tried to bring the stimulus of great events into the Concord life by writing stories, of which I would report the progress to my one or two confidantes. My father overheard some vainglorious boasts from my lips, one afternoon, when the windows of the little library where he sat were open ; and the small girl who listened to me, wide-eyed, and I myself, proud and glad to have reached a thrilling dénouement, were standing beside the sweet-clover bed, not dreaming of anything more severe than its white bloom. A few minutes afterwards, my father hung over me, dark as a prophetic flight of birds. " Never let me hear of your writing stories ! " he exclaimed, with as near an approach to anger as I had ever seen in him. "I forbid you to write them!" But I believe this command only added a new attraction to authorship, agreeably haunting me as I beckoned imaginary scenes and souls out of chaos.

An oasis bloomed at remote seasons, when we went to visit Mr. and Mrs. Fields in Boston. My mother writes of my reviving, and even becoming radiant, as soon as a visit of this fragrant nature breathed upon me. I joyously begin a letter of my mother's with the following greeting: "*As soon as we got to Boston. My dear, dear Papa. We will write to you very promptly indeed. We have got here safely, and are also very glad to get here. We had some rich cake and sherry as soon as we got here. —* [My mother proceeds:] Annie glided in upon us, looking excellently lovely. Heart's-Ease [Mr. Fields] appeared just before dinner. He declares that the 'Consular Experiences' is superb. — I write in the deep green shade of this wood of a library. We all went to church through the hot sunshine. Mr. Fields walked on the sunny side, and when Mrs. Fields [Mrs. Meadows was the playful name by which we called her] asked him why, he said, 'Because it makes us grow so. Oh, I am growing so fast I can scarcely get along!' Mr. Fields said it made him very sleepy to go to church, and he thought it was because of the deacons. — He says the world is wild with rapture over your 'Leamington Spa.' He did not know how to express his appreciation of it. — We met Mr. Tom Appleton at the gallery, and he was very edifying. There is a good portrait by Hunt. Mr. Appleton called it 'big art,' which took my fancy, it being so refreshing after hearing so much said about 'high art.' There is a portrait of Hunt by himself, which has a line about the brow that is Michelangelic; 'the bars of Michelangelo.' A head of Fremont was handsome, but showing a man incapable of large combinations. He looks eagle-like and loyal and brilliant, but not wise. We felt quite glorious with the war news, and were surprised to see so few flags flying. To breakfast we had Mr. Dysie. It was pleasant to hear his English brogue — a slight excess of Henry Bright's Lancashire accent. To tea we had Mr. and Mrs. Bartol, and Mr. Fields was so infinitely witty that we all died at the tea-table. Mr. Bartol, in gasps, assured him that he had contrived a way to save the food by keeping us in convulsions during the ceremony of eating, and killing us off at the end. Annie had on a scarlet coronet that made her look enchanting, and Mr. Fields declared she was Moses in the burning bush. Oh, do delay the acacia blossoms till I come! Give a sky full of love to Una and Julian."

My father also tasted the piquant flavors of merriment and luxury in this exquisite domicile of Heart's-Ease and Mrs. Meadows.

And at The Wayside, too, we had delightful pleasures, in the teeth and front of simplicity and seclusion, sandy flower-borders, rioting weeds, and intense heats. Concord itself could gleam occa-

sionally, even outside of its perfect Junes and Octo-
bers, as we can see here in the merry geniality of
Lousia Alcott, who no more failed to make people
laugh than she failed to live one of the bravest
and best of lives. In return for a package of
birthday gifts she sent us a poem, from which I
take these verses : —

> " The Hawthorne is a gracious tree
> From latest twig to parent root,
> For when all others leafless stand
> It gayly blossoms and bears fruit.
> On certain days a friendly wind
> Wafts from its spreading boughs a store
> Of canny gifts that flutter in
> Like snowflakes at a neighbor's door.

> " The spinster who has just been blessed
> Finds solemn thirty much improved,
> By proofs that such a crabbed soul
> Is still remembered and beloved.
> Kind wishes ' ancient Lu ' has stored
> In the ' best chamber ' of her heart,
> And every gift on Fancy's stage
> Already plays its little part.
> . . . .

> " Long may it stand, the friendly tree,
> That blooms in autumn and in spring,
> Beneath whose shade the humblest bird
> May safely sit, may gratefully sing.
> Time will give it an evergreen name,
> Axe cannot harm it, frost cannot kill ;
> With Emerson's pine and Thoreau's oak
> Will the Hawthorne be loved and honored still ! "

My mother's records, moreover, in letters to her
husband, refer to the humble labors that almost
filled up her devoted year (her daughters tried to
imitate her example), and these references indi-

425

cate the difference we felt between Europe and
home : —

Rose raised all the echoes of the county by
screaming with joy over her blooming crocuses,
which she found in her garden. The spring intox-
icates her with "remembering wine." She hugs
and kisses me almost to a mummy, with her raptures. Little spots of green grass choke her with
unutterable ecstasy.

September 9, 1860. Julian illuminated till tea-
time ; and after tea I read to both him and Rose
a chapter of Matthew, and told them about Paul.
— Rosebud has been drawing wonderfully on the
blackboard recognizable portraits of Mr. Bennoch,
her beloved Charlotte Marston, and Julian. Ben
Mann appeared with a letter from dear Nona
[Una] ; and with one from Bentley, England, modestly asking of thee a book, to publish ! — The
weeds in the garden now exceed belief. There is
not a trace to be seen of the melon or cucumber
vines, or squashes, or of the beans towards the
lane. All are completely overtopped by gigantic
plants, like the Anakins overrunning the Israel-
ites. Such riot of uninvited guests I never imagined. I shall try to do something, but I fear
my puny might will not effect much against such
hordes. The wet and heat together produce such
growths as I never saw except in Cuba. There
is a real forest at the back door, between the
house and the terraces. The greenness is truly
English and Irish. — I picked forty ears of corn

to-day. — We all met at the Alcotts' at tea-time.
It was a clear, frosty air that bit me as I went in
through the sunset. We had a delightful visit.
Mr. Alcott was sweet and benign as possible, and
Mrs. Alcott looked like Jupiter Olympus. — General Hitchcock has been gone about an hour.
Baby had got me some exquisite roses from Mr.
Bull's, of various shades from deep crimson to
light pink, and I arranged a flat glass dish full on
the Roman mosaic table, and a tall glass on the
white marble table, and a glass on the Hawthorne
tea-table, while the illuminated crocus [a vase]
was splendid with dahlias and tiger-lilies beneath
the Transfiguration. So the drawing-room looked
lovelily, and a fine rose-odor was diffused. All the
blinds were open and the shades up, and a glory
of greenness refreshed the eyes outside on the
plumy, bowery hill and lawn. In this charming
apartment I received my General. The most
beautiful light of life beamed from his face at
my recognition of his ideas, and at any expression
of mine which showed a unity with his ; or rather
with truth. His quiet eyes have gathered innumerable harvests, and his observations are invaluable because impersonal. [He had made a study
of the alchemists, and all mystical philosophy.] —
Elizabeth Hoar spent the whole of yesterday morning with me. We talked Roman and Florentine
talk. She thought our house the most fascinating
of mansions. She is always full of St. Paul's charity. On the Roman table was a glass dish of
exquisite pond-lilies, which Una brought from the

river this morning ; and out of the centre of the lilies rose a tall glass of superb cardinal-flowers. On the white table was a glass dish of balsams of every shade of red, from deep crimson through scarlet to pale pink, over to purple and up to white. — Una returned to-day from Boston. She has had a nice visit, and seen many persons, all of whom expressed to her unbounded adoration of you. "Why mamma, how everybody loves, *adores* him!" said she. Of course. — I had a call from the dancing-master, a most debonair individual, all smile and bow and curvets. I wish you could have seen the man. It was the broad caricature of elegant manners. How funny things are! I can hear you say, "Natur' is cur'ous." — I looked in upon Edith Emerson's party, and she had a large table spread with flowers, cake, and sugar-plums, beneath the trees, and a dozen children were running and laughing round a "pretty Poll," who scolded at them all. Mrs. Emerson was flitting like the spirit of a Lady Abbess in and out, in winged lace headdress and black silk. Your letter was a bomb of joy to me last evening. — I have taken heaps of your clothes to mend. What a rag-fair your closet was — and you did not tell me! Mrs. Alcott brought me some beer made of spruce only, and it was nice. Thou shalt have thy own beer, when you come home. — Bab went to see Mrs. Alcott, and I resumed weeding. At seven I heard thirteen cannon-shots, and did not understand it. Then I possessed The Wayside all alone till near eight of the evening. Not a sound but birds' last notes was to be heard. It was strange and sweet. I thought of you in a sea-breeze with felicity. At about eight I heard little feet racing along the Larch Path, and Baby came to view. She read aloud to me some of your "Virtuoso's Collection," and then to bed, celestial. — A letter came from Mr. Bennoch. He wails like Jeremiah over our war, and longs for a letter from you. He sends *cartes de visite* of himself and his wife. He looks uncommonly dumpy, with a pair of winged whiskers of astounding effect, and the expression of his face is blandly seraphic.

[From my mother's diary.] *January* 1, 1862. Letter and wine from General Pierce. I heard Mr. Emerson's lecture on War. Furious wind. — There is a lovely new moon ; a golden boat. — Papa read "The Heart of Mid-Lothian" aloud in the evening. — I wish I knew whether the lines of my hand are like those of Sir Thomas Browne's. — My husband has made an anagram of my name : "A hope while in a storm, aha !" — General Pierce arrived at noon. I went to the Town Hall to hear the Quintette Club play the Fifth Symphony of Beethoven. Mrs. Alcott came with us. Bright moonlight at midnight. General Pierce remained all night. — My husband made an ana-gram of the General's name, "Princelie Frank." — My husband read aloud to me "Sir Launcelot Greaves." Papa read "Anne of Geierstein." — I prepared Julian for acting Bluebeard ; and Ellen Emerson lent me the gear. We worked hard all day. — We received the photographs of Una and myself. Mine of course uncomely. — Mr. Ticknor came to dine; and Mr. Burchmore [son of Stephen Burchmore, whose tales at the Custom House were so inimitable] also came. — My husband is not well. I have been very anxious about him; but he is better this evening, thank God. — My right hand is so bad that I have to bathe it in arnica all the time, for I have worn it out by making shoes [and other ornamented articles for a masquerade to which her children were to go].

[The letters to my father continue.] Ellen and Edith Emerson took tea with Una, and they went home early, at about eight. At ten I heard a man's step and a ring at the door-bell. I went to the door, and not opening it, in a voice of command asked, *"Who is it?"* No reply. I again fiercely inquired, "WHO IS IT?" "Is Ellen here?" pleaded the surprised, quiet voice of Mr. Emerson! I immediately unlocked my portcullis, and in the lowest tone of woman begged the Sage to excuse my peremptory challenge. — The Masquerade was worth the great trouble taken in preparing for it. Una was quite gorgeous with her glittering embroideries of silver and gold, and her exquisite turban gleaming with precious stones and pearls. The most delicate roses bloomed in her cheeks, and her eyes were like two large radiant stars. She danced with Sir Kenneth of Scotland, personated admirably by Edward Emerson, in armor of black and gold, severe and simple. — [My sis-

ter adds her own delighted reference to my mother's.] " Oh, father ! I did have the most awfully
jolly time at the Masquerade that ever anybody
had. It was the most perfectly Arabian Nights'
scene, and the Princess Scheherezade [herself] at
last saw in very fact one of the scenes that her
glowing fancy had painted ; but being now freed
from the fear of death, her mind had lost its terrific stimulus and returned to its normal condition,
or perhaps was a little duller than usual from being so long overtaxed ; at all events, she did not
compose a new story on the occasion, as might
have been expected. A great many people spoke
to me of the splendor of my dress. Mamma was
so delighted with the becomingness of my black
velvet jacket, that she has bought me a splendid
dress of the same, and has sent for a bushel of
seed-pearls to trim it with. The little bill for
these items is awaiting you on your desk. I shall
set up for a queen for the rest of my life, and if
you are still going to call me Onion, you must
find out the Persian for it."

[The diary resumes.] My husband read to me
his paper on his visit to Washington. Dr. George
B. Loring and Mr. Pike [of Salem] came to tea
in the evening. Mr. Thoreau died this morning.
— The funeral services were in the church. Mr.
Emerson spoke. Mr. Alcott read from Mr. Thoreau's writings. The body was in the vestibule,
covered with wildflowers. We went to the grave.
Thence my husband and I walked to the Old

Manse and Monument. Then I went to see
Annie Fields at Mr. Emerson's. — Fog and sul-
try. Brobdingnag dropping from eaves. — Superb
morning. My husband transplanted sunflowers
[of which he was immensely fond, though lilies-
of-the-valley were his favorites]. — My husband
and Julian went to Boston; and Julian walked
home in eight and a half hours [twenty miles]. —
Una's party took place to-night. Papa illuminated
it with his presence. — Pleasant day. Papa mag-
nanimously picked some strawberries. — I went
on the hilltop with my husband all the morning
[of a Sunday in June]. — Our wedding-day. It
is very hot and smoky. We think it the smokes
of battles. — Very warm and fine. Mr. Alcott
worked all day, lacking three hours [in constructing a rustic seat at the foot of our hill]. I went
on the hilltop with my husband for a long time.
Ineffable felicity. — A perfectly lovely day. I
read "Christ the Spirit." Rose had a discourse
from the Sermon on the Mount; the four verses
about giving alms. We have very nice discourses
[my mother's]. Una went to church. — Mr.
George Bradford came to see us. Una and Julian
went to the Emersons' in the evening. — Read
again "Leamington Spa." Inimitable, fascinating. — Thanksgiving Day. We invited Ellery
Channing, but he could not come. — Julian and I
went to Boston. When I came home I found
my husband looking very ill. Julian has gone
on a visit to the Fields's. — My husband quite ill.
Everything seems sad, when he is ill. I sewed

all day. — My husband seems much better. He
went up on the hill. Papa and the children played
whist in the evening, while I read Charles Reade.
— Celia cleared the old attic to-day. I found my
dear hanging astral, that lighted my husband in
his study at the Old Manse, and also Una's baby
socks. — Judge Hoar came to invite my husband
to tea with Mr. Eustis and Mr. Bemis and Mr.
Emerson. He would not go. — I read ominous
news of the war, which quite saddened and
alarmed me. I read "Christ the Spirit." — I read
about Alchemy and Swedenborg. Ellery Channing came to tea and spent the evening. He
asked me if he might bring General Barlow to
tea on Tuesday.

It was almost immediately after our return home
that the first notes of the requiem about to en-
velop us fell through the sound of daily affairs,
at long intervals, because my father, from that
year, began to grow less and less vigorous.

There are many references in my mother's diaries and letters to my father's enforced monotony,
and also to his gradually failing health, which, by
the very instinct of loving alarm, we none of us
analyzed as fatal; though, from his expression of
face, if for no other reason, I judge he himself
understood it perfectly. Death sat with him, at
his right hand, long before he allowed his physical decline to change his mode of life. He tried
to stem the tide setting against him, because it is
the drowning man's part, even if hopeless. He

walked a great deal upon the high hill-ridge behind the house, his dark, quietly moving figure
passing slowly across the dim light of the mingled sky and branches, as seen from the large
lawn, around which the embowered terraces rose
like an amphitheatre. A friend tells me that,
from a neighboring farm, he sometimes watched
my father in an occupation which he had undertaken for his health. A cord of wood had been
cut upon the hill, and he deliberately dragged it
to the lower level of his dwelling, two logs at a
time, by means of a rope. Along the ridge and
down the winding pine-flanked path he slowly and
studiously stepped, musing, looking up, stopping
to solve some point of plot or morals ; and meanwhile the cord of wood changed its abiding-place
as surely as water may wear away a stone. But
his splendid vigor paled, his hair grew snowy
white, before the end. My mother wrote to him
in the following manner from time to time, when
he was away for change of scene : —

September 9, 1860. My crown of glory. This
morning I waked to clouds and rain, but for myself I did not care, as you were not here to be
depressed by it. There was a clear and golden
sunset, making the loveliest shadows and lights
on the meadows and across my straight path [over
the field to the willows, between firs], and now
the stars shine. — The way in which Concordians
observe Fast is by loafing about the streets, driving up and down, and dawdling generally. No

one seems to mourn over his own or his country's
sins. Such behavior must disturb our Puritan
fathers even on the other side of the Jordan. — In
the evening Julian brought me a letter. "It is
from New York," said he, "but not from papa."
But my heart knew better, though I did not know
the handwriting. I dashed it open, and saw "N.
H.," and then, "I am entirely well," not scratched
out. Thank God! . . . The sun has not shone
to-day, and there is now a stormy wind that howls
like a beast of prey over its dead. It is the most
ominous, boding sound I ever heard.

March 15, 1862. The news of your appetite
sends new life into me, and immediately increases
my own.

July. I am afraid you have been in frightful
despair at this rainy day. It has flooded here in
sheets, with heavy thunder. But I have snatched
intervals to weed. I could see and hear everything growing around me in the warm rain. The
army corn has hopped up as if it were parched.
The yellow lilies are reeling up to the skies. Pig-
weed has become camelopard weed. . . . Alas
that you should be insulted with dried-apple pie
and molasses preserves! Oh, horror! I thought
that you would have fresh fruit and vegetables.
Pray go to a civilized house and have decent fare.
— I know it will do you immense good to make
this journey. You should oftener make such visits,
and then you would "like things" better. Your
spirits get below concert pitch by staying in one
place so long at a time. I am glad Leutze keeps

you on [to paint Hawthorne's portrait]. Do not
come home till the middle of September. Just
remember how hot and dead it is here in hot
weather, and how you cannot bear it. — I do not
think I have a purer pleasure and completer satisfaction, nowadays, than I am conscious of when I
get you fairly away from Concord influences. I
then sit down and feel rested through my whole
constitution. All care seems at an end. I would
not have had you here yesterday for all England.
It was red-hot from morn to dewy eve. We burned
without motion or sound. But you were in Boston, and not under this hill. If you wish me to
be happy, you must· consent to spend the dog-
days at the sea. — After a cool morning followed
a red-hot day. It seemed to me more intolerable
than any before. You could not have borne such
dead weather. The house was a refrigerator in
comparison to the outdoor atmosphere. — We
have had some intolerably muggy days. That
is, they would have been so, if you had not been
at the sea. — You have been far too long in one
place without change, and I am sure you will get
benefit under such pleasant conditions as being
the guest of Mr. and Mrs. [Horatio] Bridge, and
a witness of such new phases of life as those in
Washington. — Splendors upon splendors have
been heaped into this day. Loads of silky plumed
corn or even sheaves of cardinal-flowers cannot
be compared to the new sunshine and the magnificent air which have filled the earth from early
dawn. The brook that became a broad river in

the flood of yesterday made our landscape perfect.
It seemed to me that I must dance and sing, and
now I know it was because you were writing to
me. Rose and I went down the straight path
[called later the Cathedral Aisle] to look at the
fresh river. I delayed to be embroidered with
gold sun over and over, and through and through.
At the gate I was arrested by the tower, also
illustrious with the glory of the atmosphere, and
very pretty indeed, lifting its nice, shapely head
above the decrepit old ridge-pole of the ancient
house. — I took my saw and went on a lovely
wander, with a fell intent against all dead and
confusing branches. How infinitely sweet it is
to have access to this woodland virtue ! It does
me measureless good ; and I am sure such air
as we have on these fine days must be the effect
of heroic and gentle deeds, and is a pledge that
there are not tens only, but tens of thousands of
heroes on this earth, keeping it in life and being.
— Your letter has kindled us all up into lamps
of light to-day. But I am wholly dissatisfied with
your boarding-house, so full of deaf women, and
violin din, and schoolgirls ! Pray change your
residence and have peace. You will curse your
stars if you have to " bellow " for three weeks,
when you so hate to speak even in your natural
inward tone. — Mary has just sent me a note,
saying that there is a paragraph in the paper
about your being at Washington, and that the
President [Lincoln] received you with especial
graciousness. Stay as long as you can, and get

great good. I cannot have you return yet. — The President has had a delicious palaver with a deputation of black folk, talking to them as to babies. I suspect the President is a jewel. I like him very well. — If it were not such a bore, I could wish thou mightest be President through this crisis, and show the world what can be done by using two eyes, and turning each thing upside down and inside out, before judging and acting. I should not wonder if thy great presence in Washington might affect the moral air and work good. If you like the President, then give him my love and blessing. — The President's· immortal special message fills me with unbounded satisfaction. It is so almost superhumanly wise, moderate, fitting, that I am ready to believe an angel came straight from heaven to him with it. He must be honest and true, or an angel would not come to him. Mary Mann says she thinks the message feeble, and not to the point. But I think a man shows strength when he can be moderate at such a moment as this. Thou hadst better give my high regards to the President. I meant to write to him ; but that mood has passed. I wish to express my obligations for the wisdom of his message.

CHAPTER XV

THE ARTIST AT WORK

I was once asked to write of my father's "literary methods," and the idea struck me as delightfully impossible. I wish I knew just what those methods were — I might hope to write a romance. But as the bird on the tree-bough catches here and there a glimpse of what men are about, although he hardly aspires to plough the field himself, or benefit by human labor until the harvest comes, so I have observed some facts and gathered some notions as to how my father thought out his literary work.

One method of obtaining his end was to devote himself *constantly* to writing, whether it brought him money or not. He might not have seemed to be working all the time, but to be enjoying endless leisure in walking through the country or the city streets. But even a bird would have had more penetration than to make such a mistake as to think this. Another wise provision was to love and pity mankind more than he scorned them, so that he never created a character which did not possess a soul — the only puppet he ever contrived of straw, "Feathertop," having an excellent soul until the end of the story. Still another method of gaining his success was to write with a noble respect for his own best effort, on which account he never felt satisfied with his writing unless he had exerted every muscle of his faculty; unless every word he had written seemed to his severest self-criticism absolutely true. He loved his art more than his time, more than his ease, and could thrust into the flames an armful of manuscript because he suspected the pages of weakness and exaggeration.

One of his methods of avoiding failure was to be rigorous in the care of his daily existence. A preponderance of frivolous interruption to a modicum of thorough labor at thinking was a system utterly foreign to him. He would not talk with a fool; as a usual thing he would not entertain a bore. If thrown with these common pests, he tried, I think, to study them. And they report that he did so very silently. But he did not waste his time, either by politely chattering with people whom he meant to sneer at after they had turned their backs, or in indulgences of loafing of all sorts which leave a narcotic stupidity in their wake. He had plenty of time, therefore, for thought, and he could think while walking either in the fresh air, or back and forth in his study. Men of success detest inactivity. It is a hardship for them to be as if dead for a single moment. So, when my father could not walk out of doors during meditation, he moved back and forth in his room, sturdily alert, his hands clasped behind him, quietly thinking, his head either bent forward or suddenly lifted upward with a light in his gray eyes.

He wrote principally in the morning, with that absorption and regularity which characterize the labor of men who are remembered. When his health began to show signs of giving way, in 1861, it was suggested by a relative, whose intellect, strength of will, and appetite for theories were of equally splendid proportions, that my father only needed a high desk at which to stand when writing, to be restored to all his pristine vigor. With his usual tolerance of possible wisdom he permitted such a desk to be arranged in the tower-study at The Wayside ; but with his inexorable contempt for mistakes of judgment he never, after a brief trial, used it for writing. Upon his simple desk of walnut wood, of which he had nothing to complain, although it barely served its purpose, like most of the inexpensive objects about him, was a charming Italian bronze ink-stand, over whose cover wrestled the infant Hercules in the act of strangling a goose — in friendly aid of "drivers of the quill." My father wrote with a gold pen, and I can hear now, as it seems, the rapid rolling of his chirography over the broad page, as he formed his small, rounded, but irregular letters, when filling his journals, in Italy. He leaned very much on his left arm while writing, often holding the top of the manuscript book lovingly with his left hand, quite in the attitude of a boy. At the end of a sentence or two he would sometimes unconsciously bow his head, as

441

if bidding good-by to a thought well rid of for the present in its new garb of ink.

In writing he had little care for paper and ink. To be sure, his large, square manuscript was firmly bound into covers, and the paper was usually of a neutral blue ; and when I say that he had little care for his mechanical materials I mean that he had no servile anxiety as to how they looked to another person, for I am convinced that he himself loved his manuscript books. There was a certain air of humorous respect about the titles, which he wrote with a flourish, as compared with the involved minuteness of the rest of the script, and the latter covers every limit of the page in a devoted way. His letters were formed obscurely, though most fascinatingly, and he was almost frolicsome in his indifference to the comfort of the compositor. Still he had none of the frantic reconsiderations of Scott or Balzac. If he made a change in a word it was while it was fresh, and no one could obliterate what he had written with a more fearless blot of the finger, or one which looked more earnest and interesting. There was no scratching nor quiddling in the manner with which he fought for his art. Each day he thought out the problems he had set himself before beginning to write, and if a word offended him, as he recorded the result, he thrust it back into chaos before the ink had dried. I think that the manuscript of " Dr. Grimshawe's Secret " is an exception, to some extent. There are many written self-communings and changes in it. My father was declining in health while it was being evolved. But yet, in "The Dolliver Romance," the last work of all in process of development, written while he was physically breaking down, we see the effect of will and heroic attempt. It is the most beautiful of his compositions, because his mind was greater at that time than ever, and because death could not frighten him, and in its very face he desired to complete the proof of his whole power, as the dying soldier rises to the greatest act of his life, having given his life-blood for his country's cause. Though the script of this manuscript is extremely difficult to read, the speculation had evidently been done before taking up the pen. I am not sure but that my father sometimes destroyed first drafts, of which his family knew nothing. Indeed, we have his own word for it that "he passed the day in writing stories and the night in burning them." Nevertheless, his tendency we know to have been that of thinking out his plots and scenes and characters, and transcribing them rapidly without further change.

Since he did not write anything wholly for the pleasure of creative writing, but had moral motives and perfect artistic harmony to consider, he could not have indulged in the spontaneous, passionate effusions which are the substance of so much other fiction. He was obliged to train his mind to reflection and judgment, and therefore he never tasted luxury of any kind. The mere enjoyment of historical settings in all their charm and richness, rehabilitated for their own sake or for worldly gain; and that of caricatures of the members of the human family, because they are so often so desperately funny ; the gloating over realistic pictures of life as it is found, because life as it is found is a more absorbing study than that of geology or chemistry ; the tasting of redundant scenes of love and intrigue, which flatter the reader like experiences of his own, — these excesses he was not willing to admit to his art, a magic that served his literary palate with still finer food. He wrote with temperateness, and in pitying love of human nature, in the instinctive hope of helping it to know and redeem itself. His quality was philosophy, his style forgiveness. And for this temperate and logical and laconic work — giving nothing to the world for its mere enjoyment, but going beyond all that to ennoble each reader by his perfect renunciation of artistic claptrap and artistic license — for this aim he needed a mental method that could entirely command itself, and, when necessary, weigh and gauge with the laborious fidelity of a coal-surveyor, before the account was rendered with pen and ink upon paper. When he brought within his art the personality of a human devil, he honored its humanity, and proved that the real devil is quite another thing. In fact, perhaps he would not have permitted the above epithet. In one of her letters my mother remarks, " I think no sort of man can be called a devil, unless it be a slanderer."

Though he dealt with romance he never gave

444

the advantage of an inch to the wiles of bizarre witchery, the grotesque masks of wanton caprice in imagination — those elements which exhibit the intoxication of talent. His terrors were those of our own hearts ; his playfulness had the merit of the sunlight. In short, he was artistically consecrated, guiding the forces he used with the reins of truth ; and he could do this unbrokenly because he governed his character by Christian fellowship. If he shrank from unnecessary interruptions, which jarred the harmony of his artistic life, he nevertheless met courteously any that were to him inevitable. Could he have written with the heart's blood of old Hepzibah if he had failed to put his own shoulder to the domestic wheel, on the plea that it was too deep in the slough of disaster to command his assistance ? He did not dread besmirching his hands with any affairs sent him by God.

"The heart knoweth its own bitterness, and a stranger intermeddleth not with its joy ; " and the joy and the bitterness of creative work are not intermeddled with as much as one might suppose by the outside weather of praise or noncomprehension, if the artist is great enough to keep his private self-respect. I am of the opinion that my father enjoyed his own indifference to his accomplished work, yet knew its value to the minutest ray of the diamond ; that he had sharply challenged the enchantment of his first conception, and heard the right watchword, yet recognized that no human conception can fathom the marvels of the superhuman. I believe that the men we admire most, in the small group of great minds, are sufficiently necromantic to look two ways at once — to appreciate and to condemn themselves. So my father heard himself praised with composure, and blamed his skill rejoicingly.

Some passages from a copy of an article in "The North British Review" of Edinburgh during 1851 were capable of filling a wife's heart with exultation, and my mother quotes: " 'The most striking features in these tales are the extraordinary skill and masterly care which are displayed in their composition. . . . It would be difficult to pick out a page which could be omitted without loss to the development of the narrative and the idea, which are always mutually illustrative to a degree not often attained in any species of modern art. . . . His language, though extraordinarily accurate, is always light and free. . . . We know of nothing equal to it, in its way [the portrayal of Dimmesdale], in the whole circle of English literature ; ' and much more in the same superlative vein."

But if my father could weigh his artistic success with the precision of a coal-heaver, who will ever be able to weigh and gauge the genius which carries methods and philosophies and aims into an atmosphere of wonderful power, where the sunlight and the color and the lightning and frowning clouds transfigure the familiar things of life in glorious haste and inspiration ? While following his rules and habits my father was constantly attended by the rapturous spirit of such a genius, transmuting swarming reality into a few symbolic types.

Another way in which he effected telling labor was to conserve his force in the matter of wrangling. He kept his temper. He was not without the fires of life, but he banked them. He did not permit disgust at others or at the adverse destiny of the moment to absorb his vitality, by throwing it off in long harangues of rage, long seasons of the sulks. There are no such good calculators as men of consummate genius. They dread the squandering of energy of an Edgar Allan Poe or of a boiling Walter Savage Landor. Temperateness implies the control of fierce elements; and in all management of volcanic power we perceive sweetness and beauty.

When my father handled sin, it became uncontaminating tragedy; when he handled vulgarity, as in "The Artist of the Beautiful," it became inevitable pathos; when he handled suspicion, as in "The Birthmark" and "Rappaccini's Daughter," it evolved devoted trust.

The frequent question as to whether Hawthorne drew from his family or friends in portraying human nature shows an unfamiliarity with literary art. Portraiture is not art, in literature, though a great artist includes it, if he chooses, in the category of his productions. To any one permeated by the atmosphere of art (though not quite of it) as I was, it seems strange that a truly artistic work should be thought to be an imitation of individual models. The distance of inspiration is the distance of a heavenly fair day, or of a night made luminous by mystery, giving a new quality and a new species of delight to facts about us. In reading the sympathetic merriment of the introduction to " The Scarlet Letter," and then the story itself, we perceive the difference between the charm of a Dutch-like realism and the thrill of imaginative creation, which uses material made incomprehensibly wonderful by God in order to make it comprehensibly wonderful to men. But, of course, the material thus transmuted by the distance of inspiration is only new and fine to men who have ears to hear and eyes to see. My father never imitated the men and women he met, nor man nor woman, and such conceptions of his way would bring us to a dense forest of mistake.

In the afternoon my father went, if practicable, into the open spaces of nature, or at least into the fresh air, to gather inspiration for his work. He had no better or stronger or more lavish aids than air and landscape, unless I except his cigar. He never, I think, smoked but one cigar a day, but it was of a quality to make up for this self-denial, and I am sure that he reserved his most puzzling literary involutions for the delicious half-hour of this dainty enjoyment.

In 1861 and thereafter he traversed, as has been said, the wooded hilltop behind his home, which was reached by various pretty climbing paths that crept under larches and pines, and scraggy, goat-like apple-trees. We could catch

448

sight of him going back and forth up there, with now and then a pale blue gleam of sky among the trees, against which his figure passed clear. Along this path, made by his own steps only, he thought out the tragedy of "Septimius Felton," who buried the young English officer at the foot of one of the large pines which my father saw at each return. At one end of the hilltop path was a thicket of birch and maple trees; and at the end towards the west and the village was the open brow of the hill, sloping rapidly to the Lexington Road, and overlooking meadows and distant wood-ranges, some of the cottages of humble folk, and the neighboring huge, owlet-haunted elms of Alcott's lawn. Along this path in spring huddled pale blue violets, of a blue that held sunlight, pure as his own eyes. Masses also of sweet-fern grew at the side of these abundant bordering violets, and spacious apartments of brown-floored pine groves flanked the sweet-fern, or receded a little before heaps of blackberry branches and simple flowers. My father's violets were the wonder of the year to us. We never saw so many of these broad, pale-petaled ones anywhere else, until the year of his death, when they greeted him with their celestial color as he was borne into Sleepy Hollow, as if in remembrance of his long companionship on The Wayside hill.

It is well with those who forget themselves in generous interest for the hopes, possibilities, and spiritual loftiness of human beings all over the world. Such men may remain poor, may never in life have the full praise of their fellows; but they could easily give testimony as to the delights of praise from God, — that which comes to our lips after little spiritual victories, like spring water on a hot day, and of which the workers in noble thought or adventure drink so deep. These representative men, if they cheer their fancy with fair thoughts of wide public approbation, choose the undying sort, that blooms like the edelweiss beyond the dust of sudden success. Hawthorne worked hard and nobly. Not even the mechanic who toils for his family all day, all week-days of the year, and never swears at wife or child, toils more nobly than this sensitive, warm-hearted, brave, recluse, much-seeing man. He teaches the spiritual greatness of the smallest fidelity, and the spiritual destruction in the most familiar temptations. The Butterfly which he describes floats everywhere through his pages, and it is broken wherever the heart of one of his characters breaks, for there sin has clutched its victim. It floats about us lovingly to attract our attention to higher things; and I am sure the radiant delicacy of the winged creature throbbed on a flower near David Swan, as he slept honestly through the perils of evil.

Every touch of inner meaning that he gives speaks of his affection, his desire to bring us accounts of what he has learned of God's benevolence, in his long walks on the thoroughfares and in the byways, and over the uncontaminated open country, of human hope. Poverty, trouble, sin, fraudulent begging, stupidity, conceit, — nothing forced him absolutely to turn away his observation of all these usual rebuffs to sympathy, if his inconvenience could be made another's gain. But he was firm with a manliness that was uncringing before insolence, and did not shrink from speaking home truths that pruned the injurious branches of the will ; yet he never could be insulting, because he had no selfish end. As a comrade he led to higher perceptions and moods. The men who chatted with him in the Salem Custom House, the Liverpool Consulate, and elsewhere, never forgot that he was the most inspiring man they had known. All this was work. The idle man, lazy in a drunken carouse, is in a world of his own. His sphere stretches out no connecting tendrils to the spheres of others ; he seems to us dead in spirit ; he will tell you he believes in no one's true friendship, and wishes for no companionship ; we do not know how to touch his heart, nor in what language to make him hear when we call, — he is in Mars. But the sentinel, still as marble, or moving like a well-adjusted machine that will not defy law — he stirs us by his energy, his laboring vigilance. His care for others would make him surrender his life at once. The trusted soldier has left selfishness and cowardice on the first tenting-ground, and works hard, though he stands statue-like. It is his business to be of use, and he is never useless. So with a great artist. He is brother to gentleman or churl. Hawthorne had not an atom of the poison of contempt. As I have said before, if he did not love stupidity, he forgave it.

He was fond of using his hands for work, too; and he had skill in whatever he did. His activity of this manual sort may be inferred from the fact that when a young man he gradually whittled away one of the leaves of his writing-table, while musing over his stories. He did not know, unpleasantly, that he was doing it. What fun he must have had! Think of the rich scenery of thought that spread about him, the people, the subtle motives, the eerie truths, the entrancing outlooks into divine beauty, that entertained him as his sharp blade carved and sliced his table, which gladly gave itself up to such destruction! When he was writing "The Scarlet Letter," as Julian's nurse Dora long delighted to tell, his wife with her dainty care in sewing was making the little boy a shirt of the finest linen, and was putting in one sleeve, while the other lay on the table. Dora saw Hawthorne, who was reading, lay down his book and take up something which he proceeded to cut into shreds with some small scissors that exactly suited him.

"Where can the little sleeve be which I finished, and wished to sew in here, my love?" said his blissful wife. Hawthorne (blissfully thinking of his novel) only half heard the question; but on the table was a heap of delicate linen shavings, and the new scissors testified over them.

His jack-knife was a never-ending source of pleasure, and he was seldom without the impulse, if a good opportunity offered, to subject a sapling to it for a whistle, or to make some other amusing trifle, or to cut a bit of licorice with a slow, sure movement that made the black lump most acceptable.

His mind was never in a stound. It was either observing, or using observations. Of course he lost his way while walking, and destroyed commonplace things while musing; and the world hung just so much the less heavily upon his moving pinions of thought.

His diligence of mind is reported of him at an early age. His sister, Ebie Hawthorne, gave me a bust of John Wesley, in clerical white bib, and of a countenance much resembling Alcott's, even to the long, white, waving hair. Its very aspect cried out, though never so mercifully, "My sermon is endless!"

Aunt Ebie, hunching her shoulders in mirthful appreciation, said, "Nathaniel always hated it!"

Why not? At four years of age he had already had enough of Wesley; and my aunt, with a rejoicing laugh, described how, not being able to induce his elders to act upon his abhorrence of the melancholy, tinted object, at last, in dead of winter, he filled it with water through a hole in the pedestal, which had revealed its hollowness. He then stood the bust upside down against the wall in a cold place, confidently awaiting the freezing of the water, in which event it was to be hoped that the puppet sermonizer would burst, like a pitcher under similar odds. But John Wesley never burst, to the disgust of a broader mind and the offended wonder of childish eyes.

CHAPTER XVI

THE LEAVE-TAKING

A FEW words from a letter of Emerson's to my mother, written after my father's death, will give a true impression of the friendship which existed strongly between the two lovers of their race, who, though they did not have time to meet often, may be said to have been together through oneness of aim : —

CONCORD, 11th July [1864].

DEAR MRS. HAWTHORNE, — Guests and visitors prevented me from writing you, last evening, to thank you for your note, and to say how much pleasure it gives me, that you find succor and refreshment in sources so pure and lofty. The very selection of his images proves Behman poet as well as saint, yet a saint first, and poet through sanctity. It is the true though severe test to put the Teacher to, — to try if his solitary lessons meet our case. And for these thoughts and experiences of which you speak, their very confines and approaches lift us out of the world. I have twice lately proposed to see you, and once was on my way, and unexpectedly prevented. I have had my own pain in the loss of your husband. He was always a mine of hope to me, and I promised myself a rich future in achieving at some

day, when we should both be less engaged to
tyrannical studies and habitudes, an unreserved
intercourse with him.   I thought I could well
wait his time and mine for what was so well worth
waiting.   And as he always appeared to me superior to his own performances, I counted this yet
untold force an insurance of a long life.   Though
sternly disappointed in the manner and working,
I do not hold the guarantee less real.   But I must
use an early hour to come and see you to say
more.

R. W. EMERSON.

If my father expected a full renewal of comradeship with American men of his own circle,
and even the deeper pleasure of such friendship
in a maturer prime alluded to by Emerson, circumstances sadly intervened.   The thunderstorm
of the war was not the only cause of his retiring
more into himself than he had done in Europe,
although he felt that sorrow heavily.   Or perhaps
I might say with greater correctness that when he
appeared, it was without the joyous air that he had
lately displayed in England, among his particular
friends, when his literary work was over for the
time being after the finishing of "Monte Beni."
I remember that he often attended the dinners
of the Saturday Club.   A bill of fare of one of
the banquets, but belonging to an early date,
1852, read: "Tremont House.   Paran Stevens,
Proprietor.   Dinner for Twelve Persons, at three
o'clock."   A superb *menu* follows, wherein can-

vas-back ducks and madeira testify to the satisfaction felt by the gentlemen whose names my
father penciled in the order in which they sat ;
Mr. Emerson, Mr. Clough, Mr. Ellery Channing,
Mr. Charles Sumner, Mr. Theodore Parker, Mr.
Longfellow, Mr. Lowell, Mr. Greenough, Mr.
Samuel Ward, and several others making the
shining list. His keen care for the health of his
forces induced him to hold back from visits even
to his best friends, if he were very deeply at
work, or paying more rapidly than usual from his
capital of physical strength, which had now begun
to sink. Lowell tried to fascinate him out of
seclusion, in the frisky letter given in " A Study
of Hawthorne ; " but very likely did not gain his
point, since Longfellow and others had infrequent
success in similar attempts.

I chanced to discover the impression my father
made upon Dr. Holmes, as we sat beside each
other at a dinner given by the Papyrus Club of
Boston more than fifteen years ago, on ladies'
night. That same evening I dashed down a
verbatim account of part of our conversation,
which I will insert here.

He passed his card over to my goblet, and took
mine. "That is the simplest way, is it not ?" he
asked.

" I was just going to introduce myself," said I.
Then Mrs. Elizabeth Stoddard sat down by me,
and I turned to speak with her.

In a moment Dr. Holmes held my card forward
again. " Now let me see ! " he said.

' And you don't know who I am, yet ? " I asked.

He smiled, gazed at the card through his eyeglasses, and leaned towards me hesitatingly. " And what *was* your name ? " he ventured.

" Rose Hawthorne."

He started, and beamed. " There ! I *thought* — but you understand how — if I had made a mistake — Could anything have been worse if you had *not* been ? I was looking, you know, for the resemblance. Some look I seemed to discover, but " —

" The complexion," I helped him by interrupting, " is entirely different."

He went on : " I was — no, I cannot say I was intimate with your father, as others may have been ; and yet a very delightful kind of intercourse existed between us. I did not see him often ; but when I did, I had no difficulty in making him converse with me. My intercourse with your mother was also of a very gratifying nature."

To this I earnestly replied respecting the admiration of my parents for him.

" I delighted in suggesting a train of thought to your father," Dr. Holmes ran on, in his exquisitely cultured way, and with the *esprit* which has surprised us all by its loveliness. " Perhaps he would not answer for some time. Sometimes it was a long while before the answer came, like an echo ; but it was sure to come. It was as if the high mountain range, you know ! — *The house-wall there* would have rapped out a speedy, babbling response at once ; but *the mountain !* — I

not long ago was visiting the Custom House at
Salem, the place in which your father discovered
those mysterious records that unfolded into 'The
Scarlet Letter.' Ah, how suddenly and easily
genius renders the spot rare and full of a great
and new virtue (however ordinary and bare in
reality) when *it* has looked and dwelt! A light
falls upon the place not of land or sea! How
much he did for Salem! Oh, the purple light,
the soft haze, that now rests upon our glaring
New England! He has *done* it, and it will never
be harsh country again. How perfectly he understood Salem!"

"Salem is certainly very remarkable," I responded.

"Yes, certainly so," he agreed. "Strange folk!
Salem had a type of itself in its very harbor. The
ship America, at Downer's wharf, grew old and
went to pieces in that one spot, through years.
Bit by bit it fell to atoms, but never ceded itself
to the new era. So with Salem, precisely. It is
the most delightful place to visit for this reason,
because it so carefully retains the spirit of the
past; and 'The House of the Seven Gables'!"
Dr. Holmes smiled, well knowing the intangibility
of that house.

Said I: "The people are rich in extraordinary
oddities. At every turn a stranger is astonished
by some intense characteristic. One feels strongly
its different atmosphere."

"And their very surroundings bear them out!"
Dr. Holmes cried, vivacious in movement and

glance as a boy. " Where else are the little door-yards that hold their glint of sunlight so tenaciously, like the still light of wine in a glass·? Year after year it is ever there, the golden square of precious sunbeams, held on the palm of the jealous garden-patch, as we would hold the vial of radiant wine in our hand ! *Do you know ?*" He so forcibly appealed to my ability to follow his thought that I seemed to know anything he wished. "I hope I shall not be doing wrong," he continued, — "I *hope* not, — in asking if you have any preference among your father's books ; supposing you read them, which I believe is by no means always the case with the children of authors."

" I am surprised by that remark. After the age of fifteen, when I read all my father's writings except 'The Scarlet Letter,' which I was told to reserve till I was eighteen, I did not study his books thoroughly till several years ago, in order to cherish the enjoyment of fresh effects, — except 'The Marble Faun,' which I think I prefer."

He answered : "I feel that 'The Scarlet Letter' is the greatest. It will be, it seems to me, the one upon which his future renown will rest."

I admitted that I also considered it the greatest.

In the above conversation I was entranced by what I have experienced often : the praise of my father's personality or work (in many cases by people who have never met him) is not only the courtesy that might be thought decorous towards a member of his family, or the bright zest of a student of literature, but also the glowing ardor of a creature feeling itself a part of him in spirit ; one who longs for the human sweetness of the grasp of his hand ; who longs to hear him speak, to meet his fellowship, but finds the limit reached in saying, at a distance of time and space, " I love him ! " I have lowered my eyes before the emotion to be observed in the faces of some of his readers who were trying to reach him through a spoken word of eagerness. Very few have seen him, but how glad I am to cross their paths ! Dr. Holmes's warmth of enthusiasm was so radiant that it could not be forgotten. It lit every word with the magic of the passion we feel for what is perfect, unique, and beyond our actual possession, now and forever.

Towards the last an unacknowledged fear took hold of my mother's consciousness, so that she gave every evidence of foretelling my father's death without once presenting the possibility to herself. This little note of mine, dated April 4, 1864, six weeks before he died, shows the truth : —

" I am so glad that you are getting on so well ; but for your own sake I think you had better stay somewhere till you get entirely well. Mamma thought from the last letter from Mr. Ticknor that you were not so well ; but Julian explained to her that, as Mr. Ticknor said in every line that you were better, he did not see how it could possibly be. I do not either."

461

From the first year of our return to America letters and visitors from abroad had interrupted the sense of utter quiet; and many friends called in amiable pilgrimage. But a week of monotony is immensely long, and a few hours of zest are provokingly short. Nature and seclusion are welcome when, at our option, we can bid them goodby. All England is refreshing with the nearness of London. In the rush of cares and interruptions which we suppose will kill the opportunity, while we half lose ourselves and our intellectual threads of speculation, the flowers of inspiration suddenly blow, the gems flash color. This is a pleasant, but not always an essential satisfaction; yet, in my father's case, I think his life suffered with peculiar severity from the sudden dashing aside of manly interests which he had already denied to himself, or which circumstances had denied to him, with the utmost persistence ever known in so perceptive a genius. He undoubtedly had a large store of *inherited* experiences to draw upon; he was richly endowed with these, and could sit and walk alone, year after year (except for occasional warm reunions with friends of the cleanest joviality), and feel the intercourse with the world, of his ancestors, stirring in his veins. He tells us that this was ghostly pastime; but it is an inheritance that makes a man well equipped and self-sustained, for all that. When too late, the great men about him realized that they had estimated his presence very cheaply, considering his worth. Should he frequently have sought them

out, and asked if they were inclined to spare a
chat to Hawthorne; or should they have insisted
upon strengthening their greatness from his inimi-
tably pure and unerring perception and his never
weary imagination? It is impossible to ignore
the superiority of his simplicity of truth over the
often labored searchings for it of the men and
women he knew, whose very diction shows the
straining after effect, the desire to enchant themselves with their own minds, which is the bane
of intellect, or else the uneasy skip and jump of
a wit that dares not keep still. As time ripens,
these things are more and more apparent to all,
as they were to him. In a manner similar to Emerson's, who spoke of his regret for losing the
chance of associating fully with my father, Longfellow wrote to my mother : —

CAMBRIDGE, June 23, 1864.

DEAR MRS. HAWTHORNE, — I have long been
wishing to write to you, to thank you for your
kind remembrance, in sending me the volume of
Goldsmith, but I have not had the heart to do it.
There are some things that one cannot say; and
I hardly need tell you how much I value your
gift, and how often I shall look at the familiar
name on the blank leaf — a name which, more
than any other, links me to my youth.

I have written a few lines trying to express the
impressions of May 23, and I venture to send you
a copy of them. I had rather no one should see
them but yourself; as I have also sent them to

Mr. Fields for the "Atlantic." I feel how imperfect and inadequate they are; but I trust you will pardon their deficiencies for the love I bear his memory. More than ever I now regret that I postponed from day to day coming to see you in Concord, and that at last I should have seen your house only on the outside!

With deepest sympathy,

Yours truly,

HENRY W. LONGFELLOW.

To go back to our Concord amusements. Mr. Bright caroled out a greeting not very long after our return: —

WEST DERBY, September 8, 1860.

MY DEAR MR. HAWTHORNE, — Of course not! — I *knew* you'd never write to me, though you declared you would. Probably by this time you've forgotten us all, and sent us off into mistland with Miriam and Donatello; possibly all England looks by this time nothing but mistland, and you believe only in Concord and its white houses, and the asters on the hill behind your house, and the pumpkins in the valley below. Well, at any rate I have not forgotten you or yours; and I feel that, now you have left us, a pleasure has slipped out of our grasp. Do you remember all our talks in that odious office of yours; my visits to Rockferry; my one visit, all in the snow, to Southport; our excursions into Wales, and through the London streets, and to Rugby and to Cambridge; and how you plucked the laurel at Addison's Bilton, and

found the skeleton in Dr. Williams's library ; and
lost your umbrella in those dark rooms in Trinity ;
and dined at Richmond, and saw the old lady
looking like a maid of honor of Queen Charlotte's
time ; and chatted at the Cosmopolitan ; and
heard Tom Hughes sing the "Tight Little Island ; " and — But really I must stop, and can
only trust that now at last you will be convinced
of my existence, and remember your promise, and
write me a good long letter about everything and
everybody. "The Marble Faun" [manuscript]
is now in process of binding. The photograph
came just as I had begun to despair of it, and I
lost not a moment in putting the precious manuscript into my binder's hands. I 've been for a
week's holiday at Tryston, and met several friends
of yours : Mr. and Mrs. Tom Hughes, Mrs. and
Miss Procter, Mrs. Milnes. The latter spoke most
affectionately about you. And so did Mrs. Ainsworth, whom I met two days ago. But *she* says
you promised to write her the story of the Bloody
Footstep ["The Ancestral Footstep "], and have
never done it. I 'm very fond of Mrs. Ainsworth ;
she talks such good nonsense. She told us
gravely, the other day, that the Druses were much
more interesting than the Maronites, *because* they
sounded like Drusus and Rome, whereas the Maronites were only like *marrons glacés*, etc. The
H——s are at Norris Green. Mrs. H. is becoming
"devout," and *will* go to church on Wednesdays
and Fridays. I want news from your side. What
is Longfellow about ? Tell me about "Leaves of

Grass," which I saw at Milnes's. Who and what
is the author; and who buy and who read the
audacious (I use mildest epithet) book? I must
now bring this letter to an end. Emerson will
have forgotten so humble a person as I am; but
I can't forget the pleasant day I spent with him.
Ask Longfellow to come over here very soon.
And for yourself, ever believe me most heartily
yours,   H. A. BRIGHT.

He writes to my mother, " Thank you for the
precious autograph letters, and the signatures of
the various generals in your war. . . . What a
pleasant account you give of Julian. Remember
me to him. What a big fellow he has become,
and formidable. I sincerely hope he's given up
his old wish to 'kill an Englishman, some day!'
Don't forget us all, for we think of all of you."
He speaks of my father's friendship as "the proudest treasure of my life."

A friend of Mr. Bright's pardons my father's
unfeeling indifference by a request : —

WALTHAM HOUSE, WALTHAM CROSS,
August 10, 1861.

DEAR MR. HAWTHORNE, — Am I not showing
my Christian charity when, in spite of the terrible
disappointment which I felt at your broken promise to come with Bright to smoke a cigar with me
about this time last year, I entreat you, in greeting Mr. Anthony Trollope, who with his wife is
about to visit America, to give him an extra wel-

come and shake of the hand, for the sake of yours
most sincerely and respectfully,

W. W. SYNGE.

I will quote two letters from Mr. Chorley, written before we left England, to show that even
writers and friends there could be a trifle irksome
in comment. My mother amused me sometimes
by telling me how she had written warringly to
this noted critic (a cherished acquaintance), when
he had printed a disquisition upon " Monte Beni "
which did not hit the bull's-eye. But the last
supplementary chapter in the Romance was due
to his fainting desire for more revelation, — a
chapter which my father and mother looked upon
as entirely useless, and British.

13 EATON PLACE, WEST, March 6, '60.

DEAR MRS. HAWTHORNE, — I cannot but affectionately thank you for your remembrance of
me, and your patience with my note. — If I do not
return on my own critical fancies about the " Romance " (and pray, recollect, I am the last who
would assume that critics wear a mail celestial,
and as such can do no wrong) — it may be from
some knowledge, that those who have lived with a
work while it is growing — and those who greet
it, when it is born, complete into life, — *can*not see
with the same eyes. I don't think, if we three
sate together, and could talk the whole dream out,
a matter, by the way, hardly possible, we should
have so much difference as you fancy — so much

467

did I enjoy, and so deeply was I stirred by the book, that (let alone past associations and predilections) I neither read, nor wrote (*meant to write*, that is) in a caviling spirit : but that which simply and clearly seemed to present itself in regard to a book which had possessed me (for better for worse) in no common degree — by one on whom (I think is known) I set no common store. — If I have seemed to yourselves hasty or superficial or flippant — all I can say is, such was not my meaning. — Surely the best things can bear the closest looking at, — whether as regards beauty or blemish. —

I repeat that, while I thank you affectionately for the trouble you have taken to expostulate with my frowardness (if so it be) — I am just as much concerned if what was printed gave any pain. But, when I look again (I have been interrupted twenty times since I began this) — did I not say that Hilda was "*cousin*" — that is, family likeness, *not* identity — though it means, what I meant, the same sort of light of purity and grace, and redemption let into a maze, through somewhat the same sort of chink. — I totally resist any idea of *mannerism*, dear friend Hawthorne, — on your part, — and as to the story growing on you, as you grow into it : well, I dare say that has happened ere this : — the best creations have come by chance : and if Hawthorne did not mean to excite an interest when he wanted merely to make a Roman idyl, why *did* we go into those Catacombs ? —

Might I say (like Molière's old woman) how earnestly I desire, that for a second edition, a few more *openings of the door* should be added to the story — towards its close?

You have been so kind in bearing with me, — in coming to me when in London, — and in remembering the *nothing* I could do here to make you welcome, as I fancied you might like best to be welcomed, — that I venture to send you this letter *out of my heart*, — and if there be nonsense in it, or what may seem spectacled critical pedantry, I must trust to *your* good nature to allow for them.

Won't you come to town again? and wont you eat another cosy dinner at my table? — And pray, dear friend Hawthorne, don't be so long again : — and pray, once for all, recollect that you have no more faithful nor real literary friend (perhaps, too, in other ways might I show it)

Than yours as always,

HENRY N. CHORLEY.

P. S. This is a sort of *salad* note, written both to " *He* " and " *She* " (as they said in old duetts) — once again, excuse every incoherence. I am still very ill — and have all the day been interrupted.

13 EATON PLACE, WEST, March 10, '60.

DEAR MRS. HAWTHORNE, — I assure you I feel the good nature not to be on *my side* of the treaty. It is not common for a critic to get any kind construction, or to be credited with anything save a desire to show ingenuity, no matter whether just or unjust. — Most deeply, too, do I feel the honor of having a suggestion such as mine adopted, — I thought when my letter had gone that I had written in a strange, random humor, and that had I got a "*Mind your own business*" sort of answer, it was no more than such unasked-for meddling might expect. I am glad with all my heart at what you tell me about the success of the tale. But we really will not wait so long for number five?

To-day's train takes you *my* Italian story : — I had every trouble in the world to find a publisher for it : having the gift of *no-success* in a very remarkable degree. The dedication tells its own story. It was begun in 1848 : — and ended not before the Italian war broke out. — Some of my few readers (within a dozen) are aggrieved at my having only told part of the story of Italian patriotism. — I meant it merely as a picture of manners : and have seen too much of the class "refugee," not to have felt how they have as a class retarded, not aided, the cause of real freedom and high morals. I should have sent it before, but I always feel, like Teresa Panza, when she sent acorns to the Duchess.

You *will* come to town, and eat in my quiet corner before you go, I know : — Perhaps, I may call on you at Easter : as there is just a chance of my being at Birmingham.

There is an old house, Compton Wingates, that I very much want to see. Has Hawthorne seen it?

Once more thank you affectionately, — these sort of passages are among the very few set-offs to the difficulties of a harsh life and all ungracious career. My seeing you face to face was, I assure you, one of my best pleasures in 1859.

Ever yours faithfully,

HENRY N. CHORLEY.

Hawthorne had returned, for the purpose of cherishing American loyalty in his children, from a scene that was after his own heart, even to the actors in it. He had hoped for quietude and the inimitable flavor of home, of course ; but this hope was chiefly a self-persuasion. The title of his first book after returning, "Our Old Home," was a concise confession. He would have considered it a base resource to live abroad during the war, bringing up his son in an alien land, however dear and related it might be to our bone and sinew; and if his children did not enjoy the American phase of the universe in its crude stage, he, at any rate, had done his best to make them love it. His loyalty was always something flawless. A friend might treat him with the grossest dishonor, but he would let you think he was himself deficient in perception or in a proper regard for his money before he would let you guess that his friend should be denounced. With loyal love, he had, for his part, wound about New England the purple haze of which Dr. Holmes spoke in ecstasy, because he had found his country standing only half appreciated, though with a wealth of virtue and meaning that makes her fairer every year. With love, also, he came home, after hav-

471

ing barely tasted the delights of London and Oxford completeness.

In Concord he entered upon a long renunciation. Of necessity this was beneficial to his art. He was now fully primed with observation, and "The Dolliver Romance," hammered out from several beginnings that he successively cast aside, appeared so exquisitely pure and fine because of the hush of fasting and reflection which environed the worker. It is the unfailing history of great souls that they seem to destroy themselves most in relation to the world's happiness when they most deserve and acquire a better reward. He was starving, but he steadily wrote. He was weary of the pinched and unpromising condition of our daily life, but he smiled, and entertained us and guided us with unflagging manliness, though with longer and longer intervals of wordless reserve. I was never afraid to run to him for his sympathy, as he sat reading in an easy-chair, in some one of those positions of his which looked as if he could so sit and peruse till the end of time. I knew that his response would be so cordially given that it would brim over me, and so melodiously that it would echo in my heart for a great while ; yet it would be as brief as the single murmurous stroke of *one* from a cathedral tower, half startling by its intensity, but which attracts the birds, who wing by preference to that lofty spot.

A source of deep enjoyment to my father was a long visit from his sister, Ebie Hawthorne (he having given her that pretty title instead of any other abbreviation of Elizabeth). I came to know her very well in after-years, and was astonished at her magic resemblance to my father in many ways. I always felt her unmistakable power. She was chock-full of worldly wisdom, though living in the utmost monastic retirement, only allowing herself to browse in two wide regions, — the woods and literature. She knew the latest news from the papers, and the oldest classics alongside of them. She was potentially, we thought, rather hazardous, or perverse. But language refuses to explain her. Her brother seemed not to dream of this, yet no doubt relished the fact that a nature as unique as any he had drawn sparkled in his sister. She was a good deal unspiritual in everything ; but all besides in her was fine mind, wisdom, and loving-kindness of a lazy, artistic sort. That is to say, she was unregenerate, but excellent ; and she fascinated like a wood-creature seldom seen and observant, refined and untrained. My sister was devoted to her, and says, for the hundredth time, in a passage among many pages of their correspondence bequeathed to me : —

My own dear Auntie, — I was made very happy by your letter this week. What perfectly charming letters you write! Now, don't laugh and say I am talking nonsense ; it is really true. You make the simplest things interesting by your way of telling them ; and your observations and humor are so keen that I often feel sorry the world does not know something of them. I never remember you to have told me anything twice, and that can be said of very few people ; but there are few enough people in the least like you, my dearest auntie. . . .

Aunt Ebie did not look romantic, or exactly mysterious, as I first saw her. But she puzzled me splendidly nevertheless. She was knitting some very heavy blue socks in our library, and her needles were extremely large and shining. I do not know why she had undertaken this prosaic occupation. Everybody was, to be sure, knitting socks for the soldiers at that time; but somehow aunt Ebie did not strike me as absolutely benevolent, and I doubt if she would have labored very eagerly for a soldier whom she had never seen. She desired to teach me to knit ; and, as I was really afraid of her, I pretended to be anxious to learn.

I had been told that it was almost an impossibility to get her to travel even a few miles ; that the excitement of change and crowds, and danger from steam and horse, made her extremely tremulous and wretched. I was the more impressed by these quavers in her because I also knew that she had sufficient strength of character to upset a kingdom, if she chose ; that she could use a sceptre of keen sarcasm which made heads roll off on all sides ; that there was nothing which her large, lustrous eyes could not see, and nothing they could not conceal. To think, then, that she trembled beside a steam-engine made her a problem.

She wore a quaintly round dress of lightish-brown mohair, which would not fall into graceful folds. So there she sat in the little library, knitting Titanically; and I sat alone with her, learning to round Hatteras at the heel in a swirl of contradictory impressions. I felt that she ought to have been dressed in soft dark silks, with a large, half-idle fan before her lips.

She quickly saw that I was a miniature mystery myself, and presently got me out into the woods. Here I came into contact with her for the first time.

She stepped along under the trees with great deliberation, holding up the inflexible mohair skirt as if it could tear on brambles or in gales, and looking around quickly and ardently at the sound of a bird-note or the glance of a squirrel-leap; her great eyes peering for a moment from their widely opened lids, and then disappearing utterly again under those white veils. Her dark brown, long lashes and broadly sweeping eyebrows were distinct against the pallor of her skin, which was so delicately clear, yet vigorous, that I felt its gleam as one feels the moon, even if I were not looking directly at her. By and by her cheeks took on a dawn-flush of beautiful pink. The perfection of her health was shown, until her last sickness, by this girlish glow of color in her wood-rambles.

Long before we had arrived at a particularly nice flower or species of moss, she knew it was to be found, and gathered it up as Fate makes a clean sweep of all its opportunities. I was almost as happy when out of doors with her as when I was with my father. She had the same eloquence in her silences; and when she spoke, it was with a sympathy that played upon one's whole perception, as a harp is swept inclusively of every string by an eager hurry of music. Still, aunt Ebie seemed to love moss and leaves as much as some people love souls, and I thought she had chosen them as the least dangerous objects of affection; whereas my father seemed most to love souls, and would have saved mine or another's at the expense of all the forests and vines of Eden.

To Miss Peabody I wrote of this visit in a manner which shows its reviving effect upon me: —

MY DEAR AUNT LIZZIE, — I like to get your letters, as they tell about everything which everybody does not do. What a pleasant time I did have with aunt Ebie Hawthorne last summer! It was last summer; and all the lovely flowers were nodding, and the sun shone with all its might, and we each took a basket and a book and stayed all the afternoon. We brought home heaps of flowers and greens. I never had such a pleasant time here in the woods. In England my nurse Fanny and I used to take long walks on Sunday through the lanes, or into the parks; and take baskets and pick baskets full of daisies, pink-and-white. Then we went into the endless lanes, long, without a single sign of house or cottage (until we came to walk so far as to come to a little village). Nobody came along in rattling gigs or carriages ; on Sunday you would not meet a person. With great ditches on each side, filled with tall grass as high as yourself, if you chose to get down into it. But I used to jump across, to get wild hawthorn and rose and honeysuckle and wall-flowers, and make great bunches of them. And then the buttercups and daisies and violets in the green grass! For in the lanes there was not a sign of earth, — all high, green grass. The sun shining so hot that you could go in your house-dress but for the properness of it. But I cannot explain and you cannot imagine; you must go to the place and look for yourself, and then you will know all about it. The parks are not level at all, but are nothing but high hills all together, — dear! — so lovely to run down and roll over on, and skip rope and jump!

My father began to express his wishes in regard to provision for our aunt in case of his death ; to burn old letters ; and to impart to my mother and Una all that he particularly desired to say to them, among other things his dislike of biographies, and that he forbade any such matter in connection with himself in any distance of the future. This com-mand, respected for a number of years, has been, like all such forcible and prophetic demurs, most signally set aside. It would take long to explain my own modifications of opinion from arguments of fierce resistance to the request for a biographi-cal handling of him ; and it matters, no doubt, very little. Such a man must be thoroughly known, as great saints are always sooner or later known, though endeavoring to hide their victories of holiness and charity. Certainly my father did not like to die, though he. now wished to do so. My mother, later, often spoke, in consolation for us and for herself, of his dread of helpless old age ; and she tried to be glad that his desire to disappear before decrepitude had been fulfilled. But such wise wishes are not carried out as we might choose. The sudden transformation which took place in my father after his coming to America was like an instant's change in the atmosphere from sunshine to dusky cold. I have never had the least difficulty in explaining it to myself.

One large item in the sum of his regrets was his unexpectedly narrowed means. It would have required a generous amount of money to put The Wayside and its grounds into the delectable order at first contemplated, to bring them into any sort of English perfection, and my parents found that they could not afford it ; and so all resulted in semi-comfort and rough appearances. This narrowing of means was caused not a little by the want of veracity of a person whom my father had trusted with entire affection and a very considerable loan, about which we none of us ever heard again. A crust becomes more than proverbially dry under these circumstances.

My mother bore every reverse nobly. She writes, after her husband's death : " I have 'enjoyed life,' and 'its hard pinches' have not too deeply bitten into my heart. But this has been because I am not only hopeful and of indomitable credence by nature, but because this temperament, together with the silent ministry of pain, has helped me to the perfect, the unshadowed belief in the instant providence of God; in his eternal love, patience, sweetness; in his shining face, never averted. It is because I cannot be disappointed on account of this belief. To stand and wait after doing all that is legitimate is my instinct, my best wisdom, my inspiration; and I always hear the still, small voice at last. If man would not babble so much, we could much oftener hear God. The lesson of my life has been patience. It has only made me feel the more humble that God has been so beyond cóunt benignant to me. I have been cushioned and pillowed with tender love from the cradle. Such a mother seldom falls to the lot of mortals. She was the angel of my life. Her looks and tones and her acts of high-bred womanhood were the light and music and model of my childhood. Then God joined my destiny with him who was to be all relations in one. Pain passed away when my husband came. Poverty was lighter than a thistledown with such a power of felicity to uphold it. With 'lowering clouds' I have never been long darkened, because the sun above has been so penetrating that their tissue has directly become silvered and goldened. Our own closed eyelids are too often the only clouds between us and the ever-shining sun. I hold all as if it were not mine, but God's, and ready to resign it."

It seemed to me a terrible thing that one so peculiarly strong, sentient, luminous, as my father should grow feebler and fainter, and finally ghostly still and white. Yet when his step was tottering and his frame that of a wraith, he was as dignified as in the days of greater pride, holding himself, in military self-command, even more erect than before. He did not omit to come in his very best black coat to the dinner-table, where the extremely prosaic fare had no effect upon the distinction of the meal. He hated failure, dependence, and disorder, broken rules and weariness of discipline, as he hated cowardice. I cannot express how brave he seemed to me. The last time I saw him, he was leaving the house to take the journey for his health which led suddenly to the next world. My mother was to go to the station with him, — she who, at the moment when it was said that he died, staggered and groaned, though so far from him, telling us that something seemed to be sapping all her strength; I could hardly bear to let my eyes rest upon her shrunken, suffering form on this day of farewell. My father certainly knew, what she vaguely felt, that he would never return.

Like a snow image of an unbending but an old, old man, he stood for a moment gazing at me. My mother sobbed, as she walked beside him to the carriage. We have missed him in the sunshine, in the storm, in the twilight, ever since.

INDEX OF PERSONS